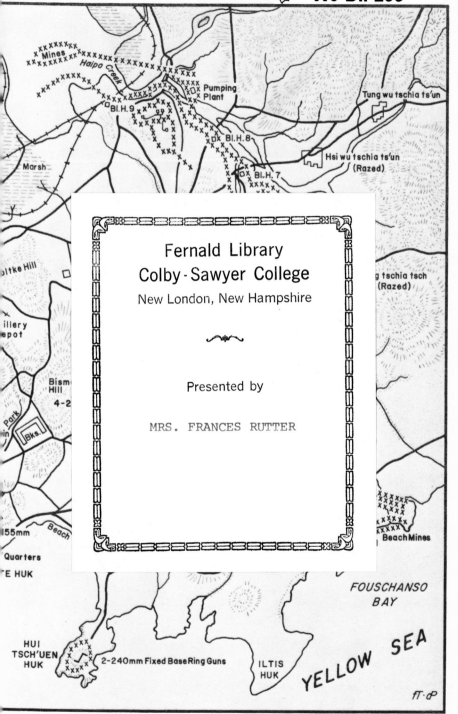

Mines
Haipo Creek
Pumping
Plant
Tung wu tschia ts'un
Bl.H. 9
Bl.H. 8
Hsi wu tschia ts'un
(Razed)
Marsh
Bl.H. 7
ltke Hill
g tschia tsch
(Razed)
illery
epot
Bism
Hill
4-2
Park
in
Bks.
155mm
Beach
Beach Mines
Quarters
E HUK
FOUSCHANSO
BAY
HUI
TSCH'UEN
HUK
2-240mm Fixed Base Ring Guns
ILTIS
HUK
YELLOW SEA

The
Japanese
Siege
of
Tsingtau

World War I in Asia

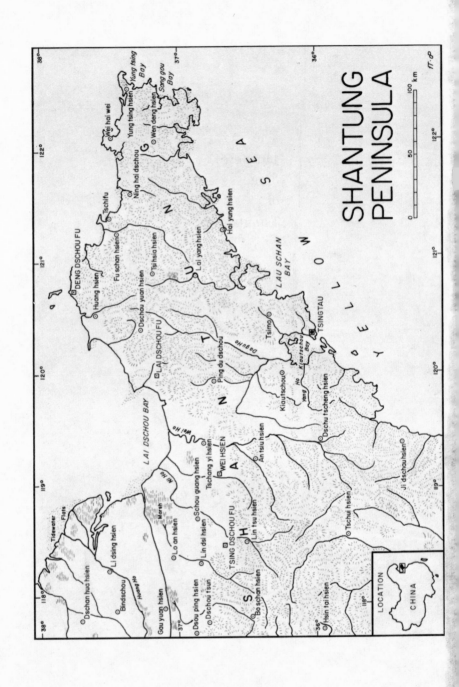

SHANTUNG PENINSULA

The Japanese Siege of Tsingtau

WORLD WAR I

IN ASIA

Charles B. Burdick

ARCHON BOOKS
1976

© Charles B. Burdick 1976
First published 1976
as an Archon Book,
an imprint of
The Shoe String Press, Inc.
Hamden, Connecticut 06514

Library of Congress Cataloging in Publication Data

Burdick, Charles Burton, 1927-
    The Japanese siege of Tsingtau.

    Bibliography: p.
    Includes index.
    1. Tsingtao, China—Siege, 1914.   I.   Title.
D572.T75B87   940.4'23   76-16073
ISBN 0-208-01594-9

for
Thomas Berberich
and
Heinrich Pfeiffer
in friendship

The German colonies will be defended before the gates of Metz.

OTTO VON BISMARCK

To explain to an Ally that her help will be welcome, but that you hope it will not be made inconvenient, is a proceeding that is neither agreeable nor gracious.

VISCOUNT GREY OF FALLODEN

The victory, which you wish to achieve in war, must be prepared during times of peace.

KAMIO, MITSUOMI

The appreciation of the Fatherland is known to you all.

GERMAN MILITARY PROVERB

Contents

Illustrations

Preface

The story of a pivotal military battle in history provides an immense challenge to any historian. In particular the search for reliable documentary materials scattered throughout the world, the location of surviving participants, and the spelling of various words create numerous difficulties. These professional requirements force the scholar to relentlessly search for the answers and to make decisions on matters often beyond his ken.

What follows is an attempt to describe a battle which has not had a wide audience. In 1914 the Japanese crowned their incredible rise to international stature with the conquest of Tsingtau. In doing so, they removed the only major European threat to their aspirations in north China, began their own dreams of empire, and started a tragic confrontation for Pacific authority. This latter endeavor, in a very real sense, opened the struggle with the United States and contributed most directly to the final denouement at Pearl Harbor.

The loss of Tsingtau destroyed Germany's colonial aspirations and empire. Certainly the defeat sharply curtailed German economic expansion and international position. Even more, however, the loss heralded the end of European influence and power in Asia. The Germans were the last to enter the field of imperialism and they were the first to leave it. Nonetheless, the struggle for Tsingtau served as the road sign for a new century of Asian turmoil, adjustment, and change.

In the course of the narrative I have tried to use the German spelling for geographic terms. They are sufficiently clear since Chinese, Japanese, and English names are very different. Additionally I have tried to utilize the ranks held by the individuals in 1914.

Any endeavor of this nature is one of some difficulty, and hundreds of people have contributed to its completion. In the bibliography I have listed some of the individuals who provided information and support for my labors. I wish, however, to recognize various persons and groups who made this publication possible. A goodly portion of my research found support through a sabbatical leave from San Jose State University, a small grant from the same institution, and a splendid award from the Alexander von Humboldt Stiftung.

Among the many archives employed for this project, I remain grateful to Agnes Peterson, the doyan of helpers, at the Hoover Institution; Colonels George Pappas and James Agnew, together with Joyce Eakin of the US Army Military Research Collection at Carlisle Barracks; John Taylor and Harry Reilly of the National Archives; Dean Allard of the US Naval Historical Center; Dr. Sandhofer of the Bundesarchive-Militärarchiv; Dr. Wagner of the Austrian Military Archives; Fregattenkapitän Heinz von Bassi of the German Mürwik Museum; Fregattenkapitän August Wilhelm Heye of the Marine-Offizier-Vereinigung; Takeharu Shima of the Japanese Military Historical Office. My good friends in the San Jose State University Library, Margaret Atkins and Christine Simpson, did wonders in searching for materials throughout the world.

While I have benefited from the help of many participants, several have been most gracious in providing information, support, and hospitality. In particular I am appreciative to Dagmar Frowein, Paul Kley, Christian Vogelfänger, Torao Kuwabara, Desmond Summerville, and the late Herman Kersten. Anyone with any knowledge of the German veterans knows of the truly incredible service of Ed Leipold. His unique attachment to his comrades, dedication to their requirements, and scholarly willingness to help others remains a major reward for this writer.

For many services which I cannot render properly in writing I am beholden to Hans-Adolf Jacobsen, Hans Ehlers, Sumi and Benjamin

Hazard, George Moore, Duilo Peruzzi, Irma von Waaden, Leslie Brand and Bea Gormley.

In the course of my various German visits many members of the Alexander von Humboldt Stiftung made life and research a joy beyond description. Knowing Erika Berberich, Barbara Goth, Inge Göbbel, Dietrich Papenfuss, and Hans Meise has provided me and my family many pleasures.

My daughter, Saral Burdick, has my warm gratitude for the tedious chore of assembling the index of this book.

Ultimately I remain deeply humbled by the generosity, aid, and friendship of my colleagues James Walsh and Gerald Wheeler. They have provided the understanding and guidance which have made all my efforts personally meaningful and rewarding. Thomas Berberich and Heinrich Pfeiffer made this book possible and necessary. Without their constant efforts I would have given the task up long ago. My dedication of this book is small recompense for their magnificent labors in my behalf.

All of the individuals mentioned above must assume responsibility for any value in this book. The errors are, alas, of my own doing.

The
Japanese
Siege
of
Tsingtau

World War I in Asia

Introduction

In August 1894 the Japanese government opened hostilities against China. This aggression terminated a decade of quiet competition among foreign powers maneuvering for influence and preferred concessions on the Asian mainland. Within a short time the attackers overwhelmed the defenders in a series of crushing defeats. These decisive victories proved that the Chinese government lacked the requisite administrative efficiency, the economic substance, and the modern weaponry required for minimal defense. The Chinese appealed to the major western powers for aid but the latter could find no collective resolution to the intervention question. They were more concerned with the possible impact of a total Chinese collapse upon their own concessions and aspirations than for any untimely entanglement.

Instead they divided their interests between desultory exchange and omnipresent observation in seeking positions for the anticipated new era ahead. Clearly the first casualty in the war was the notion of China as an independent power. The Japanese underscored the end of an age when they terminated the conflict in the Treaty of Shimonoseki. Under the victor's prod, the Chinese recognized the independence of Korea, ceded Formosa, the Pescadores Islands and the Liaotung Peninsula to Japan and agreed to a large war indemnity. The blatant example of an Asiatic people displaying tendencies normally associated with European politics created a flurry of excitement in Europe. That a non-European country was acting unilaterally, assuming power prerogatives, and displaying grandiose pretensions was totally unacceptable behavior for European minds.

Suddenly galvanized into action the diplomatic representatives of Russia, France, and Germany presented notes to the Japanese foreign office "recommending" that Japan disgorge the Liaotung Peninsula. The Japanese recognized the real danger involved in this collective demand and acquiesced by returning the area to its rightful owner, China. They saved honor by increasing their indemnity demands upon the helpless Chinese. In addition to these territorial demands the Japanese required a number of economic concessions from their continental neighbor which further opened the trade possibilities for foreigners in China. The amended treaty terminated the conflict, heralded potential extinction for the Chinese national government, and alerted the world's powers to China's potential for exploitation.

The Europeans, in a manner comprehensible only within the context of the current imperialistic immorality, hurriedly demanded "compensations" from the Chinese. Like vultures circling in military formation each one swooped down for an assault upon the decaying Chinese territorial imperium. The French began the lengthy procession seeking "spheres of influence" as they extorted mining grants, economic concessions, and railroad rights in the south. Russia obtained the authority for a rail line across Manchuria to Vladivostok with a spur line into the Liaotung Peninsula, general supervision of Chinese finances in the north, and, eventually, occupation of the Liaotung Peninsula itself. The Germans emerged a poor third in this race for privilege with minor trading concessions and some economic advantages. In 1897 they found the required moral pretext for further action and seized the rich Kiautschou area of the Shantung Peninsula. Obviously the British could not overlook this activity and they extracted financial advantages, leaseholds on Shantung (Weihaiwei) and the mainland opposite Hong Kong, and control of certain Chinese administrative posts. In short, the Europeans threatened the Celestial Empire from all sides. Even this obvious cornucopia of concessions did not fully satisfy the Europeans.

As the greedy exploiters sought additional security, they demanded, and the Chinese provided, assurances that certain territorial regions would not be surrendered to a third party. The result was a series of "nonalienation" territorial assurances. The first of these unusual promises went to France about Hainan island; the second to Great Britain about the Yangtze valley; the third to France involving Indo-China; and the fourth to Japan respecting Fukien provence. This scramble for selfish gain forced massive adjustments among the concerned parties. Perhaps three major forces emerged from this chaotic situation: (1) the Chinese reform movement; (2) the entry of the United States into Pacific imperialist politics; and (3) the beginning indications of the jealous rivalries inherent in overly-tense competition.

With the increased international bickering and flagrant disregard of China's territorial integrity, many Chinese turned to reform movements. These people divided their intense, emotional hatred between two enemies. One was the ruling monarchy for its numerous failings in many social, political, and philosophical areas; the other was against the increasing foreign presence in the country. The result was a general rising in north China known as the Boxer War. These violent demonstrations culminated in the siege of the diplomatic legations in Peking. Acting under this sudden pressure the foreign powers utilized military force to defend their nationals and to maintain their privileged authority. The foredoomed result humiliated the Chinese, brought new indemnity payments, and removed various sovereign rights. China's claim to recognition as a free and independent country suffered further erosion.

The grievous product of this struggle was further complicated by a new participant's entry in the game—the United States. America came into the Pacific as a trading power rather than as an aggressive imperialist. Nonetheless, the exaggerated American pride, increasing international awareness, and broadening economic power altered the quiet business involvement. The 1898 war with Spain triggered a massive American expansionistic thrust. As a result of this conflict the United States acquired the Philippines and Guam, annexed Hawaii, and acquired a portion of Samoa. While the Americans might preach platitudes about morality and democracy, the colonizing powers found this territorial aggrandizement a more meaningful behavioral indicator.

Concurrently the American diplomats began extrolling their Open Door efforts. They wanted equal trade and access opportunities for everyone in China rather than a general division of the country into national colonies. Somehow China's territorial sovereignty, no matter how carefully papered over, must be protected for the economic benefit of all. Europeans, after witnessing the Americans grabbing territory at a record rate were not easily convinced about these proposals. With the exception of Russia they eventually agreed to the principle of the American position, but none of them evidenced sincere commitment. They accepted the idea so long as it cost them nothing. Besides, they required time and stability to further their own ambitions.

The most serious of these aspirations centered in St. Petersburg. In the aftermath of the Boxer difficulties the Russians absorbed more of Manchuria and completed their general occupation of the entire area. They obviously intended an indefinite stay, an action posing an immediate military threat to Japan and China. The resulting ferment precluded any collective understanding. A further contributing complication was the pressure generated by European difficulties elsewhere. All of the major countries, unable to perceive the world's shift from a pre-Columbian flat surface to the modern globe, undertook policies of opportunism and immediacy, searching for cheap gains at low cost. The resultant flux within a known system and the plethora of short sighted goals portended future trouble.

For a brief time the major powers sought bilateral understandings with each other. These agreements often brought powers together who belonged to opposing alliances in Europe. Ultimately the British and Japanese signed an alliance in 1902. Operating from this tradition-shattering power base (the British had given up their isolationism, recognized an Asian partner, and joined against a fellow continental power) the Japanese seized the initiative and opened hostilities against Russia in 1904. Japan's spectacular victory stabilized great power relations in East Asia for a time because the triumphant Japanese simply overawed everyone. A world, long accustomed to a centralized European center with an American link, confronted a new authority, necessitating new considerations, understandings, and operative rules. A Japanese drive for empire could only gain momentum through the destruction of Western colonialism and the elimination of Western dominance in Asia.

Clearly the Japanese had thrust themselves forward into a challenger's role while, following their humiliation of the Russians, alerting the nationalistic feelings of Asians. A new age was at hand.

Surely the most notable fact of this time was the speed of these changes. In contrast to the measured, orderly comprehensible tread of the past, these revolutionary adjustments occurred within a few years. They interrupted tradition, destroyed continuity, undermined belief. No country nor leadership was prepared psychologically, institutionally, or materially for these changes.

The genesis of this new time was clogged in uncertainty. As the Japanese savored their victory and discovered unexpected strengths, the Europeans spent their energies trying to fit the new oriental power into the old, antiquated system. They could not foresee a new millenium which portended a total change in the human condition. European diplomats understood that an emerging Japan must institute profound changes in Europe but they could find no human apparatus for understanding or exchange. Even the Chinese revolution of 1911 which terminated the Manchu dynasty, the last symbol of imperial stability, could provide no basis for new endeavors seeking human understanding. Clearly the Eurasian land mass was undergoing basic change. Activities at either extremity of the continent would have a basic impact upon all countries. For the moment a tenuous balance existed between the two pillars. Any removal of the European involvement in Asia would leave only two participants in the power conflict, a resident Japan and the powerful United States.

In 1913 the major players in this drama participated in an insightful war game at Tientsin. The British organized the affair, ostensibly against a possible Chinese assault. They served as one of the major assault forces and performed in fine fashion beyond confusing some signals and loitering too long in the country club. The Germans, participating both with the British force and as the play enemy, marched everywhere in close order formation, followed directions explicitly, and returned home at the scheduled time. The French displayed general lethargy despite their pride in their colorful blue uniforms which were visible for some distance; the other participants wore khaki. The French did provide the major excitement, however, when they charged the Germans posing as the local enemy. Fixing bayonets they ran through the frightened Germans screaming, "Every man a victor over the eternal German foe." Thereafter the

French liberated several chicken roosts and, with the squawking hens tied to their packs, strolled home. The Americans appeared in total field attire with their great coats tied across their chests in bandoleer fashion. Everyone was amazed at their fulsome dress; the troops found the exercise a lengthy affair. Additionally the Americans had the only available field telephones for rapid communications. They rolled out the wires in all directions and wasted many hours chasing the Chinese peasants who busily rolled up the wire for sale to the Japanese. The latter served as the chief umpires, led one assault group, and conducted the final critique. Throughout the exercise the numerous Chinese impassively watched the foreigners' strange activities. This singular effort was the only one attempted by the foreigners but the Japanese clearly had achieved a significant role in group affairs.

Obviously the Japanese had joined the Asian power structure. In the world of 1913 they possessed geographic location, powerful momentum, and a new political sophistication. The French and British had economic interests, political influence, and the traditional strength born of empire. They did not have a potent military presence in North Asia. The Russians, still hurting from their Japanese experience, maintained their concern. While their appetite remained great, their teeth were of poor quality. The Germans, despite their tardy arrival in Asia, owned a fine economic foundation for future growth and a powerful military bastion in Kiautschou.

The German leasehold in Kiautschou provided a constant proof of achievement through industriousness. Although they had arrived in Shantung in 1897, they had, by 1913, achieved impressive results. The colonial authorities had created a throbbing economic metropolis from a group of pastoral villages. With Tsingtau as a headquarters German merchants, mining concerns, banking firms, railroad engineers, and industrialists fanned out over north China. As a result commercial activities flourished and new industrial strength flowered within a few years. The local German administration created a viable political administration with an enviable political system, modern schools, adequate sanitary standards. Clearly German capital, ability, personnel, and organization had laid down the foundation for this development. If they could maintain the needed payments in interest, treasure, and manpower, their authority in Asia would grow with geometric haste. Clearly their attitudes and successes made the Germans the leading competition for a Japanese drive seeking continental influence. In 1913 the Germans believed that they would continue their expansion without question. They had few qualms about sending the requisite materials in terms of either money or manpower.

I

Tsingtau:

A *Casus Belli*

Umspult vom gelben Meere, an einer kleinen Bucht Da liegt ein Stuckchen
Erde, durchzog'n von mancher Schlucht. Kiautschou ist sein Name und
Tsingtau heisst die Stadt, Wodrinn so mancher Deutsche die zweite Heimat
hat.

Fr. edrich Blaschke "Tsingtau 1913"[1]

Daylight, on February 21, 1914, brought the cry "Land" from the
lookout on the Hamburg-America streamer, *Patricia*. The hundreds
of passengers heard the announcement, after a sea voyage of some
forty-one days, with genuine relief and sudden expectency. Furthermore, they were on the brink of an entirely new experience. For the
next two years they would form part of Germany's garrison in Tsingtau, China.

   With the announcement that the ship had reached landfall, the
eager replacements stampeded to the ship's rail. Through the mist
and haze they could see the tips of two small mountains on the
horizon. In response to their hurried pleas for identification the
amused crewmen replied "Max" and "Moritz," two renowned comic
strip characters at home. For the youthful, impressionistic naval
soldiers the humorous response carried little significance. They had
all their senses attuned to their destination. Tsingtau, after all,
carried many colorfully descriptive titles in the travel literature, i.e.,
"the Asian Brighton," "the Eastern Riviera," and the "Pearl of the
East."

As the early mist rolled away, the expectant sailors watched the emerging coast line. Even at their considerable distance the skyline provided a foreboding image—rough, high, jagged. The ship moved closer inshore, and the crew members pointed out the tip of Arkona Island, explaining that it had been the original Tsing tau (literally "green island").[2] Then the ship turned into the entrance to Kiautschou Bay.

The men crowding the rails watched as the *Patricia* slipped easily through the spacious entrance. On their left was Cape Jaeschke, a large promontory on the shoulder of the Bay; on the right was T'uan tau, the tip of the peninsula guarding the other side. The entrance was somewhat less than two miles wide. The ship moved directly into the inner harbor, past two welcoming warships, the light cruiser *Emden* and the heavy cruiser *Scharnhorst*, and tied up at the impressive pier. They had reached their destination.

For the inexperienced travelers the first sight of Tsingtau was a memorable one. To be sure, they had heard many tales about the inscrutable Orient, with its "yellow peril" and "bamboo curtain." Now they could see for themselves. What they saw was a crystal-clear, cloudless sky, the towering, rugged terrain, and the brilliant, almost jewel-like, landscape. All the visible hills sprouted green trees which offset the red-and-orange-tiled rooftops like berry bushes in full fruit.

Around the *Patricia* swirled the activity of a busy port. There were, although they could not see them perfectly, three harbors in all. One sheltered the innumerable Chinese junks and other small coastal craft; another held the smaller ship repair facilities; and the third was the main harbor, a completely man-made, horseshoe-shaped breakwater. Inside the main harbor were two straight concrete and granite piers, the principal wharves for the port. There were berths for many vessels, as well as two rail lines, several warehouses, and all the latest equipment for onloading and offloading ships. It also contained a modern 16,000-ton floating dry dock, one of the best in the world. Clearly the facilities were new, efficient, and highly functional. At first glance Tsingtau seemed little different from a European harbor.

This initial observation did not last long. On the wharf was a large, mixed crowd of people assembled as a welcoming party for the new troops. The band of the III Naval Battalion broke into a boisterous rendition of "Alle Vogel sind schon da." Shortly after the musicians had played this piece for the second or third time, the Governor of Tsingtau, Captain Alfred Meyer-Waldeck, gave a brief welcoming address. Tall, with a forceful, confident manner, he made an immediate impression upon the new arrivals. He greeted them with words more notable for their perfunctory nature than their emotional fervor. Clearly he was a sturdy professional man rather than a clever politician. Immediately after his brief presentation, the cadre busied themselves with disembarking the troops by prearranged groups.

The first stop for the long line was the Chinese custom station, a tiny, nondescript shack lost among the more opulent structures.[3] While the resident official did little more than wave briefly to each man, whether in a welcoming or a permissive gesture remained unclear, his action provided a reminder of the Chinese presence. He was the first Chinese the new arrivals encountered on land.

Once through the official formalities the men formed into loose march columns and moved out behind the brass band, starting the annual replacements' march. The men walked more than they marched, although they received active encouragement, not always politely, to remember their military professionalism. But curiosity made discipline approximate. The noisy band served as a directional guide and led the loose formation from the harbor to Tapatau (big-dry-fish island), the exclusively Chinese quarter. Here the marchers could see the bureaucratic efficiency of their countrymen. The wide streets, spacious sidewalks, and manifest cleanliness provided the first of many surprises. To be sure, the Chinese wore different clothing, and many men had the traditional braided pigtail, but otherwise the quarter provided an image of European order.

At Shantung street the column turned left and moved through the Chinese district, where the street signs were marked in Chinese characters as well as in German script. They moved past Tsimi, Kiautschou, Kaumi, and Haipo Streets at a quick step. Before the men had barely adjusted to these surroundings, they reached a small square which opened onto Friedrich street. Immediately they turned into a truly impressive boulevard some forty feet wide.

As they started down the main street of the city, the band strutted with increased vigor and enthusiasm. Along the sidewalks numerous pedestrians greeted the marchers with pleasantries obviously learned in Germany. Tsingtau was clearly a small part of Europe rather than of China, as they could see from the streets (Berliner, Bremer, Prince Heinrich, and so on), the continental architecture, and the dress styles. When the column reached the bottom of the street, two officers standing there sent the soldiers off in various directions. As relief troops they had no claim to quarters until their displaced colleagues boarded the *Patricia* for home. The first residence for many men were the attics of various barracks, the little used ancient Chinese barracks, or spaces in private homes.

Under such crowded conditions the men had the next few days for their own devices. For the most part they spent their time getting acquainted with the members of the garrison and with the geography of the area. Each day provided a new adventure. They strolled through the city like a vast human herd, gawking at the natives in their strange dress, the unusual items displayed in the shop windows, and the omnipresent rickshaws moving in all directions. Despite the whirlpool of activity, the majority spent their time strolling up and down Friedrich street. Here they could find the better stores, the desirable restaurants, and the miscellaneous places for relaxation.

The one required stop was a photographer's shop run by one T. Takahasi for a portrait photo. Takahasi was renowned for his ready wit, knowledge of German cultural mores, and infectious good will. His photographs were of the highest quality and his picture post cards of the area provided superb souvenirs. Takahasi was a municipal institution.

There were other curious stores worthy of inspection. The European establishments were little different than those at home but the Chinese firms were a curious melange of conflicting styles and smells. They carried a formal Chinese designation on the store front but they also displayed a German slang caption on a window card. The origins of these curious titles were often confused, but the owners were proud and jealous of them. The senior shoemaker was "Pill" and his competitor, "Pill 2." In view of his voice the tailor was "Rooster" and his assistant, a master in turning clothing inside out, "Turning Can." The barber was "Soapsuds" and the butcher "Ox." These honorifics went on and on and reflected a friendly association of long duration. After visiting all the shops which their purses might permit, the novitiate colonialists would drink a glass or two of beer at the Sailors' Home and then return to their barracks for tall talks about Tsingtau and Germany's acquisition of the territory.[4]

In November 1897, they learned, a local group had murdered two German missionaries, Franz Nies and Richard Hende, in the Shantung area. Whether robbers, religious fanatics, or simply disgruntled citizens were responsible for the act remains a matter of historical controversy. In any event, the incident had answered some fervent prayers by various German naval leaders, who desired an outpost in China.[5] With unwarranted promptitude the German Emperor, Wilhelm II, had telegraphed Admiral Otto Diedrichs to occupy the Kiautschou area. With three small warships, *Kaiser, Princess Wilhelm*, and *Cormoran*, Diedrichs had moved into the harbor on November 13, 1897. The next day, at 2:30 P.M., a twenty-one-gun salute had announced the hoisting of the German flag.

Thereafter the Germans had rapidly consolidated their position. They forced the Chinese into a hastily consummated contractual agreement which gave the Europeans numerous commercial advantages, an area encompassing some 500 square kilometers, and an unencumbered 99-year leasehold. Within the briefest of time they had established their dominance over the Kiautschou protectorate. Since it was, beyond the highly desirable bay, not an overly appealing area, the Germans had immediately started improving their new holding.

They transferred the villagers in the designated area to a neighboring town and then razed the buildings located in inappropriate places. Without human obstacles German engineers had laid out the city according to the most current European designs. They had started with a modern sewer and water system to guarantee Tsingtau the healthiest conditions in all Asia. From that foundation, the native work crews, under German supervision, had rapidly constructed wide streets, useful promenades, and an enviable electric system. Throughout the building period the responsible officials had emphasized careful urban planning as the basis for all decisions. They wanted a city which incorporated the best of everything. They were successful.

In order to properly honor the original occupation, the local authorities had erected a large commemorative tablet on a small hill. Under the Imperial Eagle, in both Chinese and German, was inscribed in stone, "For him who won for Kaiser and Country the land all around, let this rock be named Diedrich stone."[6] In the intervening years the rock became a much-visited symbol of German authority in China.

A more meaningful reminder of the German position, however, was the incredible building activity. Several business organizations had erected their Eastern headquarters within the city, and their employees had followed with their own dwellings. The construction authorities had also imported thousands of trees to combat erosion, to add beauty, and to camouflage fortifications. Since the Kaiser had granted his naval leaders unique authority over the protectorate, they sought the highest qualitative standards. Certainly they could, by 1914, be proud of their accomplishments.

Beyond these commercial endeavors, the Germans had developed the huge, semicircular, white sand beach into a popular spa. With the sea winds, acceptable temperatures, and clean accommodations, Tsingtau provided a scenically attractive and sensually pleasant bathing strand for all Asia. The tourist trade became an important part of the city's activities. Certainly it was a happy place where everyone, including the men far from Germany, could enjoy himself.

Once all of the men had become familiar with their surroundings and had visited the city sufficiently, the officers began shifting from the easy-going freedoms toward military responsibilities. The first requirement was saying "goodbye" to those men completing their Asiatic service. The *Patricia* remained in port for some ten days reprovisioning, cleaning, and preparing for the return voyage. When the crew had completed the preparations, the men scheduled for relief marched aboard.[7]

The *Patricia* was soon crowded with the returning passengers. From the masts fluttered handmade pennants listing the names of the departees. Several musical groups, both aboard ship and on the wharf, competed with each other in noisy renditions of familiar tunes. Shortly after 11:00 A.M. the *Patricia* moved back from her land tie and turned for the open sea. The departees lined the rail waving goodbye to old friends, happy memories, and Asia. Their optimism over returning home precluded any other thoughts. None of them knew that fortune was on their side. They would be home before international events overwhelmed the tiny colony.

So the *Patricia* faded away and replacements turned to the first real challenges of military obligation. They quickly transferred their belongings to the regular barracks, and soon discovered the realities of their service obligation. The romance quickly disappeared in the drill, drill, drill! They soon learned the proper drills, the required rifle exercises, and the essential military courtesies demanded by precise, exacting officers. In addition they discovered the less than friendly noncommissioned officers, who, while they normally played fairly, were the rigid enforcers of military discipline. Overnight military life became much more rigorous and formal.

In addition to training demands, the men soon discovered the less pleasant aspects of the weather in Tsingtau. From April through July and from mid-September through November the weather was reliable and favorable for most activities. But in July the rainy season began and lasted through early September. While the duration was brief, the waterfall (normally about sixteen inches per year) was heavy. During the rainy season the five rivers flowing through the protectorate filled or flooded; otherwise they were dry, sand-filled cuts in the rough terrain.

The major inconvenience, however, was the humidity, which challenged human patience. For many weeks the men experienced the unpleasant problems of breathing and perspiring in a laundry-like environment. Each one also quickly learned about mildew, which spoiled the best leather goods and ruined sensitive items like photographic plates. In view of these problems the officr held many inspections to make certain that weather did not impede preparedness nor cleanliness.

Since the heat often became oppressive, the authorities provided a different training program from the normal routine in Europe. Each day the men started before dawn and moved quickly through their assigned tasks. By 11 o'clock formal obligations ended with lunch and an obligatory rest period. Thereafter, excluding those individuals with special duties such as sentry duty, kitchen details, or punishment tours, everyone was free to follow his own inclinations. The training periods were brief but hard, realistic, and continuous. Meyer-Waldeck, who believed in a constant state of readiness, created a state of preparedness not practiced in many stations of the German armed forces. Sentries for key installations received five live rounds, including one with a shot-gun scatter effect, with instructions to use them. Additionally there were constant alarm drills, all timed with a watch. The losers received extra duties.

The normal training lessons included discipline, arms, tactics, and military courtesy. Beyond these subjects, Meyer-Waldeck insisted on language lessons. which included simple Chinese phrases and place names. As Governor he wanted his men to understand something of the area, its customs, and its people. He insisted on proficiency tests in every endeavor, together with fulsome reports concerning failure. He was a difficult, but, in the eyes of his men, a fair taskmaster.

For instructors Meyer-Waldeck had outstanding soldiers. He relied upon the two traditional groups: the professional noncommissioned officers and the officers. The noncommissioned officers were a highly professional and proficient group. They served in the colonies for long periods, received higher pay than their colleagues at home, earned more rapid promotion, and obtained higher retirement pay. In addition to these advantages, they had better housing, servants, and prestige; they had the pride of greater independence because of distance from Germany; and they had better prospects for civil service positions after leaving the military. After long years of duty together, they were a closely knit, totally competent group with a fine esprit de corps.

The officers, collectively, were less impressive. Unlike the long-serving noncommissioned officers, they served on detached service in the colonies; they would return to their own national regiments rather than continue in the naval infantry. Their commitment, both personal and professional, was not an enduring one. Additionally many served in the colonies because of indiscretions at home, domestic problems, personal curiosity, or eager imperialism. Their reasons were many and, collectively, served to create a high sense of individualism rather than any unifying spirit. Their quality varied a great deal as did their dedication to the job at hand. For garrison duty they possessed sufficient abilities. In time of conflict they could not do as well.

The key official in the protectorate was Meyer-Waldeck, the Governor General of Kiautschou. He was a naval officer, subordinate to the German Minister for the Navy. Under the terms of his assignment he had responsibility for the general management of the executive, judicial, and military affairs in the leasehold. He also supervised all the officers and officials. In sum, he possessed total authority over the entire district. Moreover, the original legislation creating the administration had provided him with an unusual autonomy from Berlin. Behind this unusual centralization of authority was the German naval leadership's desire to create a model colony which was economically prosperous, politically well administered, and militarily useful.

The man who carried this heavy responsibility was Alfred Meyer-Waldeck, the main character in the drama opening in Tsingtau. Born on November 27, 1864, he was the tenth child of the Professor of German at the University of St. Petersburg, Clemens Friedrich Meyer von Waldeck (the title of nobility came from Tsar Alexander II). The father retired when his son was ten years old and moved the family to Heidelberg where he gave private lessons in literature. After two semesters studying history at the University the youthful Alfred joined the navy. His service time was divided between ship's duty and staff work until 1908, when he received orders for Tsingtau. He served as Chief-of-Staff from then until 1911, when he became Governor. Given his lengthy colonial service his remaining time in this position was clearly not very long. He could anticipate an important assignment. In 1898 he had married Johanna Ney, daughter of a Prussian officer, and they had two daughters and one son.

Certainly he was an imposing figure. Standing 1.90 meters with a large, barrel-like chest (he was a superb and enthusiastic swimmer and rider his entire life), and powerful limbs, he obtained prompt attention from everyone under all circumstances. A grey-flecked goatee gave him the appearance of a Russian admiral and offset the gentle blue eyes. He was extremely quiet and reserved, albeit he thoroughly enjoyed small witticisms, intellectual discussions, and social gatherings. His voice was sonorous, direct, and carefully enunciated, the product of a man who thinks about each term before articulating it. When angry, however, the timbre changed abruptly to a gratingly intimidating tone which no one suffered without remembering it. Meyer-Waldeck sought, throughout his lifetime, to control this temper but never fully succeeded. Another significant trait was his devotion to detail. He was almost pedantic in his attention to little things, to responsibility, to correctness, to punctuality. Should any of his subordinates err in such areas, he could expect an immediate sharp rebuke. Meyer-Waldeck did not delay retribution for any delinquency or infraction. Certainly he was open and fair with his subordinates, but they never had the slightest doubt about who was in charge of Tsingtau.

On the military side of his responsibilities, the Governor's authority rested upon his rank, his role as the fortress commander, and his power as the chief military bureaucrat. His extensive staff for implementing these requirements included a general Military Bureau which coordinated the activities of the Governor's personal staff, the Fortification Department, the Mine Department, the Ordnance Department, the Signal and Wireless Telegraph Station, the Observatory, and the Naval Bureau.[8] This structure served as the administrative base for the military organizations.

These forces, built on the III Naval Batallion, consisted of four companies (each with about 210 officers and men), one mounted company (140 officers and men), a field artillery battery (six quickfiring 7.7-cm cannon and 133 officers and men), an engineer company (108 officers and men), and two horse-drawn machine gun detachments (totaling 12 machine guns and 77 officers and men), for a total of some 1300 men. With them was the Fifth Naval Artillery unit with about 750 men. Another 180 men with military requirements were scattered elsewhere.

In addition to these formations, the Governor had some responsibilities for the East Asiatic Naval Detachment. This unit, headquartered in Tienstin, served as protection for the German diplomatic mission and business representatives in China. It had some four infantry companies, each with 100 officers and men, and a machine gun detachment (fourteen machine guns and sixty officers and men).[9] The command of all these forces in addition to the civil authority provided a formidable responsibility for a single man.

The naval infantry battalion and the East Asiatic Naval Detachment contained only land troops, despite the "naval" designation. The duties of the officers and men, the tactical rules, and the service regulations were those of the army. The reason for adopting this peculiar organization came from the structure of the German military system. Since the navy was the Imperial Navy, it came under the Empire. The army, however, belonged to the federal states, each of which controlled its own resources. The political authorities in Berlin feared, therefore, that if the garrison of a military post, especially one in the colonies, were entrusted to the army, there would be administrative complications and tactical confusion. Also the Imperial Diet appropriated funds for troops sent abroad. It was easier to meet this expense via the general naval budget than through individual justifications. The ranks, uniforms, and traditions of the German troops in China were naval; the training and missions were army. This same confusion over control, responsibility, and doctrine permeated the military requirements within the protectorate.

The geography of the Shantung area created some transportation and communication problems for the military leaders. Tsingtau was located at the extreme southwest corner of a long peninsula stretching out into the Yellow Sea. This area ran back toward the east into a massive, craggy, and multifolding mountain termed the Lauschan, with heights reaching above 1,000 meters. Towards the west the ground sloped down to the sea and formed generally parallel lines of heights, the altitude and extent of which decreased in the direction of Tsingtau. These mountains were (1) the line Kaiserstuhl-Litsuner Heights (around 400 meters in altitude); (2) the line Prince Heinrich Hill—Kuschan (100-300 meters); (3) the line Iltis Hill, Bismarck Hill, Moltke Hill (80-200 meters). The mountains were sufficiently rough that any group travel, much less military activity, except along the various roads, was impossible.

Outside the German protectorate the roads scarcely deserved such designation. They were narrow paths of uneven quality which followed the land contours, running through a ravine, dropping into a hollow, or following a dry river bed. For the natives they were difficult, but bearable, for transporting produce and goods. During the dry seasons movement was restricted only by the falling rocks. When it rained, however, the water rushed down from the hills and fields into the depressions, turning them into raging torrential streams within hours. These flash floods halted all movement immediately and further deteriorated the road beds. These deep, sand-bottomed cuts with their straight, steep sides were extremely dangerous should an unwary person be caught in them during a storm.

If a wanderer could reach Tsimo, the travel prospects improved immediately. Tsimo had a population in excess of 5,000 and served as something of an emporium for the surrounding countryside, and therefore as the central point for several good roads. In particular its transportation links with the German-held territory were excellent.

The surrounding fields, planted with potatoes, peanuts, and millet, were flat and well-drained. As a result of this cultivation transport wagons could move over the fields in dry weather. From Tsimo to Tsingtau, and within the protectorate, the roads were excellent and always in good repair.

Other communication means included the railroad, the telegraph, and the cable. The Shantung railway, operated by a German company, ran from Tsingtau to Chinan, where it connected with another system, under German influence, to Tientsin. There were other lines, but all were short and of local interest only. The main line was modern, efficient, and well run.

The telegraph lines ran parallel with the rail lines. There were forty-two offices under Chinese control and forty-eight offices under joint Chinese-German supervision. Since the work force for the telegraph was essentially Chinese, however, the Chinese would have greater influence in time of war.

There were two underwater cable lines; one to Tschu-fu and the other to Schanghai. They were, obviously, most vulnerable to any sea power. As partial support for communications, the Germans had a single wireless station which allowed exchange with other stations in China and with a German station on Yap island.[10]

For the new arrivals these details were interesting, but not as directly important as their individual duty stations. Meyer-Waldeck made certain that each man had ample opportunity to acquaint himself with his various responsibilities in the field, and all the new arrivals soon learned a good deal about Tsingtau's defenses. Many installations possessed a lengthy history.

In 1896 the Chinese had established a naval station in Tsingtau and started constructing a fortress with positions for sea defense. When, shortly afterwards, the Germans assumed control, they found that the former occupants had made amazing progress in constructing various batteries. The Tsingtau Battery, situated on a height at the northwestern promontory on Auguste Victoria Bay, was complete. The Hsiaunwa Battery, on the point southwest of Tai hsi tschen, and the Yunuisan Battery on T'uan tau, were in a half-completed state. Subsequently the Germans finished the latter installations.

Thereafter the Germans had not, surprisingly, undertaken any major construction activity until 1907. At that time, after long discussions, careful investigations, and political intrigue, the various authorities accepted a general construction plan as well as a defensive concept.[11] The financing for new fortification came through a "one-time" seven million marks award by the German Reichstag. This impressive sum was not all that it might seem on paper. It was spread over several years, included some important supply functions (depots and ammunition), and made no provision for inflation. Of the original sum only M2.5 million remained for new construction and most of that went toward the land defenses.

The defenses were, by 1914, essentially complete. They provided a mixed impression for any professional observer. Among the seaward defenses the new Hui tschuen Huk battery was the most impressive installation. It had three modern, quick-firing 15-cm cannon and two 24-cm cannon, which were part of the booty from the Boxer Rebellion of 1900. They were mounted in superb ferroconcrete installations in heavy steel cupolas. This battery also possessed a lift-mounted searchlight for night illumination. On the Bismarck Hill were four 28-cm, modern, carefully emplaced guns. They lost a bit of range from their location but could function against anyone trying to rush the Bay. The old Tsingtau Battery possessed four 15-cm guns of different construction types in open positions. All of them were somewhat antiquated by 1914 gunnery standards, as were the guns in the old Hsiauniwa Battery, four 21-cm guns from the Chinese wars. They were, however, in well-constructed and carefully protected turrets. Scattered along the inner harbor and other key points were seven 8,8-cm guns. Nonetheless, in sum, the sea defenses were understrength, old, and poorly located for modern warfare. There were several uncovered areas where a Naval attacker could avoid defensive fire while bringing his own guns into action. Tsingtau's naval artillery provided nice photographs for a privileged few able to visit the emplacements, sufficient activity for their gun crews, and a powerful image for the uninitiated observer. Realistically they were less potent than they seemed.

The basic defensive organization was toward a land attack by the Chinese. The 1907 agreements called for a string of positions fully prepared for instant occupation without extensive mobilization and able to withstand a direct Chinese assault. Given such instructions and their own available manpower, the engineers in Tsingtau had decided to build the defenses where the tiny peninsula which formed the city broadened out abruptly into the Shantung area. They built a series of five redoubts across this narrow land neck. These installations varied in size and shape because of the terrain's configuration but each one had positions for light field pieces and machine guns. Each one had, as well, a kitchen, bakery, power station, sleeping quarters, ammunition magazines, and other requirements for 180 to 200 men. Trenches, six feet deep, covered, and well-constructed, connected them to each other. They had numerous firing loopholes, which were neatly concealed from external view. Each trench carried painted instructions concerning the troop capacity, various range distances, and miscellaneous combat information.

Some 250 yeards in front of the redoubts was a carefully constructed slope which moved up to an embankment reinforced by a masonry wall three feet thick. This wall was painted white on the redoubt's side, and divided into sectors marked with six foot-high black letters to facilitate artillery ranging and the use of search lights.

At the base of the wall was a ten-foot-wide ditch, running from sea to sea and filled with barbed wire entanglements supported by sharp stakes. The wire was extra strength and the barbs set closely together, making cutting a challenging job for a professional. Their stakes were heavy, imbedded in concrete, and not easily removed. For the roads the Germans had carefully prepared "porcupines," heavy objects of iron and barbed wire, which could be locked into place on short notice.

Forward of this defense line was a rudimentary set of hasty field defenses. They were dominated by Prince Heinrich Hill, a high, crescent-shaped, rough peak dominating the eastern side of the peninsula. From its crown, reached only after a long, arduous climb, an observer had a panoramic view of the surrounding countryside. The neighboring hills would serve as advance strong points, providing an early warning system, and channelizing the advance of any enemy. There were various positions scattered along this line, but there were no plans incorporating them into the defensive operations. It was the natural place for a defense of Tsingtau, but its ten-mile length demanded an extensive military force. Curiously, no one apparently had considered building an installation on the Prince Heinrich Hill.

Throughout this area the soil was rocky and the slopes covered with boulders. There were numerous small ravines (called nullahs) with an average width of thirteen meters and a depth of six to twelve meters.

The Chinese, even with an extensive farming effort, could do little more than survive. They lived in small villages, normally of some 200 stone houses surrounded by stone walls. Certainly they provided no impediment to an army's advance.

In establishing the positions for artillery support the Germans suffered serious deficiencies. The allocated funds simply did not allow the construction of ferroconcrete gun positions nor the acquisition of sufficient modern artillery pieces. The best positions were on Iltis Hill where there were two 10,5-cm guns and six 12-cm guns from the Chinese wars. The latter were not overly trustworthy and often gave a flatulent "pfaff" as they misfired. Moltke Hill possessed two 10,5-cm guns. There were, beyond these pieces, some six old 12-cm, twenty-two 9-cm and twenty-two 3,7-cm cannon scattered about the area. They were stationed in twelve open gun pits. Since the majority were on siege carriages, mobility was difficult at best, and many of the cannon were trophy relics from the 1870/71 war with France. In sum this artillery could provide some noise for morale purposes but could not promise any military support.

The same pessimistic observation held for the entire land defenses. Against a Chinese assault, the defenses were clearly sufficient; against a more formidable army or navy, they were much less impressive. A parsimonious home government did not provide the modern weapons, the required munitions, or the resident manpower for a properly organized defense.[12] Tsingtau was an economic trading post and a tourist rest center, but it was not a formidable military bastion.

On June 2 the *Patricia* arrived again with more replacements— over one thousand sailors for the Asiatic fleet.[13] The new crew members quickly discovered that they had some educational activity ahead of them. Their commander, Graf von Spee, was a well-known figure throughout naval circles. His reputation for responsibility, keen intellect, and strategic understanding was approached by few other naval leaders. Furthermore his high qualitative standards, aggressive spirit, and quiet self-confidence made him a respected commander. Anything less than the best performance from his subordinates put fire into his normally serene eyes and fireworks into his normally temperate tone of voice. He was beloved, respected, and feared.

Spee let his new replacements know immediately about his standards and expectations. They would learn, and learn quickly. But, instead of moving directly to sea for training, as was both his desire and his custom, von Spee had to make the preparations for an unwanted and unexpected visit by Vice-Admiral Thomas M. Jerram, the British commander-in-chief of their China squadron. While the various naval units in Asia exchanged visits fairly often and the leading officers were acquainted with one another, at the moment von Spee had an untrained crew aboard his ships. He found a sudden pleasure call totally out-of-place and highly inconsiderate. Nonetheless, he could not readily decline, and he postponed his departure despite his displeasure over the inopportune call.[14]

On June 12 the British armored cruiser *Minotaur*, flying Jerram's flag, moved into the harbor. She bore visible signs of careful preparation for the visit—the ship glistening clean, the men in spotless uniforms, the equipment in perfect order. After an exchange of salutes the British vessel moved to her designated berth next to the *Scharnhorst* and across from the *Gneisenau*. The Harbor-master had a new flag positioned where the *Minotaur*'s bridge should rest. To everyone's surprise the pilot made the precise location without error; the first time in history for such success. The pilot received a prompt commendation from Jerram.

That afternoon there was an almost continuous exchange of duty calls between Jerram, von Spee, and Meyer-Waldeck. The obligatory visits over, they attended a formal dinner and dress ball aboard the *Gneisenau*. All day the Germans had scrubbed and decorated their ship. They had draped canvas curtains along the afterdeck and created a delightful dance floor with bunting, plants, and electric lights. In response to a local appeal, a goodly crowd of young ladies appeared to make the festivities a grand success. Few noticed that the major supports for the decorations were the turret guns.

The following day the Germans and their guests participated in various sport contests, including foot races, polo, boxing, gymnastics, and a soccer match. For the latter event, which attracted a highly enthusiastic crowd, von Spee had a splendid silver cup for the winner. The contest determined the strength of both sides as well as their respective military strengths and weaknesses. Early in the match the lighter, quicker Germans simply outran their heavier, slower opponents and built up a 3:0 advantage. As the contest progressed, however, the Englishmen overpowered the host group and won the coveted prize, 4:3. Certainly the sporting endeavor reflected the reality of their respective strengths; as von Spee subsequently observed to Meyer-Waldeck.[15]

For those visitors unconcerned with athletics, there were numerous opportunities to visit the city, to use the local beaches, or to make brief jaunts into the hills. These strolls were a favorite pastime for everyone. The local Mountain Association had carefully marked the many trails and paths throughout the hills, using distinguishing paint marks of different colors and combinations. At junctions and prominent points the same group had cut directions into the rock.[16] The visiting sailors made many lengthy walks through the hills. In fact their numbers disturbed the Germans who were not prepared for so many alpinists. On June 14 Admiral Jerram and his senior officers made a day-long automobile excursion into the countryside.

The next day terminated with a grand ball aboard the *Minotaur*. For the Germans it was an impressive affair. Jerram's men had erected a huge striped tent, with Japanese lanterns, wood carvings, and some Pacific native war implements. This spectacular ball was the final official event and Jerram departed the next day with full honors.[17] In the wind fluttered the signal flags of both squadron chiefs, "Live well and goodbye until we meet again."[18]

With the *Minotaur*'s departure, the impatient von Spee hurried his own preparations for sea and left shortly after the British. His mission, in addition to educating the crew, was the showing of the flag throughout the German islands in the Pacific. Sometime in September the squadron would return to Tsingtau. During von Spee's absence Commander Karl von Müller, of the *Emden*, would assume the role of station commander until July 8, when he would leave for Shanghai. In all events, Tsingtau could now revert to its quiet, isolated position, far removed from German and world events.

The people in the city, military and civilian, did exactly that and returned to their normal activities. Into this quietude came the news from Sarajevo on June 29. The cold-blooded murder of the Austrian Archduke, Francis Ferdinand, stirred every European in the city. The majority of them assumed that Austria-Hungary would undertake some counteraction. Nonetheless, while virtually everyone took part in the memorial services, no one altered his accustomed activities.

This peaceful attitude lasted until July 7, when von Spee, in response to the European news, ordered the *Emden* to stay in Tsingtau pending clarification of the European scene. At the same time, von Spee asked von Müller for a careful review of all German naval units in Asia, their precise locations, and their state of preparedness.[19] These instructions did increase the concern of some interested officers but they made no noticeable change in traditional exercises, leaves, or activities.

As the current of news coming from Berlin grew more ominous, von Spee made additional changes in his dispositions. He moved his squadron to the Eastern Carolines without public announcement and asked von Müller to arrange the quiet shift of the few gunboats operating on the rivers of China. They should seek out locations nearer to possible escape routes.

The first general warning for the public came on July 22, when the old Austro-Hungarian cruiser, *Kaiserin Elisabeth*, appeared off the harbor entrance. Clearly her visit was not a courtesy call. The ship, built in 1890 with a displacement of 4,000 tons, was unarmored, and her guns (six 15-cm) were not a serious military threat to any modern naval unit. On paper she could make nineteen knots but her engines were of an age where full speed was a dangerous dream.[20] Her chief purpose was showing the red-white-red flag overseas as a sign of authority and fostering Austrian business activities.

On June 29 the *Kaiserin Elisabeth* had been in Tschifu. She had just completed a long trip, including calls at Hong Kong and at several Japanese ports.[21]

That day the ship's captain, Linienschiffskapitan Richard Makoviz, called his entire crew together and reported the assassination of Franz Ferdinand.[22] Makoviz devoted the next few days to memorial services and to collecting all his personnel from shore obligations. He was, therefore, fully prepared when he received orders on July 21, "Unobtrusively and with economic speed to go to Tsingtau; there to await further instructions." The *Kaiserin Elisabeth* departed the port quietly and without fanfare.

Once at sea, Makoviz ordered the ship's engineers to get as much speed as possible from the old engines. The entire ship soon shook with the unaccustomed strain. Concurrently the crew moved to action stations and practiced their firing exercises with considerable interest and energy. They had not had so much excitement since their original departure. The ship reached the Tsingtau harbor entrance in the late afternoon of July 22, exchanged honors with the local salute gun, and dropped anchor at 6:30 P.M. It had been a fast, exhilarating trip.

Early the next morning Makoviz exchanged visits with Meyer-Waldeck. While Meyer-Waldeck could not add any new facts about European events, he could commiserate with the Austrian, whose ship needed shelter and support against war.[23] With her arrival in port, everyone paid much closer attention to the news dispatches. Certainly the *Kaiserin Elisabeth* was seeking a haven for serious reasons. The next few days would clearly be important ones in their lives.

II

War Is Declared

Und fragt ihr, warum man D. U. sie gennannt?
So woll'n wir die Deutung euch weisen:
Aus "D"eutschlands "U"rkraft nach Asien gesandt,
Das sollen die Zeichen euch heissen.
Im "D"ienst "U"nermudlich, so nennt man sie
Mit Fug wohl und Recht: die D. U. - Kompagnie

Friedrich Blaschke and others[1]

As Governor Meyer-Waldeck prepared for lunch on July 27 an out-of-breath sailor interrupted him waving a sealed envelope as his excuse. Meyer-Waldeck quickly demanded an explanation for such an abrupt intrusion. The apprehensive messenger suggested that the missive should contain the justification. Without a further word the Governor opened and glanced at the paper which contained instructions that he should immediately decipher the message himself. With a terse apology to his table guests and a brief word to the messenger as well, Meyer-Waldeck left the room.

After laboriously deciphering the message, a task which he neither enjoyed nor did very often, he understood the urgency. Austria-Hungary and Serbia had broken diplomatic relations with each other. The Berlin naval authorities warned him that the international situation was uncertain and that he should be on the alert for new developments.[2] Meyer-Waldeck returned to lunch, and, tactfully, said nothing about the interruption to his guests. Afterwards, however, rather than taking his customary rest, he alerted his staff about the message and its significance for them. At the same time, he asked his subordinates to begin quietly looking into their manpower strengths and military preparedness. Should there be a war they would need every possible advance warning and preparation.

Meyer-Waldeck could not know the impact of a European centered struggle on his remote bastion. Nonetheless this isolation made him doubly cautious about the future. Events were moving much too quickly for anyone to gain any perspective, and a sudden coup de main remained a dangerous possibility. Both the British and Japanese had already established their willingness to engage in surprise attacks; an historical fact not lost on the Governor. While there were no immediate foes looming on the horizons, Meyer-Waldeck demanded every professional preparation against all contingencies. He saw no reason for unnecessary risk.

With this strong warning, the staff officers began recalling men on leave in China. They also sent off a message to Lieutenant Colonel Paul Kuhlo, commander of the East Asiatic Naval Detachment in Tienstin, the largest German force in Asia outside the protectorate.[3] Concurrently Meyer-Waldeck ordered the small naval units in the harbor to initiate an informal, but constant, patrol of the harbor's entrance. They should know who came into the harbor and who departed the city. The same instructions went to the Chinese police for the unobrusive control of people visiting the protectorate from the land entrances. As a further precaution, he activated several Chinese secret agents who should investigate popular opinion, new developments, and other matters of German interest among the Shantung residents. He wanted information on the developing situation every place.[4] The Germans were far from the diplomatic scene and easily cut off from home but Meyer-Waldeck wanted to avoid surprise.

While a telegram the following day indicated Berlin's confidence that the political situation would not bring international difficulty, Meyer-Waldeck did not alter his instructions.[5] His normal preciseness, concern for all eventualities, and personal caution precluded any halt in these informal preparations. If nothing else, he thought, the activity provided a useful training exercise. The Governor demanded surveys of Tsingtau's defensive power, potential military situation, and war-readiness. He wanted more information on the number of German nationals in Asia, as well as the location of all

German naval units, pending their possible recall. While Berlin might adjust easily to the fast-changing diplomatic tides, he refused to take any risks for his isolated command.

On July 30 he received a further notification from home announcing the outbreak of hostilities between Serbia and Austria-Hungary. This event intensified the political uncertainties between the other great powers. International conflict was clearly a possibility now. Meyer-Waldeck immediately sent off instructions to Kuhlo, ordering him to prepare for the transfer of his men and their equipment to Tsingtau. At the same time he spoke with Baron Yasumasa Fukuschima, the Japanese Governor of Kuantung, who was in Tsingtau on a long-term study of the German civil administration, about the changing political situation. Fukuschima, together with his staff, had been deeply involved with an investigation of the entire German bureaucratic apparatus. With genuine regret Meyer-Waldeck suggested that the Japanese might return home, pending the resolution of the diplomatic issues. Once the European diplomats clarified the problems and restored order, which he was confident would prove the case, the Japanese could return and complete their activities. Fukuschima agreed immediately and started his departure proceedings. That same evening the two men attended a festive dinner provided by the officers of the garrison, exchanged friendly speeches, and said nothing about their earlier discussion.[6]

For Meyer-Waldeck the party was more difficult than for his Japanese visitor. Throughout that day he had received messages reflecting the deteriorating international situation. The key items were, "Undertake measures for security" and "Immediately bring the East Asiatic Naval Detachment under the pretext of maneuvers to Tsingtau." War was clearly a possibility.

The next day he held an early conference with his civil and military administrators, in which he carefully informed them of the increasing threat of war and the need to avoid offending their departing visitor. They should, nonetheless, continue improving their military resources. A telegram, arriving immediately afterward, reported the imminent prospect of conflict with Great Britain, France, and Russia. Later that same day the Governor learned that the Kaiser had ordered full mobilization for August 2. The news cleared away any uncertainty as to whether Tsingtau should prepare for war or not.

While the direction from which the attack would come remained uncertain, there was now unquestionable purpose to their preparations.

Promptly Meyer-Waldeck undertook several steps to meet the challenge. The first was the immediate security of Tsingtau. He ordered portions of the infantry companies to occupy the five infantry redoubts, small units to be stationed in various observation points, and the general improvement of guard stations everywhere. Additionally he demanded a careful night watch over the city's exits and over Kiautschou Bay. He wanted especially to control the Chinese traffic, which he anticipated as a major concern for the future. They could serve as spies and saboteurs for an opponent with virtual impunity. He knew, as well, that the Chinese provided the essential manpower for his labor force. Finally, he required the completion of a communications system between Tsingtau and several points in the hills. In time of war the colony would be cut off from news of the outside world. The complete system included a series of horse stations and heliographic stations, together with sailors qualified in the use of signal lanterns.[7]

Together with these preparations, Meyer-Waldeck ordered the long-range endeavors for war. The responsible officers made surveys of all installations and started receiving the munitions, foodstuffs, and medical supplies needed for combat. They issued the field equipment, supplementary arms, live ammunition, and field rations to the troops. In the course of their frenetic activity, they discovered that the troops did not have sufficient uniforms, other than their normal white dress. A dye works was quickly established to change the white into green or blue. Finding a standard variety of either color proved impossible; when the dyeing was completed, the troops appeared in several hues. It was the first breach in uniformity of dress, but not the last.

Meyer-Waldeck's second requirement was mobilizing all German troops in China. He issued orders to Kuhlo in Tientsin to bring the East Asiatic Detachment to Tsingtau, sent out the general mobilization orders, and started preparations for receiving the influx of reservists. To accommodate the reservists, he established a reception station in the Bismarck barracks with instructions on assigning the incoming troops. Since the reservists in Asia were under the administrative control of their home military districts, he had no precise way to estimate their numbers. Using a few consular estimates, he proposed a working figure of 500 men.

During these preparations, Meyer-Waldeck complained to his staff that his defensive plans remained highly general, since the specific enemy or enemies remained unknown. But his doubt did not last very long. On August 2 came the news about war with Russia, followed the next day with the announcement of hostilities with France. In both cases Meyer-Waldeck found no cause for undue alarm. The Russians were the only power with troops in Asia, and alone they were not a formidable threat. While they had a sizeable contingent in Vladivostock (the German estimate was an exaggerated 80,000 men) no one believed that the Russian officers would quickly exchange a warm garrison bed for a hard field duty. Likewise the Russians lacked both the material and the understanding for an amphibious operation. They posed no serious threat to the tiny colony. Great Britain and Japan were the countries that might pose a serious threat to Tsingtau, and Meyer-Waldeck did not believe that either of them would go to war.

His erroneous assumption did not last long. On August 4 a telegram arrived with the report that war with Great Britain was imminent. That evening a confirming message arrived. The next morning the British vice-consul, R. H. Eckford, tears in his eyes, visited Meyer-Waldeck and quietly showed him a laconic dispatch from London, "War, ask passport." As a close acquaintance and golfing partner of the Governor, Eckford expressed his genuine regrets over the conflict. He would cherish his long association with the Germans in Tsingtau, he said, whom he hoped to see once more when the unfortunate circumstances were in better order. Meyer-Waldeck reciprocated in like language, indicating that the war was a deplorable tragedy. He wished Eckford every good fortune.

Shortly after the Englishman's departure, the Governor confirmed the news to his staff. Britain's participation increased the precariousness of the protectorate's situation many fold. Given the powerful authority of the British fleet, the availability of colonial troops, and the accessibility of supplies, the British confronted Tsingtau in a much different light than would the French or Russians. Meyer-Waldeck suggested that they must count upon a blockade and a siege. He added a quiet thought that Britain's intervention made Japan's role far more uncertain.[8] They could only prepare for all eventualities and trust to good fortune. His words did not inspire great optimism among his listeners.

The Governor's staff had little opportunity for contemplation. The continuous demands pressing upon them from all directions precluded the time for thought. There were simply too many challenges and action eliminated contemplation. The first major requirement was the mobilization of all available manpower. For the moment the basic concern was moving the East Asiatic Detachment out of Tientsin and safely bringing it to Tsingtau. Part of them were already in the city, thanks to their earlier warning. Meyer-Waldeck had a trustworthy person, Lieutenant Colonel Paul Kuhlo, charged with the responsibility for the movement. Kuhlo, a huge hulk of a man towering well over 6 feet tall and weighing close to 250 pounds, was known as a punctilious, somewhat officious officer among the foreign community. Nonetheless the foreign troops, especially the British, found him great fun on maneuvers, on the parade ground, and on the dance floor. His massive bulk and happy, extroverted social attitudes made him a required guest at all social functions. He was, nonetheless, a meticulous man, with much experience in Asia, who fully understood his precarious position.[9] His first decision was that men were more important than the unit's equipment. He had, somehow, to shift them before the neutral, but constantly alert, Chinese could intern them for the duration of hostilities. He initially favored a sea route, and he alerted the local representatives of the Hapag Lloyd shipping line, who rerouted the steamer *Longmoon* into nearby Taku harbor on July 30. She stood ready as an emergency transport. But, even as the ship made preparations for such service, Kuhlo reversed his decision. The potential entrance of Great Britain into the war would block any water movement in the narrow Tschili Gulf. He must use the land route. The danger with this approach was twofold: (1) the probable Chinese opposition to the movement of armed foreigners through their neutral territory; and (2) the Japanese strong point near Tientsin, which was fully capable of halting their movement. Kuhlo, after careful study, could find no alternative action within the certain time constraints.

When the anticipated orders arrived, from Meyer-Waldeck, to move his troops to Tsingtau, Kuhlo obeyed them with promptitude. He paid no real attention to the instruction concerning the use of informal maneuvers as a cover for the movement; all Tienstin antici-

pated the German departure.[10] Most native opinion maintained that
the Germans would use the *Longmoon*. At 7:00 P.M. on August 31 the
German started a night exercise using different routes. The local
spies watched them march out with light field equipment and
remarked, "On foot, in such equipment, the Germans cannot walk to
Tsingtau."[11] Other men moved all the equipment out a little-used
barrack's entrance or aboard sampans on an adjacent stream. A heavy
rain made the departure difficult for the men, but covered their
movement. They quickly boarded the waiting train, engineered by
Julius Dorpmuller. As he headed the engine down the track, several
German civilians destroyed the nearby telegraph lines.

They reached the outskirts of Tientsin the next morning, well past
possible Japanese interference. Kuhlo, anticipating trouble with the
local bureaucrats, had decided against continuing on as a single body.
He would divide his force into small groups of ten to twenty men. To
his dumbfounded surprise, he learned that the Chinese functionaries
had already approved the rail movement of the armed troops. Their
sole condition, which they set without explanation, was that the
Germans use the rail cars of the North Manchurian Company. This
organization, operated by several unruly Irishmen, who disliked
their British employer, acceded to Kuhlo's request without difficulty. The men quickly shifted trains, picked up some reservists at
Tsinanfu, and hurried to a tumultous reception in Tsingtau on August
2.[12]

In his concern to get his men to Tsingtau, Kuhlo had not had time
to worry about how to move his heavy equipment. In particular the
artillery pieces (three 15-cm howitzers and three 8-cm field guns)
were essential to the Tsingtau garrison. But others were concerned
about saving the guns. The Tsingtau Chief-of-Staff, Captain Ludwig
Saxer, was in Tientsin on personal business when the mobilization
orders arrived in the city. Just before leaving for his duty station he
intervened in the artillery problem. Certainly Saxer did so on his own
initiative. He was the only person who thought about the possibility
of getting the weapons to Tsingtau. He called upon a noncommissioned officer, Otto Prange, who possessed an enviable reputation
for accomplishment. Saxer told the startled Prange that he should
bring the guns and ammunition to Tsingtau and then asked, "When
will the guns be ready for transport?" Slightly overwhelmed, Prange
could barely muster a promise to do his best. He "borrowed" the

twenty-five Austro-Hungarian consulate guards, and they, working forty-eight hours without rest, dismantled the weapons and packed them for travel. They labeled the boxes "machine tools."[13]

Still fearful of discovery, Prange decided to send the howitzers by a different route than the field pieces. But the observant British-French military authorities, anticipating the German endeavor, persuaded the Chinese authorities to shunt the four railway cars with the howitzers off onto a little-used siding. For two days the French and Chinese representatives argued about the ownership of the "tools." Finally, under the guise of shunting the cars to another siding, the Germans, with Chinese cooperation, pulled them on to the mainline. Under full steam they headed for Tsingtau, with the angry shouts of the outraged Frenchmen spurring them on. The latter took some solace in blocking the passage of the field pieces.[14]

As the troops moved into the city, they encountered a surprising human spectacle. Tsingtau teemed with activity like a vast ant hill gone beserk. The mobilization from all over Asia brought an unexpected number of new reservists to Tsingtau by foot, rail, or sea. They came from Korea, Japan, the Philippines, Siam, the Pacific islands, and deepest China.[15] They arrived in strange dress and with an assortment of weapons, ranging from museum pieces to machine guns. The most valuable were the rifles and thousands of bullets for them. Since each man furnished or paid for his own transportation, compliance with the mobilization order was not a simple matter. There was the impetus of the threat of imprisonment for the tardy ones, but there was also every indication of an intense, enthusiastic support among the German community in Asia.

Certainly there were sufficient romantic tales to prove the collective patriotism. One man, Lieutenant Otto Steinbrinck, came from Indo-China with his beard and eyebrows shaven and an artificial pigtail added to give him a dubious Oriental appearance. Together with a Chinese friend, who did all of the talking for the two "businessmen," he reached the city. Five others came dressed as itinerant priests, with long beards and flowing gowns. Their Chinese guide carefully pointed out that their oath of quietude precluded all speech. In almost all cases the arrivals could report an adventuresome occurrence. The enemy searched for them with care, and not all the neutrals allowed them passage.[16] Nonetheless, over 1,000 men streamed into the city.

Normally the new troops came to Tsinanfu first, where the local German rail authorities made a cursory security examination of the arrivals. The latter often seized the opportunity for a last encounter with the prostitutes who had deserted Tsingtau at the first hostile indication.[17] It was indeed a last encounter; for the Germans the next such possibility would be six years in the future. Afterwards they boarded the local train for Tsingtau. In the city they received a loud and enthusiastic reception. A brass band played march music (normally the "Friederikus Rex" or "Alte Kameraden"), followed by welcoming speeches, free beer, and, eventually, the inevitable visit to the reception station. At the station the overworked officials tried to investigate each individual's talent and background before assigning him a position. Many men reported with their civilian friends, asking to stay together. Others belonged to gun clubs, which gave them a claim to unity and an expertise not shared by others. Some had had military training, others had no experience whatsoever. Social relationships suffered as business employees proved senior in military rank to employers. It was a chaotic introduction to military existence. Because of the haste of their induction and their totally unexpected numbers the quartermaster people quickly ran out of uniforms. The result was a potpourri of ill-fitting, strange colored uniforms, which added to the regular soldiers serious qualms about the reservists' qualities.

The human tide coming into the city encountered an equally busy group within Tsingtau. Meyer-Waldeck understood the difficulties accruing from a call-up of all the civil servants, merchants, and able-bodied manpower, even though he had not had any experience in meeting such a contingency. Given the nature of the complex problems he decided on different solutions. Some individuals, in particular those associated with transportation and communication, were not called up at all. Others received mobilization orders, obtained their ill-fitting uniforms, and then returned to their normal occupations.[18] At the end of their working day, they reported to designated points for training and military instruction. In view of their advanced age, increased girth, and general inexperience, they did not present a very threatening appearance. Others simply closed their businesses, giving away their open stock and storing the remainder. It was a carnival spirit for many.[19]

Despite the accelerated municipal tempo, the strange uniforms,

and the uncertain future, there was an exhilaration and purposeful-
ness in this activity. Everyone from the newest arrival, through the
regular soldiers, to Meyer-Waldeck's staff prepared for war without
complaint. There were innumerable tasks for everyone and the
Governor never left any doubt that he wanted everything accomplished within the shortest possible time.

In the area of naval defenses, the outbreak of hostilities caught the
Germans by surprise, their naval units scattered over a wide area.
The *Scharnhorst* and *Gneisenau* under von Spee were en route to
the South Seas. Of the three light cruisers in the squadron, the
Nurnberg, which had been off the Mexican coast, had orders to join
von Spee at Samoa, the *Leipzig* was en route to relieve the *Nurnberg*, and the *Emden* was in Tsingtau for security reasons. The
Emden's captain, Commander Karl von Müller, was the senior station officer in the absence of the senior officers. In time of mobilization, he would assume responsibility for supplying the squadron,
furnishing information for von Spee, and preparing for active operations.

The station craft of the squadron were scattered as well: the
gunboat *Jaguar* was on the Yangtse; the gunboat *Luchs* was at
Shanghai; the gunboat *Tiger* was at Tsingtau, as was the gunboat
Iltis, which was undergoing a major overhaul. Of the river gunboats,
the *Tsingtau* was on the West River, while the *Vaterland* and *Otter*
were on the upper Yangtse. The torpedo boat, *S-90*, was in Tschifu,
preparing for sea. In the Tsingtau repair sheds was the old, unarmored cruiser, *Cormoran*, undergoing a complete overhaul. In
short, at that point in time the naval craft were incapable of coordinated action.

On July 7, in response to the European events, von Spee had
ordered the *Emden* and the *Tiger* to stay in port. As the situation
deteriorated, von Spee instructed von Müller to make additional
changes. The latter complied quickly, shifting the smaller vessels.
The *Vaterland* relieved the *Jaguar* which proceeded for Shanghai,
the *Luchs* departed immediately for Tsingtau, and the *S-90* also
prepared to return to the German colony.

With the arrival of the news of war on July 31, von Müller hurriedly ordered all the vessels home. At the same moment, he took the
Emden to sea as protection against possible entrapment. His com-

mands to all the gunboats went out quickly but they could not comply with equal dispatch.

As the instructions reached Lieutenant Erich von Moller, of the *Tsingtau*, he was tied up next to a British gunboat, the *Teal*. The coded message about probable hostilities placed von Moller in a difficult dilemma. His communications gave him the news ahead of his colleague, whose vessel lacked a wireless set, and the two men had a hunting date the following morning. Moller visited the Englishman, showed him the message, and asked his advice about the next morning. The Englishman responded without hesitation, "We'll go hunting anyhow. Should the worst happen, and war should be declared, give me half an hour to get ready, and then we shall do what is expected of us." They did go hunting, and returned empty-handed to a discussion of international problems over a drink. That evening von Moller slipped away quietly.[20]

On August 3 von Moller, his ship securely tied to a buoy in Canton, told his crew that they could not escape the other British gunboats along the river. They must pack their belongings, leave the ship, and try for Tsingtau. That evening he assembled the crew and spoke quietly, "We are dependent upon ourselves. You know, as well, that we cannot undertake any action against the enemy in our small ship. . . .You should try to get through to Tsingtau. . . .Go with God!" In the early morning hours he bade each man farewell and supervised their departure in small boats. His men escaped detection by the surrounding British and French warships and, three weeks later, somewhat the worse for their trials, they reached Tsingtau. Moller himself set out for Germany rather than following his men. With five companions he crossed the Indian Ocean in a small boat and landed on the Arabian coast. About 200 miles from Constantinople, marauding Bedouins murdered all of them.[21]

The *Jaguar*, under Lieutenant Commander Luring, experienced an equally arduous adventure. With the arrival of the sailing orders, Luring shifted his ship to Shanghai. There he received instructions on July 31 for return to Tsingtau.[22] That evening Luring and two sailors went ashore with great fanfare. He had already surrendered command to Lieutenant Erich Mathias.

Surreptitiously the new captain took on a pilot and drifted the *Jaguar* into the current of the Wangpoo River. Without lights they headed for the open sea. As they dropped their frightened pilot, who had not volunteered for such risky navigation, the apprehensive sailors could see the dim outline of the Russian cruiser, *Askold*. The ship slipped past the cruiser, whose crew's voices were clearly audible. Once at sea with a full head of steam, Mathias ordered full military preparations. The crew feverishly carried ammunition to the guns, sharpened swords, loaded all hand guns, and prepared for action. They disposed of their souvenirs and all combustibles by quietly pushing them into the sea.

Once they lost sight of the land, Mathias brought the *Jaguar* about and started for Tsingtau. The next afternoon, an astonished lookout reported the *Askold* nearby. As the Russian cruiser turned, Mathias ordered two recognition shells fired as a deception. The trick apparently succeeded since the *Askold* moved off without further challenge. Fearful of further difficulties, Mathias moved the *Jaguar* inshore where, with a storm and a mere five meters of water, he felt safer.

The next morning they reached Tsingtau. Suddenly Mathias screamed, "Battle stations!" Moving quickly, the crew manned their stations and implemented his firing directions against an incoming enemy torpedo boat. Just before the order to fire, one observer noticed that the target was really a jagged piece of rock. As everyone exhaled in relief, the Tsingtau pilot hailed them from the other side of the ship; no one had observed his approach! They arrived in the harbor exhausted from the pressures of danger, but happy over their good fortune. [23]

In Tsingtau the naval personnel were too busy to join in the festivities for new arrivals. They obtained immediate assignments to an extensive number of shore installations. The most active at the time was the so-called "Etappe" service.

In 1912 the German naval authorities had created a highly secret organization for active hostilities. Its object was a supply system, using neutral harbors, for naval units. As a "harbor-poor" navy, the Germans fully realized their vulnerability in time of war. Müller, as the senior officer, had already started the necessary machinery to implement the "Etappe" concept. On July 31 he held a major conference with the various ship commanders in the harbor. They agreed to place Lieutenant Commander Fritz Sachse in charge of the "Etappe" agency, to draw up a list of personnel freed from the demobilized gunboats for use on auxiliary cruisers, and to help with the establishment of other "Etappe" centers in Asia. Müller could do little more than establish these guide lines. Under the official regulations governing the "Etappe" (the mission was the dispatch of coal and supplies to predetermined points for von Spee), he could do no more until Berlin declared a state of imminent danger of war. At that time he would have sufficient authority to command ships.

With the arrival of the message that conflict was indeed inevitable, Sachse moved quickly. He supervised the rapid reconditioning and loading, with drinking water, provisions, and general supplies, of the steamers, *Gouverneur Jaeschke, Longmoon, Markomannia, O.I.D. Ahlers, Staatssekretar Kratke, Senegambia, Frisia*, and *C. Fred. Laeisz*. They soon had 19,000 tons of coal, 120 tons of machine oil, and a massive amount of other supplies for von Spee's squadron.[24] The activities supporting these efforts filled the entire port with the hastily improvised preparations.[25] Sachse had all the directions for starting his service, but no plans for the necessary methods of accomplishing the charge. That he did so so quickly and efficiently amply testified to his ingenuity, persistence, and *Emden*, because of von Müller's fears of entrapment, put to sea during the evening of July 31. He set out for the shipping lane from Nagasaki and Vladivostok. On August 4 the *Emden* came upon the Russian steamer, *Rjasan*, of 3,500 tons. Following a brief exchange, von Müller put a prize crew aboard his captive and headed back for Tsingtau. The two vessels slipped quietly into port on August 6. After a hasty discussion with Meyer-Waldeck, von Müller ordered the *Rjasan* placed into commission as an auxiliary raider, renamed *Cormoran*.[26]

At the same time the mail steamer *Prinz Eitel Friedrich*, which had arrived in Tsingtau from Shanghai on August 1, completed her outfitting as an auxiliary cruiser. Lieutenant Max Thierichens, from the *Luchs*, ussumed cmmmund. She left Tsingtau, together with the *Emden*, shortly before dark on August 6 for a rendezvous with von Spee's units. The new *Cormoran* followed on August 9, the last vessel out of the harbor.

Left in the port and placed at Meyer-Waldeck's disposal were the *Jaguar* and the *S-90*. In addition the *Kaiserin Elisabeth* was still there, and, despite her highly uncertain role, Captain Markovz insisted that he would support the Germans. The lack of any official statement from Vienna placed him in a highly confusing position.

With such a limited force, Meyer-Waldeck had to rely completely upon his land-based defenses against sea assault.

These installations were in good repair, giving the defenders some cause for confidence. They were in closed, reinforced concrete and bomb-proof installations with sufficient splinter-proof shelters for everyone. The single weakness of the sea batteries was the Hai hsi peninsula, where the Germans had no fortifications. The earlier parsimonious attitude in Berlin had precluded any construction, thereby making the city vulnerable from the opposite shore. While this shore was also subject to German gunfire, it was still a readily accessible base for enemy guns and observation points for enemy naval units. The various inlets and bays behind the hills of the peninsula, itself provided superlative firing areas for heavy ships. From them the battleships could lob shells into Tsingtau with little interruption. It was the Achilles heel of the defenses.[27]

When the mobilization orders arrived, the naval artillerymen quickly and effortlessly occupied the batteries. They possessed the confidence created by much practice. Once they had shifted into their new stations, the officers started the required improvements for war. The first step was establishing security. Meyer-Waldeck quickly ordered tighter security control over the harbor entrance. Earlier he had darkened the city lights visible from the sea. Now he demanded the removal of the buoys, floating lights, and all navigational markers. His men established a floating barrier that closed off the entrance completely. To accompany this action, the minelayer *Lauting* put down a mine field across the harbor entrance, and, together with several smaller boats, took up watch positions. As observers an officer, Lieutenant Paul Cordau, and two men took up quarters in the tiny police station on Cape Jaeschke. They had signal lamps and carrier pigeons for communication and sufficient supplies for several weeks.

Once the artillerymen completed their portion of these chores, they found themselves assigned new obligations. The first was the destruction of possible marking points for enemy naval guns. They labored day and night in removing the lighthouses along the coast, the visible signal and flag masts, and the unusual smoke stack or tower. While they could not get rid of every one, they did destroy all except the most essential installations. They also tried to create a single color tone along the entire seacoast. Here they planted all the available trees and bushes, emptying all the nurseries in the process. Where such plantings were impractical, they dynamited the exposed area or simply painted it green.[28] Beyond that the troops filled sand bags, strung miles of barbed wire, and practiced firing exercises.

The gunnery practice, under the guidelines imposed by the threat of real war, confirmed an earlier voiced fear. The artillery stations were not in the best locations, nor did they possess sufficiently modern weapons. If the enemy had modern battleships, he would remain outside the German range and drop his shells on the city without interruption. This sudden revelation supported an idea expressed earlier by several gunnery experts that the sea defense guns should be available for use against a land foe. Only Bismarck and Hsiauniwa could fire in both directions. A rapid survey indicated that the other batteries could fire against land targets, but that the Iltis and Moltke hills were in the way. After further study, the responsible officers under Commander Boethke determined the flight paths for each gun's shells. They quickly divided a map of the city and the protectorate into minutely delimited grid squares. This simple method furnished the basis for all subsequent artillery firing tables and observation activity in Tsingtau. Once the gun crews learned about the possible patterns for their guns, they quickly adjusted the gun carriages to allow their pieces a better field of fire. While the job was not complicated the work was hard. Once the men had completed their labor, Boethke supervised a controlled firing exercise which proved that the guns could fire on land targets if they exercised some care. This discovery improved the defensive possibilities and general morale.[29]

In sum the sea defenders were confident of their position. Their guns were more accurate and possessed better observation than any ship-based weapons. With the two known limitations, the neighboring inlets and the range difficulty, they could keep any enemy at bay.[30]

For the land defenses, Meyer-Waldeck was less certain about his resources. To be sure, he did have the experiences from a detailed war game held in November 1913. At that time the civil authorities responsible for the construction work had transferred control of the infantry defenses to the military leaders. After the exercise the civilians had answered, in fulsome detail, all the complaints raised by their military colleagues over the various construction deficiencies.

Meyer-Waldeck had scheduled another war game for November 1914 as a means of finally solving the unreconciled issues. In view of the detailed positions advanced by all the participants, the various commanders possessed extensive knowledge of the fortifications in terms of their strengths and weaknesses.

The five infantry works were modern, well-appointed, and defensible installations. Their major limitations involved the open areas in front of them, their communications with each other, and their vulnerabilities to sea bombardment and to observation from Prince Heinrich Mountain. The fortifications were not impregnable. Moreover, they lacked the connecting trench systems, the closed, protected, forward gun posihimns, the proper advanced observation posts, the illumination equipment for night operations demanded by modern warfare.

Even more serious was the curiously serrated terrain, resulting from Chinese cultivation of the inhospitable soil. The farmers, in terracing the area, had created a goodly number of hiding places for an attacker. A further complication was that the fields of fire from each work did not overlap each other, allowing an observent opponent many advantages.[31] With these disturbing obstacles, Meyer-Waldeck simply ordered all necessary adjustments, changes, or additions completed by August 21. He allowed three weeks for satisfying the requirements of war, by any standard a short time. Still, with proper manpower, the governor hoped that he might mount a professional defense.

They possessed the normal complement of men for the garrison (108 officers, 2990 men) in the five companies, the Naval Asiatic Detachment, the engineer company, and the mounted naval artillery (termed the riding mountain navy by the citizens), together with a few related units. With them was the growing reserve influx (a group which eventually would total 76 officers and 1400 men). The latter served as replacements and as the basis for two new units, the sixth company and a unit of comparable size for general duty, the Seventh. In the former were a conglomerate group of people—the members of some paramilitary organizations in China, the Tsingtau gun club, and various other associations. They were men with useful civilian skills and experiences, most of whom had had some contact with military life.[32] The seventh company, which functioned more as a general reserve, contained men with military experience and understanding.

They were somewhat older, and untrained as a unit, but they could give a good account of themselves.

While each redoubt commander received orders as to improving his own installation, Meyer-Waldeck insisted upon general changes along the entire line. Captain Ernst Soldan, commander of the engineer company, directed this endeavor. He was a short, wiry man with a reputation for physical fitness, personal decisiveness, and unique knowledge. Each day he reported to Meyer-Waldeck about the day's activities since the governor wanted precise knowledge of these changes. He would not delegate this portion of his command function. The man in general charge was Lieutenant Colonel Friedrich von Kessinger who had control of the land front. Kessinger was not beloved by the troops because of his harsh demeanor, his personal distance, and his unforgiving attitude. He refused promotion to anyone who had the slightest tarnish on his record, and he was quick in meting out punishment for minor infractions. The troops seldom encountered the difficult von Kessinger, but they saw the active Soldan a good deal.

The initial decisions concerned the general defensive omissions pointed out by the 1913 study. Here Soldan and Meyer-Waldeck decided that they would concentrate their labors rather than spread them out along the entire line. They started with the right flank because it was most vulnerable to sea bombardment; if naval guns ever opened fire the Chinese labor force would disappear overnight. They also hoped that they might better sustain the proper development of a transportation and communication system for the defensives by using a single starting point; i.e., the vulnerable right flank.

The general construction program included several new developments. The work parties expanded the barbed wire and carefully integrated its use into the defensive plan, producing a veritable sea of the heavy wire. At every fifty meters the engineers put in contact wires which, when moved, rang bells or horns in key locations. They also rigged automotive lamps to give a sudden blast of light when someone crossed the trip wires. Throughout the planners carefully coordinated every aspect of their plans to assure a carefully integrated and controlled system.[33]

In order to maintain proper fields of fire, Soldan supervised the leveling of several wooded areas in front of the defenses. The troops cut the trees off close to the ground, sharpened the stumps, and wrapped barbed wire around them. For the same reasons, after lengthy staff discussions, Meyer-Waldeck approved the destruction of two Chinese villages which were in the way. The Germans removed the natives, overruled all protests, paid the owners for their estimated lossss, and burned everything.[34]

As they cleared the ground, the engineers laid an extensive mine system along the front. The mines included a wide variety of sizes, ages, and reliability, but all the available mines were presssd into service. There were few optimistic thoughts about their success. The authorities had known about the deficiencies for some time but had planned for a comprehensive mine renewal in 1915. As a resupt of these mangled plans there was a shortage of fuses (as well as the experts to adjust them), inadequate casings, and limited powder supplies. Substitute materials were in short supply. But, since there was still an adequate Chinese work force and a superabundance of dynamite, Soldan created various simple designs for expedient construction. They produced some 500 land mines, weighing from twenty to fifty kilograms. Suspecting that the Chinese would reveal the locations, the Germans did all of the planting themselves. Given the rocky soil, the long carrying distance, and the numerous manpower demands for other tasks, the labor was arduous.[35]

Behind the front, Soldan's men carefully supervised the hasty construction of trench lines and the hurried erection of nine blockhouses between the five redoubts (three between the water on the right flank and the first redoubt—one each in the next three intervals, two between works 4 and 5, and one between the latter and the bay). The blockhouses, housing a minimal dozen men, were small, half-buried in the ground, carefully camouflaged, and connected with adjacent trenches for a circular defense. The strongest one was the first one, facing toward Fouschanso Bay. Between them and the redoubts were lookout towers, of which about one foot projected above the ground line. Because of the general fear about an amphibious landing, the engineers put some energy into the installation, for which the sixth company then assumed responsibility. They extended the barbed wire entanglements into the water well beyond the low tide mark, planted mines, and created, within the assigned time limits, an impressive fort.[36]

Along with these limited strong points, the defenders added some eighteen batteries from various sources, including training pieces,

ships' guns, the Tsientsin howitzers, and four old 8,7-cm guns which
had served for salute purposes since the original occupation. For
some of these guns there were positions, carefully dug in with
concrete or stone revetments; for others there were hastily built field
positions which inspired little confidence. The artillerymen began
assembling a railway battery as a further surprise for the enemy.
They placed two 8,8-cm guns on a railway flat car, which an engine
could then pull into position. The gun crews could only fire the guns
one at a time, since a full broadside threatened everyone's safety.

The engineers managed various permanent covers for the ammunition, but they did not do as well for the guns. A professional land
siege could lead to a serious threat from enemy counterbattery
activity. Eventually the Germans assembled some ninety guns on the
land front, most of them small calibers. As a partial deception to an
opponent, they constructed several false guns and positions from
wood, straw, and stove pipe.[37]

With all of this new construction activity, Soldan did not forget the
key problems of communication. He supervised the distribution of
wires throughout the fortification zone. These lines went forward to
several observation posts in front of the barbed wire and then connected the redoubts, block houses, and observation points in the
main resistance line. With these links were other wires going back-
wards to command centers. Because of the haste to lay the wire, no
one could properly inspect the wire's quality nor its waterimpervi-
ousness. Since the troops could not bury all of it in the rocky terrain,
there were numerous breakdowns.[38] Meyer-Waldeck could ask no
more of Soldan, who, like his men, worked fourteen-hour days to
accomplish what they could before the scheduled deadline.

As additional information collectors, Meyer-Waldeck possessed
two balloons and two Rumpler Taube aircraft. They had arrived in
Tsingtau only a few weeks before the alert. For the balloons the
defenders had great hopes at first. The engineers had built a splendid
hall for the big "yellow sausage" or "floating watchtower," as the men
termed them. After completing the construction and running out the
cable to 1200 meters, they had discovered that the location was a poor
one. Thereafter they had shifted the balloons about, looking for a
better, albeit protected, spot. They finally concluded that there was
no satisfactory place and that the observer could not see into all the
corners of the protectorate. While all the maneuvers went off well,

the pessimists pointed out the lack of opposition. The garrison must rely upon the aircraft.

Few people believed that the rickety aircraft could accomplish much in Tsingtau. The narrow area for facilities, the unpredictable air currents, and the harsh terrain augured ill for the miniscule airforce. Because of the space concerns the engineers built the hanger on the Iltis sport ground, where all the sports events, horse racing, and garrison group activities took place. It was some six hundred feet long and two hundred feet wide, filled with uneven places, and surrounded by hills. The field might qualify as an emergency airfield in Germany, but no more.

The unsuitability of this location for aircraft received vivid confirmation when Lieutenant Friedrich Müllerskowski started off for his first flight on Augush 2. It was late afternoon and the other pilot, Lieutenant Gunter Plüschow, warned him about the faulty air currents. Müllerskowski took off anyway, cleared a small stand of trees at the end of the runway, and then apparently panicked. He pulled the aircraft up too high, and it turned over, crashing into the ground from a height of some forty meters. The aircraft was a total loss, and Müllerskowski, suffering from multiple fractures, was in the hospital for a long stay.[39] With one pilot out of commission, all the pressure was upon Plüschow.

He was an unusual man with iron nerves, extreme self-confidence, professional experience, and an incredible joy in living. His energy, decisiveness, and optimism won him the love and respect of everyone. He rented a villa next to his aircraft, acquired an automobile and several animals, and quickly became the city's star social attraction. His aircraft was new, but scarcely practical for the Asian environment.[40] The Taube was a strange craft, looking more like a da Vinci sketch than an operational machine. In view of his aircraft's needs and general appearance, the Chinese coolies nicknamed Plüschow "The Bird Master of Tsingtau." The unusual wing construction gave the aircraft a strong resemblance to a bird in flight. He provided Tsingtau's hope for observation over the protectorate.

In spite of all these developments and adjustments, Meyer-Waldeck faced the additional problems of a possible siege. A pitched battle would have been a much less complicated affair. He had to investigate the state of preparedness, organize his resources, and decide upon their effective employment. Such activity demanded much attention and care, since the knowledge of military resources in the protectorate, was, despite some exceptions, not good.

The Governor set out to clarify this uncertain issue with his normal exactitude. As a first step, at July's end he created a new command structure for the defenses. All responsibility and final authority rested in his office. Lieutenant Colonel von Kessinger assumed control over the land defenses. To direct the city itself in both civilian and military matters, Meyer-Waldeck selected a naval officer, Captain Wilhelm Timme.

In order to give these men sufficient authority he proclaimed, on August 1, martial law. With this declaration he could close the port, mete out serious punishments for various crimes, and more precisely control the population.[41] The extralegal powers, likewise, permitted a realistic survey of the military resources available for the defense. Officials could investigate business records, inventories, and warehouses without using peacetime legal regulations.

Many surprises came from these studies. The first was not a pleasant one: there was a most serious shortage of shrapnel shells, the most effective artillery weapons against advancing infantry. None of the guns had an even remotely sufficient supply. Each of the big guns on Bismarck Hill had twenty shells, while those on Hsiauniwa possessed five.[42] There were more explosive and armor-piercing shells, but they too were insufficient for a lengthy action. As a partial substitute, the reserve ammunition stores from the fleet were available, since von Spee's ships would not be able to use them. But this welcome addition to the supplies was not without a price, since the firing rings on the large-caliber shells were about 2 millimeters too thick, and would not pass into the tubes of the land guns. Also the equipment for unloading the shells was not available, and the munitions depot personnel were forced to file the rings by hand, a dangerous undertaking. For the smaller-caliber shells they had a single apparatus for the retooling process. The personnel used it on a twenty-four hour basis, with resultant breakdowns.

Together with these changes the depot people emptied the training shell casings and filled them with new powder drawn from the fleet's stores. The naval powder was of better quality than that ashore and burned faster, thereby making the firing tables approximate rather than realistic. It was some time before the artillerymen discovered this error.[43]

An equally serious concern, of a somewhat different nature, was the money supply in the protectorate. As the news of imminent war reached the citizens, many merchants halted credit, raised prices precipitously, and began hoarding their supplies. Even more threatening was a furious run on the Deutsch-Asiatische Bank. The frightened Chinese depositors demanded full payment in Mexican dollars. The Bank's efforts to pay them in bank drafts or in the normally acceptable "silver shoes" failed completely.[44] Confronted with this inexhaustible demand, the Bank put out guards and curtailed its working hours. Fortunately it could obtain the needed funds through its affiliates in Tsinanfu, Tientsin, and Shanghai, as well as through the funds deposited by incoming reservists.

After some frantic days, reports filtered back into the city retelling horrible stories of robbers who seized the silver, withdrawn from the bank, often killing the owners in the bargain.[45] This news quickly sobered the populace and slowed withdrawals until they ceased altogether. For the administration this change was extremely important, because it reflected the renewal of popular trust, provided a supply of liquid funds for purchasing supplies, and removed the most serious threat of general panic.

The money saved went into prompt circulation, as the Government's concerns over transportation and communication required substantial funds. Few people, Chinese or European, with whom the government did business were interested in promissory notes. The first efforts in transportation and communication came easiest. A number of skilled buyers hurried into the hills and purchased all the ponies and mules they needed from native handlers. While the prices rose appreciably, they did not exceed the official estimates. As the animals descended upon the city, the owners surrendered them to experienced reservists whose civilian experience had included animal tending.

More significant to the defenders were the vehicles in the city. The Government reached rental agreements with the automobile owners in the city, requisitioned all bicycles, confiscated all gasoline supplies, and shifted all of these vehicles and supplies into a military motor pool.[46] Of particular value were four trucks, one of them discovered by accident still crated on the pier, which served as the major transport means. All the vehicles were promptly brought into service for command purposes, shifting supplies, carrying wounded, and scouting missions. Again the Government employed reservists who were auto mechanics in their civilian occupations. They brought their own equipment and tools, made a careful inventory for the bureaucratic records, and started work.

The communications issue was not resolved as easily as the transportation question. They were certain to be cut off from Berlin. MeyerWaldeck realized that the protectorate was vulnerable in this area and gave Captain Waldemar Vollerthun full authority over it. Vollerthun was Chief of the Kiautschou Office for the German Navy in Berlin. He had started for home after completing a three-month stay in July, but now he had a much different assignment. As expected the British interrupted the two cable lines. On August 14 the British cable ship *Patrol* picked up the Shanghai cable and, not long afterward, found and cut the Tschifu link. German information sources would be less reliable in the future.

Vollerthun sought various solutions. Initially he created a secret mail system, in conjunction with the Chinese authorities, for transporting letters in and out of the protectorate. The system involved a long series of foot messengers who moved along the railway, transferring their missives secretly. The trouble with this idea was that the Chinese were uncertain of their role in a nonneutral action, their loyalty was highly suspect, and the system demanded a sophisticated control mechanism beyond the grasp of the participants. While some communications passed along this route—most of them in hollowed-out bamboo stalks—the service did not repay its required human and economic investment. [47]

From the very beginning, however, Vollerthun understood that the wireless was his sole hope for effective communication with the outside world. He arranged initially, through the help of the German military attaché in Peking, Captain Rabe von Papenheim, for the use of the official Chinese station in Peking. But this arrangement did not prove successful, since the Chinese would not fully cooperate. They could not decide the question of their neutrality. An agreement with an American professor, Fuller, in Tientsin failed for the same reasons. The best solution was with the small coastal steamer, *Sikiang*, in Shanghai. As luck would have it, she had a new wireless aboard for delivery to the Chinese. Since they had not completed the transaction, the Germans took it for their own use. The *Sikiang*, using English as a guard against possibly offending their hosts, transmitted all the world's news to Tsingtau.[48]

For military information Vollerthun worked closely with the various police administrators in the protectorate. He found that the customs agents, German and Chinese, worked well together. Through them, he established an intricate system of clandestine agents throughout Shantung. Their chief locations were Lungkou, Tsimo, along Lauschon Bay, and in the British possession, Weihaiwei. The reports came by foot messengers, who used little-known mountain paths, small boats which drifted along the coast, and carrier pigeons.[49] From these diverse sources Vollerthun provided his superiors with an amazingly precise and continuous flow of information on events in Shantung, China, and the world.[50]

The chief function of Timme, who was in charge of the city, was the compilation of a food survey. He was able to report a pleasant discovery—there were sufficient supplies for at least six months. To make doubly certain, however, Timme's staff began purchasing all the straw, hay, nonperishable foodstuffs, cattle, pigs, and so on, in the protectorate. His office also assumed the responsibility for halting, on August 1, the American merchantman *Hanametal*, bound for Vladivostok with a mixed cargo of cattle, cement, and Chinese passengers. The officials bought the cattle at the market price.[51]

Most of the livestock purchased from citizens lacked space and sufficient protection against the elements. Timme, in addition to serving as a purchasing agent, then became a rancher. He quartered his livestock in and around the municipal slaughterhouses. In view of their hurried acquisition he was not surprised that hoof and mouth disease broke out almost immediately. But he was mystified, as was the harried naval veterinarian, by the sudden departure of the disease. Timme acquired sufficient foodstuffs to increase the reserve supplies for a year.[52] No one would go hungry.

Throughout these hurried military preparations the most noticeable change in the city itself was the quickening tempo of activity. When the European news arrived in Tsingtau, the city was filled with vacationers from all over Asia. The hotels were full, the bathing beaches were occupied, und the few pleasure spots were doing a thriving business. But, as the threat of hostilities grew, the tourists emptied the hotels in their rush for home or their reserve stations.

The few French nationals (about thirty) sold their business interests with little personal loss and left almost immediately after the Archduke's murder. There were very few Russians (approximately fifty) in the city. In fact, Kropatscheck, a German who served as the acting Russian consul in Tsingtau, gave up his official position in favor of his German mobilization assignment. The fifty British nationals stayed on, hoping that the war clouds would blow away. Meyer-Waldeck assured them that, if they took an oath not to bear arms against Germany, they could remain indefinitely without fear of reprisals. But on the day before hostilities the British departed for China or Japan, at great personal financial loss.[53] Throughout this activity the Japanese watched with keen concern, but did not sell off their holdings. They did not purchase any of the sale properties, either.

The most obvious response to the impending war came from the Chinese. In addition to removing their savings, they fled the city in large numbers. They mobbed the train station and seriously impeded the incoming reservists. At first the rail officials instituted special trains in an effort to expedite the departing crowds. Then they reversed their cooperative attitude and, under strict orders from Meyer-Waldeck, initiated strong controls through restricted ticket purchases. The refugees were part of the city's labor force, and their massive departure threatened the work base.

The first suggestion for preventing the workers' departure was the erection of concentration camps. Meyer-Waldeck turned it down. While part of his reasoning was humane, he also suggested that proper work opportunities combined with high wages assured greater productivity than did any compulsory hotel. Therefore, he directed the creation of a central work office with one branch in the Market place, and the other in Taitungtschen. These offices arranged all work assignments, conditions, and wages. Wages increased geometrically until they stabilized at 50 cents for laborers, 75 cents for craftsmen, and 10 cents for all meals. There was a 10 cent per head reward for the labor contractors. These wages, combined with the bank's payment of its obligations and the lack of open hostilities, brought the frightened Chinese back to their jobs. They insisted, nonetheless, on prompt payment. For the majority this meant settlement at noon and at night. Others received immediate payment. The coal carriers carried their coal buckets on bamboo poles up one side of a ship, dumped them into the hold, and collected their copper coins on the way back. These measures kept the work force intact.[54]

In such ways the bastion and its garrison made ready for war. The exhilirating activity, the ever-evolving international situation, the constant adjustments charged the atmosphere. For the new arrivals the passing days and weeks blended into a wild melange of overlapping images. The Tsingtau which they had observed from the *Patricia* was gone. In place of a toy-like green forest, storybook mountains, and colorful block houses was a grim fortress, foreboding in its strength.

No one escaped the frenetic activity. In the few free hours the men crowded into hotels and taverns. The uniforms with their many colors and curious fittings, clothed a motley crowd. The men's different physical shapes, diverse ages, and varied bearings reflected their mixed military heritage. The sole common denominators were their enthusiasm and their fantasies.

The news from home was of victory after victory. Supposedly America's neutrality assured Tsingtau's security, since the British would undertake no action threatening that country. The Japanese, in the German view, counted for little. In fact, the universal prediction was a general peace by Christmas. Many men volunteered for special leave in order to get back to Germany before the peace ended hostilities. If a new telegram arrived, the messenger quickly sprang onto a nearby chair or table and shouted, "Quiet! Information from home!" Then in the immediately tomb-like quiet, he read his report. Normally the listeners followed the reading with three "hurrahs," a verse from "Deutschland über Alles," and a rapidly raised beer glass.

The exhilaration was, of course, collateral with wild rumors, unreal dreams, and colorful theories. Many self-created experts preached authoritatively to attentive audiences on America coming to their aid, on Japan's certain neutrality, or on an all-out British assault. These dreams, written in air, helped spawn additional notions which moved from club and bar through the barracks to the defensive works. The channels for such thoughts, narrow and ill-defined, precluded any official dam; the rivulets of the mouth quickly found a new channel. The stories were believed, disbelieved, discarded, recreated.[55] Throughout this strange world of make-believe, however, the key concern, sometimes mentioned, sometimes a major theme, sometimes muted, was of Japan's attitude. Everyone was concerned, no one knew the answer.

Almost everyone assumed that Japan would remain neutral. The reports of Japanese reaction to departing German reservists, the Japanese newspaper accounts of German victories in Europe, the mutually satisfactory military cooperation, and the long-term friendly relations between the two states provided grounds for optimism. There was, likewise, a general belief that the Japanese could not involve themselves in a major war because of economic problems. But, on August 7, Meyer-Waldeck received a report that his just-departed guest, Baron Fukushima, was in Harbin, discussing diplomacy with the Russians. The message, from trusted sources in Mukden, suggested that the two parties were talking about spheres of interest in China as well as a Japanese assault on Tsingtau.[56]

For Meyer-Waldeck the news was highly disturbing and confusing. He promptly sent out pleas for information on Japan to the German consulates in Yokohama, Kobe, Schimonosecki, and Nagasaki, as well as to the embassy in Peking and consulate in Shanghai. The answers, returned as promptly, reflected a general fear that the Japanese intended war, without any proof for this supposition.[57] At something of a loss concerning the Japanese position, Meyer-Waldeck sent Vollerthun to Peking. The latter found the German representatives positive that "Japan, under all circumstances, would make Tsingtau a casus belli. . . ."[58]

Even as Vollerthun started back for Tsingtau, other events changed the optimistic German attitudes. The small Japanese colony, about 250 persons, abruptly began closing their businesses and started moving out. Their bank closed without warning, and the staff disappeared with the funds. Throughout Asia the Japanese press abandoned its pro-German position in favor of a highly anti-German stance. The editorials angrily recounted German transgressions against Japanese citizens and retold the history of German sins against Japan.[59] They underscored the dangers to Japan of a German naval squadron in Asia, the problems of von Spee's squadron for the Anglo-Japanese alliance, and the continuing uncertainty of German designs in the Pacific.

New reports from consular agencies in Japan added new details on Japanese intentions. They recounted ship movements, troop concentrations, and travel restrictions. A still uncertain Meyer-Waldeck dispatched the much-traveled Vollerthun to Tokyo in search of final clarification. But the latter only reached Tsinanfu to find a telegram ordering him back to the city.[60] There was no longer much doubt concerning the immediate future.

The expected note had reached Meyer-Waldeck on August 16 in a terse telegram from Tokyo, summarizing the Japanese demands. They simply asked that all German warships withdraw from Chinese and Japanese waters and that Germany surrender its entire protectorate, without condition or compensation, by September 15. The deadline for a response was August 23. A copy of the text followed shortly thereafter.[61] The Governor called an immediate staff meeting and reported the demands. He decided in favor of suppressing the news for two days, pending clarification. At the same time, there was no question concerning their response to the Japanese demands. They had another eight days for their military preparations, which would be helpful. There was no disagreement from Meyer-Waldeck's staff.

Besides discussing about their now more difficult circumstances, Meyer-Waldeck wanted to make a ringing public statement reflecting his determination and strength. There were many rumors about German efforts to return the Kiautschou district to China. With the concurrence of his staff, the Governor then sent a terse message to the Emperor, "I guarantee the utmost fulfillment of duty." That could leave no doubt concerning his position.[62]

The response from Berlin was prompt and equally direct. On the next day the naval authorities at home dispatched a succinct, "His Majesty has ordered the defense of Tsingtau to the bitter end."

On August 23 the period allowed for a response by the Japanese ran out. It was a Sunday, and the church services—the Protestants in the Bismarck Barracks and the Catholics on the Iltis Platz—attracted goodly crowds. Meyer-Waldeck appeared at both ceremonies. At the end the Protestants sang "Ein feste Burg ist unser Gott," while the Catholics concluded with "Herr mach uns frei." Immediately afterward the bells of the Christ Church sounded the end to both services.

Afterwards Meyer-Waldeck had two proclamations distributed in the city. One of them was directed towards the general public. Its tenor was best rendered in a sentence, "If the enemy wants Tsingtau, he must come and take it." The Governor exhorted the peoples' love of their area and their obligation to emulate their heroic countrymen at home. The second, which included some of the same paragraphs, went to the troops. It reflected his determination and called upon the men to remember the heroes of their glorious past and to do their best.[63]

At the same time his messages were being circulated, Meyer-Waldeck revealed the text of a message from home. It said, "God be with you in the difficult struggle. I think of you, Wilhelm." Their position was clearly not an enviable one.

III

The Japanese Land

Die Zeit verging, es kam der Krieg, der Deutschland
   sollt vernichten.
Für Tsingtau gab es keinen Sieg, nur eisenharte Pflichten.
Stolz lauschten wir im fernen Land der Heimat Rumestaten,
Doch deckten auch den gelben Sand viel junge Seesoldaten.

Friedrich Blaschke[1]

The terse note from the Kaiser reflected the exposed, vulnerable
position of the German garrison. They were thousands of miles from
home. The homeland was at war with three formidable opponents
and could not provide any help. In Tsingtau there had never been
adequate military preparations for a major struggle. Given these
realities, there could be no doubt concerning the result of the coming
battle. At best the troops could give a good account of themselves,
but they could not hope for success. They could maintain their
military honor, tie down enemy forces for as long as possible, and
pray for an early end of the European war. Clearly they had no reason
for optimism.

Still, the Japanese ultimatum cleared up the Germans' uncertainty, eliminated the rumor mills, and identified their foe in a single
moment. The generalized plans against all possible foes could now be
adjusted and concentrated on more concrete dangers. Meyer-
Waldeck fully understood this advantage and sought to develop it.
He believed that the Japanese would take one of two actions. If they
did not emulate their 1904 surprise coup d'main against the Russians
(a possibility given much credence in the German staff, they would

mount a full-scale traditional siege. They would not negotiate nor take a middle approach. While no one could anticipate the size of the attack force, the Japanese would, unquestionably, make it a very powerful one. They could not afford the embarrassment of defeat or undue delay.

Given such assumptions, Meyer-Waldeck decided in favor of a short-term continuous alert as the ultimatum ran out, and a long-term preparation against the enemy's best avenues of approach. For the continuous alert, there was no need for particular efforts. For the long-term preparation, he assigned his staff various studies. From them they deduced that the most vulnerable points of the defenses were the two flanks, where the gaps between the fortifications and the water were too wide, and the area between the infantry works IV and V, where there were several hidden zones, inaccessible to German observation. In all three cases the enemy could move forward through the numerous ravines and gullies without detection. He would not even require normal field spades for digging approach lanes. Defending these areas would be extremely difficult.

Meyer-Waldeck studied his position with this information in mind. He readily accepted the paradox created by two facts: (1) that his position was untenable and (2) that he would give battle. The fundamental issue, in the Governor's mind, was whether to wait for the Japanese within the city's defenses or to attempt battle at the protectorate's frontier. His peacetime thinking had always envisaged, because of the weak garrison, a totally defensive position. But with the strength increase of the East Asiatic Detachment and the reservists, he had an adequate manpower source to provide a full complement to every installation.[2] Beyond these units, however, he had another mixed-bag of formations. These included the mounted company (often termed the Kauliang—a local millet crop—husars, because they enjoyed cross country riding), ten horse-drawn guns, four mobile howitzers, two horse-drawn machine gun units, and some miscellaneous machine guns. To this equipment pool he could add some men without damaging the general readiness level.

Morale was an additional consideration. For the Japanese the easy conquest of Tsingtau's approaches would, unavoidably, boost their spirit's greatly. By the same measure, the easy surrender of German territory would have a debilitating effect upon the impatient defenders. They knew their desperate situation and could not maintain a high sense of commitment under continuous frustration. Meyer-Waldeck decided in favor of the advanced defense which, if nothing else, would disrupt the enemy's approach, channelize his advance, provide an opportunity for defensive success, and give the defenders needed experience. He would advance some troops into the protectorate. His decision emerged only after a long and open exchange with his staff. In particular, von Kessinger opposed the distribution of the weak forces, arguing that they could accomplish nothing while risking a good deal. If the Japanese moved quickly they might crack the entire defensive line with a single powerful thrust.[3]

Once he reached this decision, the next issues were those of time and place. Since Tsingtau could not mount a serious naval threat, the Japanese possessed the answers to both questions. The Germans thought that there were three potential landing areas for a Japanese amphibious operation. The best was Schatsykou Bay, which was within the protectorate and beyond the range of Tsingtau's cannon. Although much more exposed to the elements, the beaches at Schantung tou were an attractive possibility in the same area. In the fall, however, both places suffered from a powerful south wind which created high waves and strong currents. Moreover, they were within the German defensive zone, which, no matter how weakly manned, posed a threat of an offensive sally at a critical moment. Given this risk of failure, Meyer-Waldeck did not believe that even the offensive-minded Japanese would attempt a landing at either point.

If he was correct, the Japanese had two other possibilities. The Lau schan Bay region proffered several landing areas, and the north coast of Shantung had some advantages. The former's sheltered position assured a protected landing area, and its location in the neutral zone created a serious defensive problem for the Germans.[4] About the north coast, the Germans had already heard rumors about a landing in Lung kou. The Japanese, through earlier pressures on the Chinese, had created, both in the city and in the surrounding territory, their own sphere of influence. A landing in Lungkou was a simple affair, because the land mass protected it against sea and wind. Its sole delimiting factor was the distance to Tsingtau. For the Japanese, movement across the peninsula would involve a serious loss of time and a discouraging logistical problem.

With these possibilities in mind Meyer-Waldeck carefully reviewed the topography of Shantung once more. When in doubt, he sent out patrols, mounted or motorized, and used the Chinese agents. After he had several reports, the Governor completed his own general survey of the possible Japanese routes. Looking outward from the protectorate, the right flank faced the steep, inaccessible Lauschan mountains. The sole path of consequence was from Wang go deschuang, over the Hotung Pass, into the German zone. It was not an easy path for a sizable group, but, after the Mecklenburg House, a well-known rest and recuperation center, there was a fine road leading directly to the city. A mule track provided a less accessible, if shorter, route through the mountains to Teng yau. There were other footpaths through this rough terrain, but they were insufficient for a military force. In fact none of them offered an appealing route for a sizable unit.

Once they landed, the Japanese, therefore, had no real alternative to taking Tsimo. It was the best supply point, the best transportation center, the best labor source. With control of Tsimo, they would, in Meyer-Waldeck's scenario, shift to their right and move down the useful secondary road to Liu ting dsi. After crossing the Pai scha ho River at that point, the enemy would drive down the narrow pass between the Lau hou schan and Tung liu schui. Once through that defile, the Japanese could shift their forces from a column into a line running along the Kouschan-Taschan-Waldersee Heights, with observation from Prinz Heinrich Mountain.[5]

With this information at hand Meyer-Waldeck insisted upon rapid action. Time was essential because, as he constantly insisted, his troop strength was, and would remain, insufficient for the defensive needs. Only through industry, planning, and promptness could they hope for the slightest success. With these probabilities formulated, he made, therefore, several adjustments in troop locations and assignments. His first shift was the East Asiatic Detachment. It already had sections posted in the hills, but he wanted a greater commitment against the probable Japanese attack routes. Since Kuhlo's men knew the Peking/Tientsin geography, but lacked experience in the Shantung hills, they required training for the new assignment. For this undertaking the Governor granted them a goodly portion of the recently requisitioned bicycles and native ponies.[6]

With his new equipment Kuhlo received instruction about shifting additional men into the hills. They were supposed to get acquainted with their new transportation during the employment. Kuhlo ordered his mounted unit into the far reaches of the protectorate, where it could patrol the boundaries and provide an early warning service. An infantry company went to the Litsun area, another to Schatsykou, and another to Fouschan hou. Given the urgency of the requirement and the lack of prior planning, the officers did not take the accommodations into consideration. The Litsuner group quartered its enlisted men in the local jail and its officers in the police station, after sending the occupants of both places off on a holiday. In Schatsykou the men survived in the field while the officers moved into an old customs post. When the ravenous mosquitoes made life unbearable for the men, they shifted to a nearby Chinese temple for relief.[7] At Fouschan they survived in several dilapidated huts.

In all areas Kuhlo ordered prompt construction of proper defenses. The men quickly tossed up temporary entrenchments, built artillery emplacements, strung barbed wire, and concealed mines. In the beginning phases they had sufficient Chinese labor for the heavy work, but as the Japanese threat expanded, the natives quietly departed for safer places. The Germans then did the work themselves. Moreover, understanding their weak position, the officers carefully prepared covered exits from all positions, reconnoitered retreat routes, and explained all of the details to the men. They wanted a high price from the enemy, but not at serious cost to themselves.

Together with these preparations for an exterior defensive line, Meyer-Waldeck required additional reconnaissance activities for specialized people. Plüschow explored the territory from the ground, picking out distinguishing terrain features for his later aerial observation. Artillery observers roved over the protectorate, doing the same thing for their subsequent requirements. The engineers sought out key points; that is, bridges, rail switches, and rocky overhangs, for future destruction. They bored test holes and collected the necessary explosive charges, and, in many cases, loaded the carefully designated boxes on carts for quick departure.

However, the Governor also demanded some offensive preparations and training. He conducted an extensive personal reconnaissance through the area around the city, explaining the key features and points to his staff. The artillery commanders, the engineer officer, and the *Jaguar*'s new commander, Lieutenant Commander

Karl von Bodecker carefully walked over the ground, discussing aiming points, inaccessible corners, rapid communications, and other issues essential to coordinating their resources. On August 17 Meyer-Waldeck supervised a major exercise for the entire garrison as a test. To the great surprise and pleasure of all concerned, the war game went off well.[8]

Within the infantry works the individual commanders pushed their own needs toward completion. The essential preparations— basic installations, available equipment, and needed manpower— were finished. There remained many other requirements, however, and the men were busy with building new trenches, adding new machine gun points, increasing observations posts, and improving their living conditions.[9] By this time the distribution of troops also required final clarification. The troops were stationed according to a definite plan. In the first work was the first company of the Naval Battalion, the newly created seventh company in works 2 and 3, the second company in work 4, and the third company in number 5. At the time the famous sixth company was busy with the construction of its own fortifications along the water. Behind this group were the reserves, the fourth company on the right flank, the fifth company and the engineers in the middle, and the East Asian Detachment's remaining men (the majority being scattered about on the frontier) and the various extra men on the left flank.[10] They were now ready for the possible Japanese surprise assault.

Elsewhere in the city the same frenetic activity continued unabated. For the expectant crews assigned to the sea defenses, the delay was interminable; they wanted action. They had no morale concerns while busy with their field activities, but once they completed this occupation, they faced the more depressing assignment of getting the installations ready for action. They had to clean the forts carefully, store adequate supplies, fill the water cisterns, and shift the needed equipment. This activity kept the men busy, but could not do so for any length of time.

A complementary problem was that of the various battery buildings themselves, which were not proper living accommodations. They were closed, crowded, areas with poor air circulation, limited illumination, and continual dampness. After a few difficult days of confining the men in the positions, the commanders decided to let the men sleep outside or even in their barracks. In order to avoid further morale concerns, they also gave the men permission to swim in the ocean, to attend amateur theatrical performances, and to borrow books from the local library. Once a week they attended a movie in one of the city's large halls, where they received free beer and tobacco.[11]

Despite these freedoms, the men did not neglect their training exercises. These firing drills were difficult and closely supervised by the officers. As reinforcement there were compulsory lectures by young officers who had served with the Japanese forces or who had just come from that country. In all cases the lecturers underscored the Japanese emphasis on fierceness in the attack, their low estimate of human life, and their ruthless dedication to victory. Their enemy was a formidable one.

Under such circumstances, that is, the intense activity and the prospect of Japanese brutality, there arose some concern among many men for their families. Fully aware of this concern Meyer-Waldeck decided that the dependents should be sent away. He had ordered the preparation of the steamer *Paklat* for this possibility on August 10, and the ship was already prepared when the Berlin authorities ordered an evacuation on August 18. Various concerned families had already taken the train to Tientsin, but there were still some 250 women and children left in the city. A small group of women would remain as nurses. On August 20 the *Paklat* departed with the dependents.[12] The captain had strict orders to stop if he encountered any enemy naval units. That same afternoon five British torpedo boats stopped the ship and ordered her to Weihaiwei. En route the British practiced torpedo runs and ramming exercises on the ship. One of the torpedo boats hit the *Paklat* and tore a large hole in the hull. Fortunately it was above the water line. In their port the British seized the crew as prisoners-of-war and loaded the dependents on a Chinese steamer (owned by a British firm) *Schenking* with a maximum capacity of eighty passengers. The women and children survived on deck and wherever they could find a resting place; the ship had cabin space for only twenty-four people, two toilets, and limited space for the crew. They reached Tientsin on August 25, after a harrowing and difficult trip.[13] The news of their harsh treatment was a great shock to the men in Tsingtau, who, for the first time, began to understand the realities of war.

There was no time left for the defenders, however, since the

Japanese deadline was expiring. On August 21 Meyer-Waldeck held a meeting of all commanding officers. He received assurances from all of them that they had fulfilled his demands of August 1. Following a brief report by each officer, Meyer-Waldeck turned the conference over to von Kessinger. The latter, using large note cards and a rough sketch map, lectured his audience over their progress, the results of the many training tests, and the resolutions of their numerous group exchanges. He spoke in a dull, monotonous tone, but he underscored their state of preparedness. They were as fully prepared as possible for the Japanese assault. After a few questions, Meyer-Waldeck made a short review of their situation, went over the proclamations he planned for the next day, and wished everyone good luck.[14] It was a solemn moment.

That afternoon and the following morning Meyer-Waldeck shifted his command post to the Bismarck barracks. He had a spacious reinforced concrete area in the basement which would serve as his siege headquarters (the troops called it the "ink barrel" because of the numerous messages issuing from it). It possessed good communications, a central location, and proper accommodations for the staff. From it he could supervise the last-minute preparations and keep everyone alert for a possible surprise action.

One of the final defensive efforts Meyer-Waldeck ordered was the laying of all but a handful of naval mines. He assumed that any surprise assault must involve a naval bombardment, and that even one successful mine explosion would throw the enemy off balance at a critical moment. On August 22 the minelayer *Lauting* ran out from Tsingtau and put down thirty-five mines off Hai hsi. Returning for the crew's noon meal, she loaded another fifty-two mines. At the table the crew learned that they would sow the last group off Tai Kung tau, with the *S-90*, which would meet them there, as a protector. As the *Lauting* ran out past Cape Jaeschke, the crew activated the mines in order to accelerate their disposal. They had few concerns about the enemy, who had not yet put in an appearance. It was, therefore, with genuine shock that they heard, at 6:20 P.M. the sound of gunfire.

The *S-90* had earlier begun a long patrol off Tscha lien tau island. Her Captain, Lieutenant Helmut Brunner, had moved his ship into the area as a security measure. Once certain that it contained no dangers, he intended to move on to the designated rendezvous. He was loitering on the searchlight stand without much thought when he observed, shortly after 6:00 P.M., another vessel's smoke on the horizon, followed by the smudges of two others. At first glance Brunner thought that the first ship was one of the coastal steamers he had often seen in Tsingtau. But immediately afterward he changed his mind and called his men to action stations. The lead vessel was clearly a British destroyer, headed in a westerly direction at full speed. Clearly she intended to cut the *S-90* off from her home port.[15]

Brunner turned his vessel immediately and ordered every ounce of speed as he tried to warn the *Lauting* and to escape the trap. After a five-minute chase the British destroyer, *Kennet*, opened fire. Her first shot was over, the second a bit short, and the third almost a direct hit. It covered the *S-90* with water, shredded the flag, and cut a stay on the mainmast. Brunner promptly altered his course slightly and ordered his gun crews into action. His hope was to dissuade his obviously superior foe through a withering, if not coordinated, defensive fire. The *Kennet* was much larger than the *S-90*, much faster, in better condition, and fired heavier guns. But the *S-90* possessed two advantages. For one thing, her limited size and low silhouette made her a more difficult target than the foe. Also her desperate, isolated situation provided some impetus. It was a matter of life and death. The engine room now delivered twenty-one knots, a speed the ship had not reached for many months.

As the two ships noisily exchanged shells, the sounds alerted the shore bound troops, who, together with their Governor, climbed every available observation point. The weather was clear and the blue water smooth, giving the entire action the appearance of some childhood game. As the two grey slivers moved over the glass-like water, only the heavy bow waves and sudden smoke puffs reflected the serious action. To the watchers, the *S-90*'s guns sounded like a puppy's yelp, while the *Kennet*'s larger guns came over like a bull-dog's angry bellow. For the Germans on shore, the war's first action was a grotesque tableau which they could only watch in curious frustration from a grand stand seat.

The *Kennet*'s heavy shells tossed up impressive water towers, but did not hit their fast-flying target. On the other hand, the *S-90*'s wild firing did substantial damage to the pursuer. Almost at the outset she managed a good hit on the *Kennet*'s bridge and subsequently made six more, one of which put a gun out of action. The *Kennet* did not pause in its pursuit, however, and rapidly closed with the *S-90*. If the British could cut the *S-90* off from Tsingtau, it would be a brilliant victory.

As they approached Tai kung tau island, the *S-90*'s position was desperate. There was little possibility of reaching the protective coastal guns in time, and there was no possibility of a successful confrontation with the enemy. Because of their various maneuverings, they were at the island before they knew it. Brunner moved past the rocky projection on its east side. The *Kennet*'s commander, Lieutenant Commander F. A. H. Russel, had the unpleasant option of passing the island on the west side if he wanted to catch the *S-90*. There were several uncharted reefs on that side, which made the dash a risky one. Russel changed course and followed his quarry around the island, losing considerable distance in the process. Once around the island, Russell hurried the *Kennet* in pursuit.

By this time the two combatants had moved much closer to the harbor's mouth. Moving past the barrier was the *Lauting*, with all but eight of her active mines still aboard, and her crew much interested in the *Kennet*'s progress. But, before either German ship suffered any damage, a 24-cm shell from Hui tschuen huk geysered the water near the *Kennet*. While it fell short, it made the required impression. Russell quickly turned about and headed for safer waters.[16] He had three dead men and six wounded, including himself. The Germans suffered no casualties. Nonetheless, the engagement confirmed the enemy's presence and made the war more real.

Early the next morning the *S-90*, the *Jaguar*, and the *Kaiserin Elisabeth* moved out to sea as a protective screen for the *Lauting*. The latter completed her mine laying shortly before 6:00 A.M. and turned for home. As she did so, there was a tremendous explosion behind the ship which threw up a water spout some 100 meters into the air. It drew the ship's bow under the water to the railing, while the concussion knocked the crew to the deck with bruising force. The motor stopped and steam poured out of various holes. A careful search of the ship proved that there was extensive, but not fatal, damage. They could steer the ship with an emergency rudder and create sufficient power to make port. One of the crew found a jagged piece of metal, marked "Portsmouth," on deck, which indicated that others were also using mines. The *Lauting* hurried into the drydock, where the repairs took two days.[17] Within two days the tiny ship had escaped twice.

This happy news for Meyer-Waldeck was offset by less pleasant developments. On August 23, the Captain of the *Kaiserin Elisabeth* had a message waiting for him as he returned from escorting the *Lauting*. Makoviz received preemptory orders from home to neutralize his ship and to move his crew to Tientsin. His government could find no reason to involve itself in Asia where it had no military force beyond the antiquated cruiser. The directive was an unwelcome surprise to both the Germans and the Austrians. In particular, Makoviz was taken aback. His secret instructions for war, contained in a sealed envelope, had succinctly told him "to operate in the best interests of the Three-Power Alliance." For a few days he had maintained a certain reserve until the protagonists had clarified their positions.[18] Thereafter he had placed his ship under German control. The *Kaiserin Elisabeth* had performed patrol duties, conducted training exercises, and prepared for war.

With the Japanese ultimatum, Makoviz had confronted another difficult question for his country was not at war with Japan. On August 17 he had a long discussion with Meyer-Waldeck, in which he articulated his political dilemna, personal uncertainty, and, pending other instructions, individual determination to give battle.[19] They had worked out various plans for the ship's tactical use. Thereafter Makoviz made several land reconnaissances while preparing his ship and crew for action.

The sudden direction to Tiensin was a highly unwelcome change. He asked his diplomatic legation in Peking for confirmation and received it on August 24. There was no possibility to disobey the order, and there was every assurance that the Germans would soon break the rail connection to Tientsin. Under such circumstances Makoviz had no alternative. While his country offered the only decoration for successfully disobeying orders (the Maria Theresa medal), he could not take the chance despite his strong belief. The men hurriedly unloaded the munitions into the artillery depot and shifted the ship to the harbor's shipyard for dismantling the guns. At the same time, they destroyed all impedimenta and unneeded equipment to preclude their loss to the Japanese. By evening they had finished the job. Makoviz ordered a small watch party of eighteen left behind, and, feeling that his ship would be destroyed in the coming siege, decided to stay himself. That evening he unhappily watched 8 staff members and 391 men leave the city.

The train trip to Tientsin was not pleasant for Makoviz's men, already depressed over their sudden departure. Along the way many observers, Europeans, Japanese, and Chinese, through obscene gestures and loud jeers, indicated that the Austrians were running like cowards from the battlefield. The refreshments served by German women along the way merely underscored the same feeling that they had deserted their friends. Once in the city, the group commander, Lieutenant Commander Georg von Pauspertl, sent off a telegram to Makoviz reporting their arrival. Forty-five minutes later the local legation officials learned from the German Consul about new instructions ordering them back to Tsingtau! A confirmation from Vienna followed shortly thereafter.[20] They must return to their original station.

The order, no matter how welcome, posed serious problems for the Austrians in Tientsin. Pauspertl demanded an immediate return before the Chinese could intern them, and ordered two groups prepared for departure that night. As the local Austrian officials discretely asked the Chinese bureaucrats about the movement, they discovered that the latter, while not opposed to small groups, would halt any mass departure.[21]

This rebuff forced Pauspertl to reconsider the options. The local Austrian officials promptly circulated a rumor that the crew would continue on to Shanghai, where the accommodations for internment were better than in Tientsin. Privately they began collecting clothing from the German community and started falsifying passports. On August 27 the news of hostilities between Austria-Hungary and Japan arrived in Tientsin, with a plea from Tsingtau for the return of as many men as possible.[22]

Under these circumstances the Austrian Consul started the surreptitious movement of small groups on August 29. The men received no notice of their impending departure until shortly before the designated time. The schedulers divided each departing group into different parts and did not allow one section to meet another before they left as a unit. They visited the clothing storage area first, where they could choose from various piles of suits, shirts, hats, and shoes. Once outfitted, they marched, in groups of ten to twenty men, for some two hours to a canal, where they boarded a small ship. On this ship they traveled until 6:00 A.M. to a remote train station. Leaving their ship singly, they tried, with little success, to lose themselves among the Chinese. This moment was the critical one, since the Chinese officials' view was neither consistent nor known to the travelers. They simply had to employ their own resources in bluffing their way through an inspection. Fortunately for those apprehended by the Chinese, they suffered only the ignominy of public arrest, and then went to their own consulate for punishment.[23] Those who managed to get aboard the train could hope for a relatively uneventful trip to Kiautschau. It was dangerous to leave the train, however, since the Japanese agents, who often employed girls, would try various devices—taking photographs, extending conversations, creating incidents, giving false directions—to make them miss the train.[24] Once they were in Kiautschau, which they usually reached at night, they slept on sampans tied up along the water's edge. The steady rocking of the small boats and the shifting of the animals aboard, together with the unfriendly darkness, was the last unsettling experience of their journey. They had a difficult struggle, merely to reach the war.

The success of these early missions persuaded the Austrians to push their luck before it ran out on them. Already the Japanese authorities were bringing sharper protests over the Austrian troop movement. In these demands the Japanese indicated that, if the Chinese could not stop them, they would do so. To overcome this opposition, one of the Austrian officers, Lieutenant Vladmir Mariasevic, visited with a Major Lugowski, the local police leader and a German citizen. The latter, pleading his fear for his job and the mounting Japanese pressure, insisted that no more Austrians would get through the Chinese control points. Mariasevic quickly pointed to Lugowski's decorations from both Austria-Hungary and Germany, knowing their value to the latter, and suggested that he could lose them for his refusal to help the Austrians. He then proposed that Lugowski report sick for a few days; an action certain to upset any coordinated effort against the Austrians. Lugowski accepted the proposal.

On September 12, 100 men left Tientsin by the usual route. The Japanese lodged an immediate protest, but, with Lugowski unavailable, the uncertain Chinese officials could not act fast enough to stop them. In Tsianfu Japanese agents pressed the local authorities to stop the train, but an alert civilian accompanying the men persuaded the engineer to leave before the scheduled departure time. They left ten minutes before the Chinese police arrived on the scene and passed through Kiautschou one hour ahead of a Japanese patrol. They were the last group to escape Tientsin, making a total of 300 men.[25]

Those men who did get through returned to their old stations. A group of them went ashore for artillery instruction, and they set up the two 15-cm guns, removed from their ship, on cement blocks in the hills. Another group formed a volunteer infantry company. Since the only clothes the men possessed were the civilian suits on their backs, they received whatever extras the Germans had in their supplies. Most of these were odd sizes or the rejects from earlier dyeing experiments. In their outlandish costumes they took up an infantry position and started preparations for the Japanese assault. In their absence, the Japanese had appeared on the scene.

While the Germans had anticipated an early, surprise assault, it did not take place. They felt certain that the Japanese would come quickly and in full force. The new American Consul, Willys Peck, wrote his brother, "In five minutes the period of Japan's ultimatum ends and everyone here expects the Sabbath calm to be slightly shattered, perhaps by the guns of five nations. It is splendid this waiting."[26] The *Kennet - S-90* action was proof that the war was a real one, but the absence of the Japanese gave it an aura of mystery. Until they appeared in the protectorate, the puzzled defenders could do little more than engage in fantasy. In the early dawn of August 27, the uncertainty came to an end. A sailor, Jakob Neumaier, had the watch duty on Iltis Hill. Having served there several times, he had learned to cope with the early morning haze, which created many strange shapes that ended in false alarms and sharp reprimands. This time the dark, small dots on the horizon did not go away. Neumaier contemplated them for several moments until certain that he was right. Then he screamed, "They're coming!" into the speaking tube. Immediately he could hear the neighboring posts shouting out the same message and adding a bit more: "They're coming! The entire horizon is swarming with ships!" On the stairs Neumaier heard the feet of the officers and their muttered dire threats about a new error.[27] They found none. This alarm was not a false one.

The barely discernible slivers grew as they closed with the land mass. The excited men on Iltis Hill counted them. There were fifteen in all, three large and twelve smaller ones. As the enemy squadron moved closer, the headquarters telephoned the sea batteries, ordering the men either into their positions or, at least, off the open observation platforms. They anticipated an immediate gun battle between the land and sea giants and did not want human targets betraying the defensive installations' locations.

As the naval force moved closer, the German guns elevated and their crews loaded them for maximum range. The Japanese advanced steadily until they reached a line some fifteen miles away. There they stopped, well out of range. Their Admiral, Sadakichi Kato, wirelessed Meyer-Waldeck, asking for permission to send a steam-launch into the harbor. He wanted a Japanese officer to interview the captain of the *Kaiserin Elisabeth* and the American Consul concerning their positions on the war. Meyer-Waldeck decided against allowing the emissary into the city, suspecting that the man would deliver a blockade declaration.[28] He was right.

Upon receiving the rejection, Kato wirelessed his blockade declaration against the entire German protectorate. All neutral vessels had twenty-four hours' grace to clear the port. Thereafter the Japanese would enforce all legal measures against violators.[29] The announcement clearly established the Japanese intent and cut off the Germans from all water-borne aid or communication. They were on their own.

A brief time after this message, shortly after 9:00 A.M., the first sounds of war reverberated across the water. As the Germans hurriedly looked out to sea, they observed two Japanese destroyers firing at the two minuscule islands offshore, Tscha lien tau and Tai kung tau, termed "Max" and "Moritz" by the sailors and "the hay stacks" by the inhabitants. They were steep, rough, and uninhabited. The Germans had already destroyed their lighthouses on the latter island and deserted it. As the Japanese fired away, the tops of the islands disappeared in smoke. After a brief, impressive bombardment, two cutters moved away from an accompanying repair ship, *Kwanto Maru*, and landed on the larger island. Once ashore the Japanese struggled to the top and raised the Japanese flag. After a few hours they pulled down the flag, much to the delight of the watching Germans.

They did not leave the island, however, until they had established an observation post and a wireless station, together with a lighthouse.

Its presence served as a guide post for the Japanese, as well as a nightly reminder to the Germans of the besiegers' presence.[30] As one German wit observed, "They had to bombard them heavily, otherwise they would never have captured them."[31]

As the Japanese celebrated their first action, two destroyers moved too far inshore, and one of the big guns on Tui tschuen huk fired a single shell. It was far short of the target, but the tower of water prompted a hasty departure by the two intruders, bringing German cheers. In such half-comic fashion the belligerents opened hostilities.

The Japanese soon established a blockade line well out to sea and started mine-sweeping operations. They quickly discovered one of the few mines laid off Tai kung tau. For the Japanese this revelation was an unpleasant one, since they had not anticipated finding them so far out at sea. Thereafter they were extraordinarily cautious as their mine sweepers plied their dangerous trade. While the tiny vessels quickly became part of the daily scenery, they also were constant reminders to the Germans of their precarious situation.

The blockade served as a catalyst for Meyer-Waldeck in another area. Obviously, the enemy would soon begin closing off Tsingtau's land communications. In particular, the Governor was concerned about the railway. He needed the link for transporting goods, foodstuffs, and men. At the same time, he heard rumors that China and Japan were discussing an agreement giving Japan an immense war zone. If they should land on the north coast, they could use the rail line in support of their advance. The mere threat was sufficient for Meyer-Waldeck; he carefully regulated all rail traffic as a security measure until August 30, when he halted everything except handcars.

Concurrently he asked his engineers for a complete report of their preparations for destroying various bridges, tracks, and key switches. Because some of these plans involved an invasion of Chinese neutral territory, the destruction of several cultural treasures, and the certain loss of Chinese good will, Meyer-Waldeck could not make up his mind about timing the required destruction. As the last train left on August 30, however, the engineers began moving out along the line, preparing their destructive charges.[32] The problem was solved by a sudden action from an unexpected quarter.

On the same day the first clouds announcing a change in the

weather arrived over Tsingtau. That night the rain poured down in a totally unexpected and unseasonal storm. The following day continued wet and foggy. As the weather cleared slightly, the startled German observers saw a Japanese destroyer (subsequently identified as the *Schiotayen*) aground on Lien tau island near Cape Jaeschke. She had gone on the rocks during the night's storm. Three other destroyers hovered nearby, trying to pull the Schiotayen off. They had already removed the crew.[33] Once more Hui tschuen huk opened fire, this time unleashing three salvos, which, while they hit nothing, drove off the Japanese vessels. The *Jaguar*, now commanded by Lieutenant Karl von Bodecker, quickly ran out to administer the *coup de grace*. He fired just over 100 shells, with excellent results: the *Schiotayen*'s mast was gone, she was badly broken amidship, and she was burning throughout. Then the daring Bodecker brought the Jaguar in close to his quarry as a trap for the Japanese. Observing his temerity, the three destroyers attacked and von Bodecker, waiting until the last moment, fled in precipitate retreat. As the *Jaguar* fled, under full steam, the Japanese fired many shells but turned off before getting into the range of the fortress guns.[34]

Even as the triumphant *Jaguar*, happy over drawing first blood, returned to the harbor, the weather closed in once more. Within a few short hours the skies opened up and the rain began falling in sheets. While no one could anticipate the future, the storm would last for two weeks. Never in recorded or remembered history had the clouds poured so much water on Shantung—especially in September, a time for sunbathing and outdoor living. The water fell in torrents and without pause. As one participant observed, "It appeared as if the weather god had wanted, in this year, to pour out the entire cup of anger upon so much human stupidity."[35]

Starting in the mountains, the water flooded everything. It filled the normal waterways almost immediately and went over the banks. Any identification of the former stream bed was impossible. Once the streams reached flood stage, there was nothing to stop their mad rush in all directions. Entire roadways, carefully and methodically built by hard work, disappeared in seconds, the heavy building stones washing hundreds of meters within a few minutes. Bridges, constructed some six feet above the highest expected flood waters, flew apart under the abnormal pressures.

Most dangerous was the sudden arrival of the surging water from a small feeder stream which suddenly broke through a restraining embankment and joined another waterway. The resulting sudden increase in the water level, like a miniature tidal wave, swept everything before it. Three soldiers were pushing a cart along one stream when a rapid flooding knocked one of them down and carried him into the main stream. As he drifted away, the second grabbed a nearby tree limb and tried to reach his friend. As the third rushed to help, he too lost his balance and fell into the raging torrent, where all three died.

The villages in Shantung suffered appalling damage. They lacked even the simplest defenses against flooding, having depended upon the visible water tracts and human memory for their protection. The natives hastily tossed up sand dikes, but the rushing water quickly eroded them and attacked the stone foundations. Within a short time the flimsy houses were careening around like whirling toys, only to collapse into soiled piles of household goods. The ruins, partially filled with sand, gave the townships the eerie unreality of another world. The Chinese must have perished in large numbers, but no one kept records.[36]

Such vast destruction precluded any German attempt to destroy communications, as well as the necessity for such action. The unrelenting storm weakened or destroyed the railway bridges, left the tracks twisted into curious shapes, and undercut the roadbed. Nature's forces far exceeded human destructive power. The same kind of damage was done to the hill roads, which the rains made impassable. All of the telegraph lines also went down as the rushing waters undercut the poles and dropped the lines into the muck. The failure of all efficient communication isolated the city from the outside world.

The storm wrought similar havoc in the defenses themselves. Despite the planning, care, and effort in construction, the works were not designed for the storm. Inside the infantry and artillery installations, the ceilings and walls streamed water. The swirling waters flooded the storage areas, food, munitions, and personal effects. The installations filled with one to two feet of water, and the small pumps available could not evacuate them fast enough. The men, in swimming suits and high boots, bailed the installations out by hand. The officers joined the men in this coolie labor forgetting all

protocol in the battle to save their installations for the coming campaign. Around them the newly dug trenches and holes were gone,
filled with sand or smashed beyond recognition. The barbed wire
obstacles were swallowed by the water. Everything was damaged or
destroyed and would require extensive repair.

Within the city the damage was also very serious. The streets
suffered extensive damage, the sewers overflowed, and several
buildings collapsed under the pressure. While all of the destruction
was unpleasant, the city water system suffered more than other
facilities. In peacetime, Tsingtau had its main water works in Litsun.
Since any besieging army would quickly occupy that area, Meyer-
Waldeck had ordered another system built on the Haipo, just in front
of Infantry Work II. A massive water wave, on September 4 and 5,
overwhelmed the key pumping points. The flood washed away most
of the pumping machinery and a thirty-meter portion of its twelve-
meter-high retaining embankment. With the enemy still a long way
from the city walls, the city residents were suddenly dependent upon
eighty-five municipal wells.

The soldiers suffered the same problems as the civilians. They
could not see two meters in front of them, could not stay dry, and
could not cope with nature's elements. The cloudbursts made the air
oppressively humid outside, and dank, sticky, and unbearable inside
the fortifications. Nearly everyone suffered from colds or bronchial
congestion. In the evening the mosquitoes rose to the attack, and
anyone caught in an area belonging to these fearsome flying daggers
had little respite. Many men looked like human pincushions and
swelled up like elongated balloons under the ferocious assault.
Attempts at humor were few and ill-received as everyone suffered
from the elements.[37]

The leaders, overwhelmed by the disaster, had to await the storm's
end until they could undertake repairs. Many of them took some
comfort in knowing that the Japanese must be suffering worse damage to their preparations and to their morale. As the attackers, they
were in the open and more exposed than the defenders. But, in the
midst of these thoughts, on September 5 came two electrifying
reports which changed everything. That morning in Tsingtau the rain
let up for a few brief hours, but the low-lying, dark clouds remained
as a pessimistic symbol. Shortly after 10:00 A.M., the sound of an
airplane propeller interrupted morning activities in Tsingtau. Sud-

denly an aircraft dropped through the clouds and swooped over the sodden defenses. No one had expected its arrival. In fact, most Germans, hearing the whirring propeller, assumed that Plüschow was enjoying an outing. Virtually everyone watched spellbound as the aircraft gracefully soared over the city. Only a few looked through their field glasses and saw the red suns painted on the wings. Then a glistening object fell from the aircraft, whistled through the air, and exploded near the Bismarck battery, making a tiny hole in the mud (50 cm x 60 cm). The pilot, Lieutenant Hideo Wade, dropped two more bombs which did no damage and then departed without difficulty, although the defenders fired a few shots after him. Nonetheless, the three explosions made a much greater psychological impact upon the garrison than did the bomb craters. The Japanese had brought aircraft with them. While they might not be effective bombers, they could certainly carry out land reconnaissance duties, scout ship locations, detect mines, and locate landing areas. This surprise, the only unexpected development of the campaign, was complete.[38] The Japanese were obviously planning a professional, complete siege.

The other disturbing news was of the long-awaited Japanese landing. On September 2 the first elements of the invasion force had landed in the north at Lungkou. While rumors involving this area as the key point had been rampant for some time, the German commanders had not seriously considered it a possibility. They thought that it was too far away for a large military force, totally unacceptable for the aggressive Japanese, and militarily of no value whatsoever. Despite these earlier comforting assumptions, the Japanese were clearly starting there, for whatever motives. The details were vague, since the information came, in part, through carrier pigeons, which managed to get through despite the poor weather. While the precise nature of the landing remained unknown, there was no question that the Japanese were bringing a major force ashore. The message indicated that the naval squadron had some twenty-six transports and thirty-six warships in the undertaking. Their arrival ended the rumors that the Japanese intended to starve the Germans out, that the Americans had brought sufficient pressure against the landing, or that the Japanese would be content with Tsingtau's neutralization. The Japanese had obviously completed their preparations.

For the Japanese the decision to wage war had necessitated as much activity as it had for the defenders. The Japanese military leaders were not prepared for hostilities. Fortunately they did not know about the incredible diplomatic activity which led to the Japanese entry.[39] They could concentrate on their military preparations; albeit against their friends and former instructors. Without question they owed a great deal to the Germans, whom they had accepted as their military model and as their actual teachers.[40] They were, however, very flexible and the military equal of the so-called more advanced western powers in general organization, mobilization speed, and professional efficiency. In peacetime the Japanese maintained nineteen divisions (two of them stationed in Manchuria and Korea) and several independent brigades. A division contained about 19,000 men and had two infantry brigades of two regiments of three battalions. Each of the battalions possessed four companies. Normal tactical doctrine suggested that a battalion, the most desirable attack echelon, attack with a three company front, leaving one in reserve. When larger units were involved, they assaulted in columns with different goals, rather than in a collective mission against a single point. Unlike Western armies, the Japanese also had considerable training in the use of combined arms, amphibious landings, and precise command structures.[41]

With the political decision in favor of war, the Japanese military leadership ordered, on August 16, the mobilization of the Eighteenth Division.[42] The command of the assault force went to Lieutenant General Kamio Mitsuomi, a highly experienced and knowledgeable soldier. He had started his career as a sergeant in 1874 and rose through the ranks to command positions. His major reputation came from his experience in China, where he had served as a military attaché, a field commander, and an observer. He had visited Europe and spoke comprehensible English. Kamio enjoyed social activities, where his charm, calmness, and broad-mindedness made many friendships. Approaching his sixtieth birthday, Kamio inspired confidence through his meticulous attention to detail, his keen knowledge of staff work, and his wide breadth of experience. His reputation was such that no one anticipated an adventuresome or sensational campaign, but no one was in the slightest doubt about the ultimate outcome.

His Chief-of-Staff was Major General Hanzo Yamanashii. He possessed extensive European experience, together with a perceptive understanding of staff work, which made him a popular figure among his subordinates. In contrast to the taciturn Kamio, he was flamboyant, emotional, and gregarious. At the same time, he lacked his commander's physical strength and was often sick. He had served in various capacities in Germany and had mastered the language. But he had neither forgotten nor forgiven the Germans for jeering at him during his 1907 attachment to their forces as an observer.

The two brigade commanders were Major General Horiuchi Bunjero for the Twenty-third and Major General Yamada Ryosui for the Twenty-fourth, both experienced soldiers with good reputations.[43] Since the campaign promised to be Japan's only military endeavor in the war, many officers sought assignment or temporary attachment in any capacity. As a result, there were many officers in the latter category, which made the entire staff structure very large and often cumbersome.

Fortunately, Kamio had tested the unit mobilization plans in various exercises. His key personnel fully understood their duties. The additional 4,000 men from the reserve formations appeared within a few days of the orders and quickly filled their assigned places. On August 24 Kamio made a short address to these new men where he indicated, "The European war has extended to the Far East. The special [independent task force] 18 Division is about to depart for the Shantung Peninsula in order to sweep away the German troops. The German Army was, hitherto, considered the best in the world. Our 18 Division is going into action as the representative of the entire Japanese Army. Now is the time for us to demonstrate wariness, courage, and energy."[44]

The military orders were succinct and to the point. An earlier General Staff study in 1913 had arranged the basic information for Kamio.[45] This plan envisaged a strong holding force south of Tsimo, which would keep the defenders securely tied down in the city. Under the cover provided by this group, the siege troops could land their heavy guns, equipment, and specialized units in Laoshan Bay. Originally the planners called for a double-pronged effort, with a small contingent landing above the Bay and pushing down the peninsula. They would be joined by a landing force within the Bay, and then jointly screen off any German sortie. Kamio's very simple instructions followed this general scheme. His program was to load in Nagasaki and Ujima, to land at Lungkou and subsequently near Laoshan, and to capture Tsingtau.[46]

The planners fully understood the geographic advantages of a direct move into Laoshan Bay, but they feared a German sortie at a critical moment. If the Germans discovered a weak covering force, they could mount an assault, which, no matter what its success, must disrupt the Japanese timing and force embarrassing delays. Additionally, their information suggested that the defenders had sown many mines in Laoshan Bay; these obstacles would require a week's labor for the navy. While they possessed assurances that the adjacent seas were clear of enemy warships, they had no assurance that the weather would be favorable. The monsoon season would not be over for some weeks, and bad weather, in particular the high waves, would adversely affect the Bay's landing potential.

In view of these considerations, Kamio decided in favor of landing his main force in the north, moving it overland while the navy swept the mines, and guarding the secondary landing with a large force. He issued these instructions on August 24. This approach would take longer but guaranteed ultimate success. Given the unusual nature of the campaign, i.e., the comparable strength of the combatants, he put victory above risk.[47]

For the Navy the assignment was equally direct. The First Squadron should protect the advanced base at Hakko-ho on the west coast of Korea.[48] All the choice assignments went to the Second Squadron, which would blockade the German protectorate, clear any mines obstructing a landing, and support the land assault on Tsingtau. Under Vice-Admiral Sadakichi Kato this Squadron would carry the basic naval responsibility.[49] The Third Squadron would keep watch over the shipping routes south of Shanghai for a possible return by von Spee.

At full speed Kato's group had moved toward Tsingtau and their assigned blockade position. They arrived at the harbor entrance and sent off their blockade declaration. With the anticipated German response, Kato sent the *Takachiho* off to cut the German cable links. The ship did so, not realizing that the British ship *Patrol*, had performed the same mission a day earlier. Then the Japanese began minesweeping, and the squadron settled down into routine patrol procedures against the harbor. This activity involved little more than controlling the movement of the numerous junks and sampans.

On September 1 the *Wakamiya Maru*, an aircraft depot ship with four aircraft, joined the squzdron, but for several days the stormy weather and some mishaps kept the aircraft from taking off. On September 5 Lieutenant Wade managed his first flight over the city. While his bombing effort proved unsuccessful, Wade's reconnaissance report provided essential information. For the first time the Japanese knew which ships were in the harbor and which ones had successfully reached the open sea. In particular, the revelation that the *Emden* was not in port alerted all the allies about her possible interference.[50]

As the Japanese marshalled their forces for the blockade, they learned that they would not be alone. Great Britain would also contribute a contingent. The question of British participation provided another challenging issue for the Anglo-Japanese alliance.[51] Behind the British military participation was a proposal by Eugene L. G. Regnault, the French Ambassador in Japan. He knew about the various Anglo-Japanese discussions relative to the war and wanted every possible advantage for his own country. On August 8 he had approached the British Ambassador in Tokyo, Sir Conyngham Greene, with a strong plea for Franco-British naval participation in any Asian campaign.[52]

The proposal demanded some careful study, because the British, at least officially, had not considered the possibility.[53] Finally, on August 12 Sir Edward Grey, the British Foreign Minister, informed Greene that British military leaders in Asia would coordinate with the Japanese whenever the latter desired such cooperation. He also proposed that the French and Russians be invited into the campaign when the British and Japanese, the two senior partners, had completed their plans.[54]

The Japanese accepted the idea of British participation without demur but they raised various questions about the extent, source, and command of any naval or army units.[55] They did come out strongly against any French or Russian participation, because they anticipated subsequent demands for territorial or economic compensation. The British, wanting French participation but realizing that the Japanese had the upper hand in Asia, accepted the Japanese position, albeit they did make a belated and fruitless effort to allow the French a token force.[56]

With the political decision on military participation a matter of joint accord, if not mutual satisfaction, the military men could initiate their necessary preparation. Their endeavors mirrored the confusion of their political leaders. On August 16 the British military authorities agreed that they would send a brigade force of four battalions (two British, two Indian) under the command of Colonel (temporary Brigadier General) Nathaniel W. Barnardiston. He would serve under the Japanese field commander.[57] The command issue was a highly significant one, since no Caucasian had previously served under an Asiatic in a field command. Barnardiston, not particularly enthusiastic about this historic possibility, sought special designation as an independent force rather than a subordinate command. From London came the clear response that he would be subordinate, and that "British troops are only engaged to show that England is cooperating with Japan in this enterprise."[58]

With this injunction Barnardiston could start developing the plans for his small force. But, even as he did so, his superiors in London telegraphed a sharp reduction in force; he would have only a single battalion.[59] It would clearly be a small escort for the flag and little else, an unpleasant arrangement for Barnardiston. The Japanese quickly seized advantage of this disproportionate representation. On August 22 they provided London with a general idea of their operational plans. In addition to pointing out their planned landing on the northern Shantung coast, they proposed that the British come ashore at Laoshan toward the end of September.[60]

The British officials accepted the proposal and began preparing for their participation. In order to assume proper coordination, the two forces exchanged liason officers. The Japanese sent Major M. Hiwatari to Tientsin, where he arrived on August 31. The British dispatched Major David Robertson, their attaché in Peking.[61] Before they could accomplish very much, however, the Japanese had to concentrate on their immediate invasion plans. Discussions of coalition warfare were clearly in order, but most important, they needed a successful landing.

Their preparations for the landing progressed with little regard for the British role. An Army officer, Major K. Takahashi, as well as several naval officers, visited the Lungkau coast. They returned to

Hakko ho for a major conference on August 30. With Admiral Kato, General Yamada, and a landing officer, the group decided upon Lungkou itself as the best landing point.[62] Their decision was a last-minute one; the orders reached the troop ships only after they were at sea.

The advance units of the Eighteenth Division had embarked on August 28 and 29 in Ujina and Nagaski for their rendezvous at Hakko ho.[63] There they received hurried instructions concerning disembarkment proceedings and methods. The troops had not had amphibious training, and they had no time for the needed education. During the evening of August 29, the advance elements departed for Lungkou. Under General Yamada, with his Twenty-fourth Brigade and a few supporting units, they were to land, to march on Pingtu, and to prepare the subsequent advance.

En route to the landing point Admiral Hikonojo Kamimura, who supervised the convoy, hastily assembled a naval landing party from his ship's personnel. He managed an uncoordinated group of four companies (approximately 600 rifles, 6 machine guns, and a composite support company). His convoy sailed without formation or organization, with only a simple order to reach Lungkou on September 1. Kanimura satisfied both requirements without incident.

As dawn broke over Lungkou, the impressive Japanese fleet was offshore. A small Chinese gunboat precipitously lifted anchor and quietly departed in haste. The Chinese steamer, *Chefu*, moved away, albeit not out of sight.[64] Because of the shallow water inshore, the Japanese anchored some two to five miles from the beach. The naval landing party left the ships shortly after 6:00 A.M. and was ashore by 7:30. Quickly occupying the southern end of Lungkou, the troops halted all external communications.[65] As they did so the rain began falling around them, although not hard enough initially to be taken seriously. Once the assault party had occupied the key areas, a small army-led reconnaissance patrol set out in search of the eventual landing areas.

The marching men viewed the rain with some humor, at first, but they soon changed their attitude, as the light rain quickly became a driving storm. Despite the discomfort, the advance party reconnoitered the immediate landing possibilities. They brought back their impressions to Yamada, who decided upon two of them, Chiming-tao and Langkao. Chiming-tao had the advantage of an easy approach for landing craft at high tide and for men and horses, wading ashore, with a low tide. It was, unhappily, some four miles over sand to Lungkou, which forced Yamada to land equipment at Langkao.

To be certain of his position, Yamada ordered an infantry battalion with four companies, two machine guns, and a cavalry troop ashore as a cover force. They quickly landed and moved some seven miles inland in a defensive circle. Behind them came an engineer battalion, which started constructing two landing piers, each about 150 meters long. By this time the rain had turned into sleet, with abnormally high winds. Despite their extreme discomfort, the men kept at their labors until they finished one pier at 3:30 A.M., and the other at 9:30 A.M., the following morning. As they finished the last project, a handful of exhausted volunteers joined a naval party in constructing a floating pier, which was ready that evening.

When General Yamada learned that there were no enemy soldiers in the area and that the 300 defending Chinese soldiers had discretely withdrawn, he went ashore himself.[66] Even so he was late, in terms of his schedule. The landing troops faced the serious challenges of loading in heavy seas (on sampans carrying fourteen men or six horses), wading some 200 or 300 meters in a pounding sea, and assembling under a driving rain. They moved inland in some disorder. On September 3 the weather forced a halt in all landing efforts.

Fortunately for the operation, Lieutenant Commander G. Haga from Port Arthur arrived and discovered an anchorage much closer to the landing beaches. At the same time, the signal troops completed a wireless station, which allowed ship-shore communications. These adjustments eased the landing, but, even so, the bad weather constantly interrupted the operation. By carefully taking full advantage of lulls in the storm, the Navy finally put the Yamada detachment—a force of 8,000 men, in addition to their equipment and horses—ashore by September 6.

On September 7 the invasion fleet had a break in the weather and quickly reached the original schedule levels for the landing. General Kamio also went ashore for the first time. His manifest pleasure over the successful day did not last long; the next day the storm returned and battered the fleet once more. That night it ripped away many landing craft; by morning, more than half of them were gone, driven away by the tides or simply smashed on the shore. The raging water washed away the permanent piers and seriously damaged the floating one. Ashore a small, inconsequential stream between the landing point and Lunkou flooded over its banks and rolled across the beaches. With the exception of a small patch about 90 meters square around the Harbor Control Headquarters, the entire landing point was a muddy torrent several feet deep.

Kamio was acutely aware that his efforts to get the invasion moving had not worked any miracles. After his arrival on September 3 he had reminded Yamada that they were behind schedule. Yamada with this suggestive prodding from above, ordered his cavalry elements (from the Twenty-second Regiment) to advance ahead of the rest of the troops, to reconnoiter the countryside, to drive back any enemy units, and to secure Pingtu by September 7. Because the weather made transporting supplies difficult, he added instructions that the Regiment would, when necessary, leave its support echelons behind and live off the countryside.

Even as the Regiment started out, an advance patrol reported that the Chieh-ho River had flooded that same day, making passage impossible. Lieutenant Colonel Chikami Tokiji, the Regimental Commander, told his men that they must reach the flooded area anyway. The cavalrymen rode only a short distance before halting, but the rain and mud ruined their uniforms, soaked their horses, and dirtied their equipment. Among the troops the watchword was, "In China the streams and roads are the same."[67] With advance in this direction so difficult, Chikami divided his scouting forces in search of alternate routes. He directed the main force to continue toward Pingtu but sent another group toward Tschauyuan.

By morning the stream had fallen and was some 150 meters wide and 70 centimeters deep. The Regiment pushed across, but progress was slow. All the roads were virtually impassable. The horses had great difficulty with the poor footing, and the men had to manhandle all of the vehicles.

An observant officer saw a group pushing a wagon laden with rifles and field packs. A sudden cloudburst turned the road bed, on which they were moving, into a moving stream. At first they kept marching, but within a short time the water reached the axles, forcing a halt. They quickly unloaded the rifles because they could not lift the light wagon over the high banks along the road. As they staggered up the incline to safety, the flood waters surged down the road, floating their loaded cart to lower country. The men could only watch in mute amazement, happy about surviving but incredulous over the swiftness of the event.[68]

The weather turned the advance into a series of fitful, chaotic jumps and halts. Yamada ordered that all troops advance as soon as they reached the shore, but compliance was more an aspiration than a reality. After crossing the Chiehho waterway, the cavalry patrols encountered the Chi-chia-chen, normally a dry creek bed. After all the rain, it held 1.5 meters of fast-moving water and was impassible for man or beast. One patrol managed a crossing but the others simply camped, awaiting a change in the water level. Then the successful group reported that the Germans were not in the area, and on the seventh all of the advance elements crossed the river.

They were a sorry sight after a week in the field, without even sighting the enemy. The uniforms were faded and full of gaping rents and holes, the saddles were sodden and damaged, the horses were covered with mud and grime. Most of the men were listless from fatigue and lack of provisions. Already the Japanese had discovered some serious problems with their cavalry mounts. Supplying fodder under such intolerable conditions was impossible, the horses themselves were not strong enough for the local terrain conditions (they were handsome beasts but lacked endurance), and the reserve horses were not able to make up the losses (already thirty percent). Their efforts had thoroughly exhausted both the men and the animals.

They staggered into Pingtu the following day, scarcely the image of victorious conquerors. In fact, they could go no farther. Chikami, on his responsibility, ordered a halt. He needed complete rest for his men and animals, an opportunity to gather stragglers, and a chance to reestablish communications with Yamada.[69]

Yamada, with the main body, suffered from the same general difficulties. At the very outset Yamada had wanted his troops moving forward as rapidly as possible, for if the Forty-eighth Regiment followed closely on the cavalry, they would assure an orderly process and provide effective support. But with the storm and the cavalry's uneven advance, his men made little progress toward their goals. On September 4 he ordered a general advance. His instructions clearly intended no more than moving men forward, and the troops, once ashore, simply marched inland. Without instructions, order, or march plans, they simply trudged along with the general flow of men.

Under such vague orders, and in the slippery footing, they were soon totally disorganized. Yamada accepted this sloppiness for the moment, because he wanted the men in Pingtu, and because there was no immediate threat from the Germans.[70]

As he personally drove his men forward, Yamada had to contend with the changing weather. Crossing the Chieh-ho was no easier for the infantry than it had been for the cavalry. A Company, moving through water up to their chests, barely survived their crossing. Shortly after they reached the opposite shore, the river flooded again (250 meters wide and 1.3 meters deep), and no one could get over it. The infantry waited a full day in the pelting rain before moving across. When they finally moved forward they did so without proper sustenance, uniforms, or supplies. Everything and everyone was mired in the mud sea.

Kamio came ashore permanently on September 7, setting up housekeeping at Peima. He soon discovered that the situation was worse than he had thought earlier. The roads were miserable, the living conditions impossible, and the rations unfit for use. Solutions, even short-term expedient ones, were difficult. North Shantung, not a rice-producing district, could not provide the main item in the Japanese diet.[71] Under such unexpected strain, Kamio ordered a general pause in the advance for September 9 and 10. The unit commanders should expand all efforts in sorting through the human mass milling about north Shantung. He wanted a semblance of order. At the same time, Kamio wanted an improvement in the food supply before morale sagged to unacceptable levels.

For Yamada these instructions provided a much-desired pause. On September 8 his men had tried crossing the Chiehho with hastily constructed rafts. The river, running 550 meters wide and 3 meters deep, completely frustrated their efforts. Moreover, the rain that day destroyed Yamada's communications with both his cavalry and advance elements. In the confusion many units did not receive Kamio's halt order, but the storm effectively imposed obedience.

On September 11, at long last, the sky cleared and the rain ceased at last. The roads were still miry, filled with deep pools and soft spots, and subject to floods as dams in the cultivated fields broke under the built-up pressure. Each unit repaired the road bed as it moved along. The infantry were forced into the new roles of road construction, baggage movement, and general support. For the cavalry, despite their pause, the traveling conditions were not much different. They had expected to advance again on September 11, but soon encountered new difficulties with the waterways. In fact, they could not move until September 13, when they found some fords over two streams. They loaded their saddles and equipment on a small Chinese boat and swam their horses across.

As they did so a Chinese runner brought a letter bearing the curious salutation "Highest from Thousands." The troops quickly brought it to Lieutenant Colonel Chickami, who scanned the contents and issued new instructions. The note was from a patrol leader, Lieutenant Nakamishi, who reported a brush with ten Germans near Tsimo, their hasty departure, and his occupation of that point. They were in the protectorate and in contact with the enemy. Chikami ordered a platoon forward to Tsimo as a protective screen. The city was too important to risk its loss to the Germans, who must quickly learn the strength of the occupation force.[71] Chikami reported the easy acquisition of Tsimo to Yamada. They had, at least, occupied their first basic goal.

Yamada, from his station in Pingtu, ordered the cavalry regiment forward into Tsimo, but with some caution. He did not want the unit too far in advance of the supporting infantry, nor did he want the horses unduly punished by an overly rapid movement. The cavalry made a rather bedraggled appearance in Tsimo on September 14, but they did ride into the city at noon. Quickly they threw up defensive works, built observation points, and sent out new patrols. One of these patrols reached Kiautschou that same day, cut the rail and telegraph lines with Tsingtau, and occupied the railroad station. There would be no movement along that line.

Behind them the infantry struggled forward in a tortuous effort to catch up. With the snarled road network, they made little progress. They reached Pingtau during September 11 to 14, but were far behind Kamio's schedule. As they arrived, however, Yamada's staff sorted them out and created a better sense of order. Nonetheless, the bad weather had forced changes in the Japanese plans.

Kamio had already reached the decision that he could not concentrate his main force around Tsimo before September 20. The muddy roads, limited supplies, and bad weather predictions provided no grounds for optimism. He communicated this view to his superiors that same day (September 14) in a brief telegram. The General Staff replied the following day with instructions to halt the troop disembarkations, and to transport a regiment by sea to Laoshun for a September 18 landing. They intended no change in their original plan to start the Laoshun landing on that date. There was no doubt in their minds that the amphibious undertaking posed some challenge because Kamio could not reach the desired defensive line to protect it. The reloading of troops, shifting them, and relanding them as a protective screen posed some risks, but they were willing to take them. However, while these risks in Tokyo were an intellectual and emotional challenge, they were practically impossible in Shantung.

About half of Horiuchi's Twenty-third Brigade was ashore, strung out along the road outside Lungkou. In view of the new General Staff orders, Kamio ordered them reembarked aboard the transports. The sea was still rough, the weather bad, the landing craft limited, and the troops inexperienced in climbing aboard ship. Nevertheless Kamio sent a Major Kurosa of his staff to Lungkou with the simplest instructions: he must get the required troops aboard ship within three days. Nothing was said about the means.

Kurosa decided that the troops ashore must simply abandon their equipment and baggage. After that quick decision, he carefully relocated the necessary transports as close to shore and to each other as safety allowed them, thereby simplifying the transportation problem. At the same time, he decreed the use of all landing vessels solely for reloading troops, thereby speeding up this activity at the expense of unloading equipment. The crews of the landing craft had learned a good deal in the intervening period and performed very well. A hastily assembled instructional team informed the troops about the best boarding procedures as they left the beach. By 2:00 P.M. on September 15, Kurosa could report his success, and the required transports left for their rendezvous in time.[73] For all the troops involved in the operation the date remained a memorable one since the weather cleared up at last.

With this change in the weather, the morale of the much-tried Yamada force was greatly improved. They advanced on September 16 with the hope that they could make up their lost time and bring the enemy to battle. Each day the cavalry reported seeing the enemy and exchanging a few shots, but they could not locate a unit of any consequence. The cavalry did establish the fact that the Germans had a scattered outpost line along the Paisha ho.[74]

For the Japanese these outpost positions represented their first genuine hope for contact. Yamada ordered a more careful reconnaissance; this time in force. Just before dawn on September 18, a force of some 150 men moved out from Tsimo. They quickly divided into platoon-size units with advance patrols. One of these parties rode toward Liu ting, reaching their designated area about 9:30 A.M., and promptly discovered a nearby German party.

Coincidently Yamada arrived on the scene at the same moment, sparing the messenger a trip. The Regimental Commander ordered Captain Suida Sakuma's patrol force down the road toward Liu ting. When they reached the village, they dismounted behind a house at the southern outskirt and advanced, on foot, through a nearby ravine. The soy bean and millet made observation difficult for both parties.

Deciding in favor of aggressive action, Sakuma advanced toward the river bank. His goal was the capture of some prisoners. But as the Japanese crept slowly around the edge of the village, one of them loosed a shot, revealing their presence. A general melee opened between the two parties as both sides underwent their baptism in fire. The small German patrol faded into the fields and the Japanese started after them. As they did so, about twenty more German infantrymen opened fire on them from their flank.

After some twenty minutes of general firing, Yamada instructed Sakuma to shift his men slightly in an effort to outflank the Germans. As Sakuma began following these orders, a wayward bullet hit him in the chest, severing an artery. He died quickly, the first man killed in action.

Even as he died, the Germans started retiring. As they did so, one of their officers, Baron Riedesel zu Eisenbach, fell, shot through both legs. Because of the Japanese strength, he ordered his men back while he covered their withdrawal. Subsequently a small party returned to the spot and found that he had bled to death.[75]

Thereafter both parties retired, under the impression that they had claimed victory against overwhelming odds, and prepared for new tasks. Given the length of the engagement and the amount of ammunition expended by both sides, the two deaths, the first of the campaign, were surprising in that more were not killed.[76]

IV

The Japanese Advance

Seh'n im Winde unsern Plüschow kreisen,
Horen schwere Schiffsgranaten heulen,
Sehen hochgewuhlte Einschlagsaulen
Und das Land besat mit Splittereisen

Friedrich Blaschke "Unser Tsingtau"

Within the city the defenders felt that curious ambivalence often characteristic of men under severe stress. They were relieved to be certain, at last, that the Japanese would mount a serious assault. At the same time, they realized that the enemy would bring an overwhelming force, which was a frightening prospect. The aircraft visit of September 5 was thought-provoking for many people. Surely the Japanese thoroughness in bringing the aircraft reflected their single goal: total victory. There could be no genuine contest-of-arms.[1]

That afternoon and night the city's inhabitants discussed the unwelcome arrival of the "evil bird," as they called the aircraft. Among the military, the officers schooled their men in preparing for the return visits. Kessinger issued detailed instructions on the proper firing routines. He demanded that all men either unarmed or busy with duties should stand still or seek cover. Those men with arms should fire supervised vollies against the enemy airplane. He added a direct order that all installation or equipment commanders (artillery, searchlight, and so on) should begin camouflaging their activities against possible Japanese aerial observation.[2] Since no one had anticipated such action, the troops were soon busy with several new activities.

The next day, as everyone sat down for lunch, the noise of the airplane interrupted the meal. Moving quickly, the men fell in with their arms and prepared their welcome. This time the Japanese pilot started over the bay and swept in over the city. As he came over the *Kaiserin Elisabeth* and the *Jaguar*, they fired their guns at him. The big land cannon followed suit, firing away with a great deal of noise. Next the infantry ranks fired salvoes at the large target. As the noise and excitement grew, individuals, military and civilian, joined the effort. They fired from windows, roof tops, the streets—in fact from any sure footing—with an assortment of weapons. It was a grand opportunity for everyone to get rid of many frustrations.

At one point, whether through pilot intent or aerial turbulence, the aircraft dropped suddenly, rose slightly, and fell again before righting itself. The thousands of observers thought surely that they had finally struck the enemy a mortal blow. Quickly the pilot disabused them, as he sought a higher altitude and circled back for his bombing run. He dropped three bombs near the German aircraft hangar.[3] None of them came close to their target, but one did strike a nearby villa. On the veranda the owner and a visitor were taking a nap, oblivious to the racket around them. After the bomb struck the veranda on which they were sleeping, sending iron fragments in all directions, there were holes in everything except the two bemused men.

During the engagement the Germans expended at least 18,000 bullets, uncounted artillery shells, and their own energy, without hitting the Japanese aircraft. Nonetheless, the activity helped morale. For weeks afterward the men spoke fondly of their joint effort, "That was really one 'Hello'!"[4]

The next morning Meyer-Waldeck received the reports on the effectiveness of his rudimentary antiaircraft defenses. Clearly the only persons endangered by this defense were those on the ground; all the falling metal and misplaced shots threatened damage to property and human lives. He needed other methods. Meyer-Waldeck, therefore, sharply restricted the number of people allowed to fire, called for shrapnel fire screens from the big guns, and suggested the development of an early warning system.

In response to the Governor's suggestion, signal troops built a high pole on the Signal Station which virtually everyone in the city could see. To this they could attach a large, red ball, which indicated that aircraft were in sight or two black balls which meant an enemy aircraft over the city. In the latter case, everyone not doing required duty was obligated to take cover. The wounding of some Chinese on September 6 during an air raid helped give the requirement authority.

Concurrently German engineers developed plans for antiaircraft guns, and the dockyard machinists built two sets from the *Kaiserin Elisabeth's* landing guns. They completed a complex firing table based upon mirrors. It worked out the aircraft's speed and altitude while providing the needed firing information. So long as the approaching aircraft held to a straight line, the system proved reasonably effective. However, the Japanese aviators did not fly in a direct line, partially through intent and partially because of the sudden air currents which provided an interesting challenge to the engineers (professional and amateur). While it allowed a defensive barrage against the enemy, and disturbed the Japanese flyers on occasion, the system did not shoot down any aircraft.[5] Despite the intensive German efforts, the Japanese never confronted a serious threat to their aerial supremacy.

The sole German aircraft was more of a counterinfluence to the Japanese airplanes than a serious aerial challenge. Plüschow could accomplish the same general missions; that is, reconnaissance and bombing. His aircraft, however, was not as well suited as the Japanese aircraft for the flying conditions around Tsingtau. In fact, he could not take off for ten days because of the weather. For that period Meyer-Waldeck and his staff depended upon the Chinese courier and spy system for their information. They had a plethora of reports, but they had no way to measure their accuracy. At last, on September 13, Plüschow took off for a quick early morning reconnaissance flight over Shantung. He flew toward Pingtu, Tsimo, and Lauschan Bay in search of the enemy.

In Pingtu he found them without difficulty. In fact, he discovered both the enemy troops and their unique fire discipline. As he came over a small hill, he saw a long, worm-like column moving along the water-filled road. When they observed him, they promptly divided into two lines, which remained motionless as though rooted in the ground. As he moved overhead, they quickly put their rifles to their shoulders and fired a withering volley. Plüschow immediately sought altitude, but his slow, underpowered craft reached 1500 meters with difficulty. The Japanese did not halt their rhythmic firing pattern. Fortunately they did not hit any key parts, but they did put several holes in his aircraft. From his first experience under Japanese fire, Plüschow learned respect for his enemy.[6]

Despite the Japanese professionalism, Plüschow brought back the first information concerning enemy movements, locations, and strengths. The news was highly disturbing. Clearly the Japanese, despite the miserable weather conditions, were moving sizable forces, including artillery pieces, through the Shantung hills. They would soon be at the edge of the protectorate. Meyer-Waldeck was not completely surprised by these details; they substantiated many of his earlier assumptions. Obviously the Japanese had sent a large, competent force. They would be a worthy opponent.

Another aspect of the Japanese advance was that it underscored the weaknesses in the German communications system. The Chinese agents and the pigeon post as sources of information were not enough; neither was the wireless link through the *Sikiang* in Shanghai. Because of these uncertain connections with the outside world Meyer-Waldeck determined to find another means for obtaining information in China.

At hand were three portable wireless sets. While their range was limited, they could provide a clandestine communications line in China. On September 13 a small party with signal troops left Tsingtau. Under a noncommissioned officer, Erich Schutte's, command the group crossed Kiautschou Bay at midnight. They had some sixty-five Chinese bearers and fifteen mules, obtained through their Chinese agents, for the expedition. The next morning they reached Wang tai, where the local Mandarin was anti-German. When the floods forced the Germans into the city, a goodly number of the Chinese bearers melted away. Replacements could not be obtained without the local leader's support. Following long haggling, Schutte persuaded the Mandarin that the equipment was for a distant war lord. With a hastily constructed note to that powerful man, Schutte won the argument and obtained the needed men and animals.

Thereafter the party made slow progress. The storm and less gullible officials conspired against movement. At last, on September 17, they set up their first installation on a remote hill and established contact with Tsingtau, some eighty kilometers away. But the celebration was tempered with a concurrent problem. Despite their efforts

for secrecy, the "Chinese telegraph" carried the news of their arrival
in all directions. The neighborhood Chinese turned out by the hundreds and ringed the expedition each day. Despite the large, unwelcome audience, Schutte left an operational crew and departed for his
next position on September 20.

Right after his departure the German vice-consul from Tsinanfu,
Emil Holzhauer, arrived with the suggestion that they stop their
activities and abandon the station. The Japanese, he said, must be
aware of their position and would be searching for them within a few
days. The crew promptly accepted the idea, assembled their equipment, sent a registered letter after Schutte, and left for a hamlet,
Fang tse. A Japanese patrol reached their old position the next day.
The Germans, learning that the Japanese were already in that area,
hurriedly bypassed it in a wild flight for Tsinanfu. They reached that
city, gave their equipment to the consulate, and fell into bed.

After a day's rest, they received orders for another remote hamlet,
T schou fu. When they finally reached there on September 28,
following severe privations, they found instructions sending them to
Peking. The bearer of the news, a German policeman disguised as a
missionary, filled them in on Schutte's team.

This group had also encountered serious difficulties. After they
had wandered for three days, a local missionary helped them obtain
six camels. With this mobility they set up the second station. They
also quickly discovered the inquisitive natives, who crowded around
them as they worked. Under this informal harassment the Germans
gave up all hope. They turned their receiving equipment over to the
Chinese (receiving a hand receipt) and hid their sending set in a
nearby missionary building. Eventually they reached Peking without
any equipment and without success.[7] Meyer-Waldeck would not
have his desired communications link with the outside world.

A second adjustment was forced on the Governor by the nature of
the Japanese advance. With the Japanese moving overland, the
threat to the protectorate was less centralized and less predictable. In
particular, the Japanese movement into Tsimo created a new interest
in geography. From that point the obvious approach would carry the
assault over the road from Tsimo over Liu ting to Tsingtau. If the
Japanese took this route, they would cross the Pai sha ho, march over
a small, flat area, and then struggle through the hilly country of Lau
hou schan, Tsan kou, and Tung lui schui. At this point the Germans

might present a strong defense and halt the Japanese for some time.

Of the other possible routes only the Hotung Pass, via the Meck-lenburg House, came into question, and it was too far, given the rough terrain, from Tsimo. The March Pass was a difficult, steep mule track, as was the Kletter Pass. No German took either of these routes seriously.[8]

This relative certainty about the Japanese approach was upset when Chinese agents reported Japanese shipping off Lau schan Bay. There were only three merchantmen and a few protective warships, but they pointed out the possibility of an amphibious landing. Meyer-Waldeck had not envisaged a Japanese attack force with such resources. Together with von Kessinger, he decided upon a more formalized defense along the frontier. They must prepare a defense for the entire protectorate despite their earlier assumptions.

On September 11 and 12 he changed assignments for the defensive force. Major Ernst Anders, from the III. Naval Battalion, assumed control of the mountain approaches running along the German right from the water to the Tung liu schui heights. For executing this assignment he received a company from the East Asiatic Detach-ment, together with a reserve artillery battery, the observation troops already in the mountains, and some signalmen. The employ-ment of these men was left to Anders's discretion and report.[9] The remaining defenses from the juncture point in the hills to the Bay, continued under Kuhlo's command with the remainder of his Detachment. He received some artillery and machine gun reinforce-ments, since von Kessinger still believed that the Japanese must come through Liu ting.

Kessinger's view received additional support in the following days, as the patrol encounters increased, as the agents reported the Japan-ese troop movements, and as Plüschow observed the massed enemy advance. Kessinger ordered additional concentrations of men for Kuhlo where he anticipated a serious threat.

The Germans grew tense with the uncertainty. They believed that the Japanese must advance over the only decent road, but their respect for the Japanese soldier, fear of losing men in a surprise action, and concern for the ratio between men and distance (1000 men to defend a line almost 32 kilometers long) gave them pause. This fear received another shock when the Japanese made a sudden foray with torpedo boats into Schatsykou Bay on September 14. They swept in, fired a quick bombardment, and disappeared before the Germans could do anything. It was little more than a show of force, but it upset the defensive calculations once more.

To settle this uncertainty, on September 15 Kuhlo ordered a major reconnaissance-in-force of the Tsimo area. The following day a large mounted patrol under Major Eduard Kellmann crossed the Pai sha ho and moved through Liu ting. A few hundred meters beyond that point they encountered a Japanese patrol, and the two sides traded shots for forty-five minutes before the Japanese withdrew, carrying some wounded with them. Kellmann did not pursue because the terrain on both sides of the road was too soft for horses. Although Kleemann also carried wounded men back, he had confirmed the Japanese presence in force.

That afternoon von Kessinger met with Kuhlo, Anders, and Lieutenant Trendelberg, who represented the Schatsykou defenders, in Litsun. They discussed the developing situation in detail. From all the reports they assumed a possible enemy operation from the north or the northeast, or via a landing in Schatsykou Bay.

They agreed that any assault on Kuhlo's force should be met in the mountains, rather than along the Pai ha so or the level area behind it. Kuhlo would deny the roads to the Japanese as long as he could and then fall back. They also agreed that Anders could not even do that well. His main assignment must be an early report of any Japanese movement and a speedy retirement before the enemy could outflank him. The same instructions pertained for Trendelberg, who would report, fire a few shots, and fall back. All were agreed that they must emphasize the mountain line.[10] With this understanding, the commanders returned to their units, not overly sanguine about their defensive positions, effective manpower, or military prospects.[11]

Behind these loosely assembled formations in their exposed frontier positions, the Germans hurriedly labored on a second defensive line. It followed their previously considered ideas. The engineers sought a rough series of interrelated (but not connected) positions running through the Kouschan and Waldersee Heights to the Prinz Heinrich Mountain. Taking advantage of the natural terrain features with the dominating position of the mountain, the line would be a strong one. Prinz Heinrich Mountain was the significant factor in this scene. If the Japanese could take it, they could easily role up the entire line and could, as well, overlook the Tsingtau defenses. In mid-September someone proposed placing an observation post on the peak. Meyer-Waldeck agreed and, on September 22, ordered the preparation of a sixty-man contingent for this undertaking. The mountain top was about one kilometer in diameter, but it rested upon almost unscalable steep walls. They were rough, deeply cut, and provided no developed pathways. The engineers made the ascent even more difficult in the days thereafter by destroying many approaches. If the Japanese should break through the defensive line elsewhere, the occupants, safe in the aerie, could still provide information despite being cut off from their countrymen.[12]

Since much depended upon this hastily conceived and equally hastily constructed position, the Germans invested a good deal of energy in it. In fact, the troops on the mountain received a surprising additional parcel of cognac, rum, and cigars for their stay. Clearly there was little official doubt about their eventual fate. The troops were truly engaged on a suicide mission. The place quickly became known as the "Eagle's Nest."[13]

In order to maintain the flow of information the Germans pushed forward several patrols on September 18. One of these led to Baron Riesedel's death; another brought news of a Japanese landing in Lau schan Bay. For the Germans this news was a blow, complicating their plans and anticipations. For the Japanese the landing served as another link in their offensive chain around Tsingtau.

The Horiuchi troops, after their successful September 15 reembarcation in Lungkou, found the trip to Lau schan highly uneventful. After they were at sea, the unit commanders had opened sealed envelopes and discovered their destination. The enclosed orders set down the landing order, the initial landing objectives (essentially a line about one-half mile inland), the need for five days' rations per man, and the requirement for haste. This was different from the Lung kou landing; the Japanese anticipated strong German resistance shortly after coming ashore.

The six transports and their escorts arrived in Pipokao, a small inlet about sixty miles north of Lau schan. Here they met the eight ships and escorts carrying the scheduled second echelon from Japan. The latter consisted of specialized troops; that is, engineers, special railway groups, heavy artillery, quartermaster, searchlight, etc.[14] Immediately Horiuchi hurried to Admiral Kamimura's flagship, *Chitose*, for a hasty conference about the landing. They listened to a report by a Major Kihara from the Imperial General Staff, who detailed his reconnaissance of the area on September 13-14. On their first visit a German calvary patrol had almost captured them. Kihara and an equally unarmed colleague had barely reached their small boat and escaped under heavy fire. The next day the Germans had caught them again, but this time the Japanese had a machine gun. With it they had driven the Germans back and retired properly. Kihara's experiences indicated that the Germans were present and would give battle.[15]

With his knowledge, Kihara proposed a landing point 0.8 kilometer south of Wang ko Chuang, which the responsible officers accepted without demur. Kihara then went on to describe the landing zone as a broad, shelving beach with a good rise and fall of tide. Inshore there was a large landing place with a fine space for parking guns, exercising horses, storing ammunition, and starting the roadbed for a light railway. Equally significant for Japanese consideration, the area would accommodate several score of ships. They could disembark troops two or three times as rapidly as they had off Lungkow.

In contrast to this optimistic view Kihara added that the anchorage possessed two drawbacks. First, there was no shelter against winds coming in from the east or southeast. In the event of waves moving in from either direction, the landing would be difficult, for the high swells would make it troublesome to get small craft onto the beach. Also, there was no available refuge for smaller craft, which would, in stormy weather, have to run for Chiangtung, some eighty kilometers away.[16]

In view of Kihara's observations and experiences, Horiuchi insisted upon getting the troops ashore quickly. He wanted the needed men, equipment, and rations ashore behind a secure defensive perimeter. After the troops had achieved these goals, they could worry about assembling landing piers, bringing baggage ashore, and sorting out misplaced men. The assembled officers agreed to his strictures, and they sailed shortly after dawn on September 18.

The day was clear, with a rough sea stirred by a strong southwest wind. At 6:00 A.M., just before the arrival of the transports, six cruisers opened fire, bombarding the hills around the landing point against German interference. Encountering no opposition, the landing party quickly occupied a height about half a mile inland, where they set up a small wireless station and opened direct communications with the ships. On their heels came the landing officials, together with special reconnaissance teams. The latter selected the best locations for piers, landing places, road sites, etc. At 8:00 A.M. the first troops, elements of the Forty-sixth Regiment, started going ashore in hastily impressed landing vessels. Since the expected barges were late in arriving from Pi pa kou, Horiuchi would not wait and forced the available tugs, launches, lighters, and Chinese shipping into service.

All went well until noon, when the winds shifted to the southeast and the resultant high swells filled the landing craft. The landing officials, after a hurried look at the scene, moved the landing point to a sandy beach about 500 meters away. It was the sole place where the combers did not overwhelm the small craft, but it was narrow, full of rocks, and had an unpleasant rip tide. At sunset even this point proved overly dangerous, and the landing officials withdrew the landing craft. Despite the various interruptions, Horiuchi's landing was a success. The major portion of his force was ashore, thereby establishing the essential prong of the Japanese attack operation.[17]

Horiuchi had already issued the orders to be distributed to the infantry units as they reached shore. His carefully written instructions, sealed in envelopes, were given to each unit commander as he moved off the beach. In accordance with these orders, a company started out for the Hotung Pass shortly after landing. The Pass, and a neighboring height, controlled the neighboring terrain. Concurrently smaller units moved out along the coast road to Tschang wa and to Wang go deschuang.

The First Company, under a Captain Kamaji, marched quickly toward the Hotung Pass. It was some eight kilometers from their landing point and ten kilometers from the German defenses. Kamaji did not have any information about the area itself, but he assumed that the Germans would not give it away cheaply. The approach path was narrow and rugged, permitting little more than a double file of foot soldiers. The steep mountains on each side towered precipitously over them. After a difficult climb, they reached a point some 700 meters from the crest, where at three o'clock, they received German fire. Since the defenders used well-sheltered trenches with loop-holes, the Japanese could only estimate that there were twenty or thirty enemy soldiers.

In reality the Germans had forty men under Lieutenant Gunther Below, a high school teacher in Tsingtau and a renowned outdoorsman. He was interested in giving battle, but he was also aware of his orders to delay rather than to stop the enemy.

Kamaji deployed his company into two basic units, a large fire base to keep the Germans busy and a smaller section to climb the rocky slopes on each side of them. As soon as any portion of the flanking group reached a commanding point, it would start firing as a cover for the main party's assault. The climbers were delayed by crags, precipices, and curiously shaped ravines until five o'clock. By that time the impatient Kamaji, afraid that darkness might rob him of his opportunity, ordered the main force forward. The two sides traded shots for an hour as the attackers inched their way along the path. At last Kamaji, tiring of this practice as well, demanded a direct charge.

As they charged the German position, the Japanese discovered that Below's men had already departed without further contesting the ground. The two sides had each fired some 500 rounds, and the Japanese had picked up some miscellaneous items of military equipment. More important, the latter had captured a carefully prepared defensive position, their first such success in the campaign. The essential point, however, was that the seizure of the pass assured the success of the landing. The Japanese could now proceed with their landing without fear of German interruption.[18]

The other units, after coming off the landing craft and obtaining their orders, fanned out in a constantly expanding half-circle. One company slipped into a village, Tu lau, just inside the protectorate. As they arrived in the hamlet, they came upon five or six Germans loitering on a small path. The surprised defenders left hastily, without attempting a shot. Afterwards the Japanese marched a short distance and threw up defensive works against surprise attacks. They were the first Japanese inside the protectorate.

A force from the fourth company started even later for their destination—the link-up with Yamada's troops. Much to their mutual surprise, scouts from the fourth company encountered a Japanese cavalry patrol that evening at six o'clock. They quickly learned from them that the cavalry regiment had entered Tsimo and had begun exploring the Pai ha sho, that the Division's infantry troops were nearing Tsimo, and that there was no need for the company to push on. They had achieved the joining of the two forces with unexpected ease.

Having succeeded at every point in their plan, they settled down for the night. The Japanese had, however, left all their equipment behind them and discovered that the mountains offered no fuel. While the day had been pleasantly warm, the night turned bitterly cold, with strong winds and freezing rains. Bivouacked in the open, the men suffered from the elements.[19] That night, despite the unpleasant conditions, the Germans gave the attackers no rest. Both at Tu-lao and in the Hotung Pass, they advanced patrols of varying size who fired several hundred rounds and departed into the darkness. They knew the ground, while the Japanese did not.

During the night Horiuchi decided to hold his positions and develop them, rather than advance further. The weather had interrupted the movement of his equipment and baggage. At the same time, he did not want a repetition of the German night harassment. On September 19, then, he ordered a local offensive action against the Germans.

In the Hotung Pass the Japanese troops searched for the Germans but could not locate them. The local Chinese all reported that the defenders had departed for areas unknown. The company started forward, after some delays, at 3:30 P.M., in a fine rain which kept up the rest of the day. While marching, the detachment commander received a report from an advance patrol. It had run into the Germans at Mecklenburg House, the health spa on the road to Tsingtau. Below's troops had reacted quickly, wounding two of the four-man patrol.

The Japanese hurried forward, arriving at the spa at 5:30. By this time their battalion commander was with them. He observed the German force and decided that they were not strong enough for effective resistance. Since the hour was late, he ordered a prompt assault. He strolled along, behind the advancing soldiers, exhorting them forward with the strongest words and gestures.

Below's men retired slowly, firing as they moved back. They carefully started prepared fires in the various buildings and removed several items of interest (including the guest book of the health spa, which they all signed before removal). They broke off action only at the last minute, often firing at the Japanese some fifty meters away.

Despite the intense fire, the anxiety and emotionalism on both sides affected their aim, limiting the casualties to two wounded Japanese.[20]

As Below fell back, his men crossed the Cicilien Bridge. This structure, about twelve meters long, was the sole crossing over a deep ravine. As the troops hurried over it, an engineer patrol, which had driven out from Tsingtau, fired the charges under the bridge and left without investigation. They were confident from their experience that the Japanese would not move farther until they repaired the bridge.[21]

With this general pullback the Germans extracted their patrols along the entire frontier. They no longer needed to search for the Japanese; the enemy possessed the initiative. As the Germans retired from Tu lau, they evacuated a pagoda which had served as their headquarters. Subsequently one of the men missed his overcoat, and Corporal Zanzinger returned for it. After picking up the coat and climbing back on his horse, he found himself surrounded by a Japanese patrol. One of them called out in broken German for his surrender, but Zanzinger shouted some choice phrases and gave his pony the spurs. As he fled, the pursuing Japanese fired at him, wounding him in the hand, shoulder, and buttocks. He rode the pony into camp near Kouyai, where he returned the overcoat and declared, "They are miserable shots."[22]

For the most part, September 19 was a day of local activity and troop adjustments for the Japanese. Horiuchi still wanted to make certain that his position was fully secure. Like Kamio, he had no reason to take unwarranted risks or misadventures. He had time. During the day he received assurances that everything was in order. Infantry units from Tsimo joined his troops, creating a firm, continuous band against the protectorate. The weather, while it continued poor, did not halt landing activities. In the course of the day all the essential units reached shore.

Kamio reached Tsimo that same day with his headquarters and assumed command of the Division. That evening he issued orders for the next day. He proposed the continued expansion of communications, the bringing up of additional troops, and the final sealing off of the protectorate before moving on. At the same time, he desired all the disorganization and confusion of the landings to be cleared up. Once he had the men in their normal places, the essential road repairs completed, and a thorough reconnaissance of the German defenses in hand, he could decide on the next step. This was a slow process, but it did eliminate unnecessary risk.

For the next few days, therefore, the Japanese busied themselves with consolidation. The various units dug trenches, prepared blocking positions, and conducted an active reconnaissance program. In virtually all cases the Germans successfully denied them access to the protectorate. Despite their limited numbers, the Germans maintained an alert, tenacious defense.[23] On the ground the Japanese made little progress. Their pressure did provide some indications of the German strength, which was most important to their planning. They did not have any worry about the locations, because they had other means for finding the German positions.

The Japanese Army Air Force arrived on September 21. Using three aircraft, the pilots started flying the same day from a small, hastily constructed airfield near Tsimo. In the following days they quickly picked out the German defenses, troop locations, and general activity.[24]

This constant pressure through reconnaissance activity and the obviously superior Japanese numbers made the Germans understandably nervous. In particular, the unexpected Japanese appearance in the Kletter Pass bothered Major Anders in his camp near Kouyai. He, with von Kessinger's approval, developed a sudden attack plan to help his men's morale and simply to give the Japanese a lesson. Quickly assembling a task force from his command (some 100 men from the East Asiatic Detachment, 30 men from the 5th Company, III Sea Batallion, 4 machine guns, and 2 artillery pieces), Anders ordered a sortie for the morning of September 23.

His instructions made clear that their action was neither a major nor a permanent effort. They would try for the saddle-like area in the Pass, where they would dislodge the enemy, do as much damage as possible, and retreat of their own accord.

The Japanese in the Pass thought that their high position was a secure one, since the steep walls made any approach difficult and vulnerable. They also made the error of accepting German lethargy as a permanent condition. The fact that the area was overgrown with small pine trees, obscuring vision and that the slopes did have some pathways did not disturb them; neither did the manifest signs of German activity, clearly visible below them.

Shortly after 8:00 A.M. a ten-man Japanese patrol started out from the camp toward the German lines. They quickly discovered that the enemy was at their own doorstep. Immediately both sides engaged in a furious firefight. The Germans, effectively using their machine guns and the tree cover, inched up both sides of the Pass. Under cover of the noise a small number of Germans pushed around the Japanese flank. Soon exhausted by their efforts they climbed a small high point and started firing. They were too far away to affect the action, but, as they opened fire, the two artillery pieces joined the fray. This combination proved most effective, and the surprised Japanese ran off in disorder. Moving quickly, the Germans picked up the spoils—a tent, some packs, and a few rifles—and marched back down the hill. The action lasted two hours and brought two wounded men on each side.[25]

The action was not a significant one, but it did buoy German spirits. They had turned on their foe, forced him to run, and returned with little harm. As one might expect, the tales circulating through the defenders of the enemy dead and the extensive booty far exceeded reality. For the Japanese the engagement was an unexpected embarrassment. The scheduled patrol went forward as planned, only a day later and with greater vigilance.

In the middle of his preparations Kamio received informal notice from the General Staff at home ordering him to occupy the Shantung Railroad. Apparently this decision had a political basis rather than a military motivation, but Kamio made no complaint. His troops had already broken the rail communication with their September 17 movement into Kiautschou.[26] He now assigned the task of a more extensive occupation to the Independent First Battalion of Infantry (under Major S. Kanazawa), wich was near Lai-chou. In view of the flooded conditions, Kanazawa moved on Yin-me (thirty-five kilometers east of Wei-hsien). He left Tien-tzu on September 23 and crossed the Wei-ho two days later. Leaving a detachment for the railway bridge over that river, he reached Wei-hsien Station that evening.[27]

This exercise did not impede Kamio's preparations for the major attack. He wanted every man, every gun in place before starting his offensive. He also wanted the long line of men coming from Lung kou and from Wang go dschuang, as well as the following siege troops integrated into his command. Along with these endeavors,

Kamio had to accommodate for the allied troops joining his command.

The British had been busily preparing for the campaign. Their first contribution was the elderly battleship, *Triumph*.[28] At war's outbreak the *Triumph* was in Hong Kong undergoing general overhaul. At that time half of her engines were in the dockyard, no stores or ammunition were aboard ship, and her crew consisted of four officers, twelve Chinese, and thirty sailors. With the mobilization declaration, the local British naval authorities had set out in search of a crew. The crews from demobilized British gunboats in China helped flesh out the ship's complement. Even the Governor of Hong Kong, Arthur May, visited businesses in the city to recruit likely looking young men. Still short of manpower, the ship's officers recruited some 100 men from the British Regiment in Hong Kong, the Duke of Cornwall's Light Infantry.[29] Following a hasty completion of the ship's repairs (she received a coat of gray paint in one night), she sailed for Weiheiwei, which she reached on August 6. Captain Maurice Fitzmaurice then sought to prepare his cosmopolitan crew for war.[30]

On September 10, while the ship was engaged with gunnery practice, he received instructions to join the Japanese Navy off Tsingtau. The ship coaled all night and left at noon the following day, arriving on September 12. Fitzmaurice found the British Naval Attaché, Captain Hubert Brand, a thoroughly professional and linguistically capable naval officer, doing liaison duty with the Japanese. Through him coordination of the two forces moved expeditiously and happily. Fitzmaurice readily accepted his role as a subordinate to Kato, and the latter treated him with every respect and consideration.[31]

The Army coordination did not do as well. Obviously the uncertainty in London over the strength, nature, and purpose of their commitment occasioned difficulty at the very outset. While the naval relationship was one of comparable equals who divided their naval roles with relative ease (giving the Japanese the basic role off Tsingtau), the land forces provided a different question. The British, confronted with a shortage of manpower in their empire and seeing the inexorable German advance into France, could not deal with the powerful Japanese on equal terms. As a result the exchanges between London, Tokyo, and Peking reflected a sense of frenetic uncertainty on the part of the British. The British units committed to the Asian campaign would not have a happy position from the outset.

General command went to Brigadier (temporary) Nathaniel Barnardiston, a man of great good looks and personal charm. From his long experience in dealing with foreigners he had an enviable reputation for diplomacy and tact.[32] Certainly his devout belief and devoted membership in the Anglican Church provided evidence of his moral temper. At the same time, he did not enjoy either a robust physique nor a love of field operations. He preferred the pleasures of the drawing room, where he was much more popular, to the harsh rigors of martial leadership.[33]

Bernardiston, despite his social interests, understood the need for a large British contribution. He foresaw the problem of a small force in the realistic terms of political commitment and military influence. A token force, in his view, could achieve no military objective and it must leave postwar political influence to the force with the larger battalions. Barnardiston resisted any indication of British weakness, but, international events gave his superiors little choice. Following some haggling, the London officials decided in favor of a single battalion from the South Wales Borderers.[34] Not liking this composition, Barnardiston proposed, as something of a last resort, the addition of half a battalion from the Sikh units stationed in China. Following a prompt refusal, the War Office had second thoughts. After determining that the colonial office would pay for the Sikhs, the London bureaucrats reversed themselves and accepted the idea.[35] Certainly the Thirty-sixth Sikh Battalion enjoyed a fine reputation.[36] With them Barnardiston felt that his manpower and prestige needs were satisfied within the limits of his expectations.

The two governments agreed on their respective contributions to the campaign. While each one would provide its own transportation, supplies and equipment, the Japanese would furnish the communication lines, the control for the rear areas, and the commander.[37] Given the disproportionate size of the two contingents, staff relationships, command questions, and mission assignments would be difficult. On September 3, the Japanese General Staff gave Kamio specific instructions to oblige their allies in every possible fashion. He should provide them the best possible accommodations, avoid their sacrifice (manpower replacement would not be easy), and be careful of difficulties through speech, race, etc.[38]

With these exchanges and arguments, the representatives of the two powers prepared for the campaign. Like the Germans, the British found the conflict a total surprise. The two designated units had had their barracks close to the Germans, and had enjoyed friendly relationships with them. In June 1914 Lieutenant Colonel Kuhlo had invited the Borderer officers to dinner. The British appeared in their dress uniforms, while the Germans, who had none, appeared in their normal uniforms. Both groups found the situation most humorous. At the subsequent ceremonies Kuhlo and Lieutenant Colonel H. G. Casson each spoke about the genuine friendship between their two countries, drank to each other's health, and joined in singing each other's national anthem.[39] The entire affair reflected the mutual esteem, real friendship, and collective understanding of both groups.

With the gradual movement toward war, the British soldiers quickly formed their civilian countrymen into the Tientsin Volunteer Force. This group replaced the garrison. They trained each morning before their business hours and again in the evening. As the Borderers departed for the siege, they gradually integrated into service as guards for the legation. Like their German counterparts, the plump, unmilitary businessmen added an impression of security as well as of good humor. They did, ostensibly, release the Borderers for their duty, but the reservists, like their German counterparts, did not inspire military confidence.

The regular troops were scheduled for landing on the second or third day at Lau schan Bay. Unfortunately, the problems at Lungkow forced a postponement. There were too many units scheduled for disembarkment. At length the Borderers loaded some 22 officers and 910 men at Tientsin on September 19; the Sikhs would come later. They boarded three chartered coastal ships, *Kwang Ping, Shao Shing*, and *Shuntine*.[40] Despite efforts for security, the British settlement learned of the departure and arrived en masse for a memorable send-off of loud music, cheers, and emotion. After the flat-bottomed vessels crossed the sand bar in front of the harbor, they joined the *Triumph* and the destroyer, *Usk*, which would escort them to Lau schan.

After a brief voyage, the convoy arrived at Weihaiwei the next day. They quickly embarked over 200 mules, picked up the *Shenking*, a vessel chartered as a hospital ship, exchanged views with the escort crews, and departed on September 21. Despite a strong rumor that they would meet a brigade from Hong Kong for a direct assault upon Tsingtau, they met a Japanese destroyer, which escorted them into Lau schan Bay.[41] The eager Englishmen were thrilled with the sight of some fifty-seven vessels in the Bay. They were going to war.

In the Bay they found the Japanese busy with their construction work. They had floated a long barrel-supported pier from Port Arthur for landing troops, and it served admirably for this purpose. They had also built a temporary stone pier to use while they drove two more substantial structures. The most interesting spectacle for the British was a special vessel fitted with a powerful crane. It unloaded the heavy-duty lighters on one of the half-completed docks. From the wooden gantry special crews moved the materials on to a narrow-gauge railway.[42] From there Chinese work crews, impressed as labor troops, moved the supplies and equipment forward with speed and efficiency. The landing operations went on around the clock, as the Japanese employed a small electric plant for night illumination. Clearly the Japanese knew what they were doing.

Barnardiston paid a duty call on Admiral Kamikura and hurried ashore, where he found an unexpected sight. In front of the landing office were crossed Japanese-British flags. While the Japanese were clearly committed to the movement of war materials inland, they quickly adjusted their transport efforts to include the needs of their allies. The British had no difficulty arranging their landing for the next morning.

Shortly after 8:00 A.M. on September 23, the Borderers began disembarking. The operation went like clockwork, and the men reached shore with ease. After their landing came the more tedious activity of unloading the animals, equipment, and supplies. The mules proved the most difficult. The landing crews first slung them over the ship's side by crane, lowered them into lighters, and moved them close inshore. At that point the crews had to force the suspicious mules into the water. Corporal George Terelt found that the easiest approach was twisting the animal's tail until he jumped into the water. Thereafter everyone employed the same method. Unloading was strenuous activity, but the men worked with a vengeance, since a vigorous effort would get them to the war a bit earlier.[43] They moved everything, including a fourteen days' food supply, ashore by the following morning.

Once ashore, Barnardiston quickly sent off Major H. G. Pringle, together with Lieutenant Colonel Everard Calthrop and the Japanese liason officer, Major Hiwatashi, to Chimo for a discussion with Kamio concerning the next steps.[44] At the same time he dispatched Captain C. D. Moore to reconnoitre the Lao Shan mountains, where he wanted his troops stationed on the left of the investment line, close to their support. Moore reported that the two roads in that area were not useful for military movement. One was impassable, the other passable only with severe difficulty.[45]

On September 25 the Borderers moved off the beach at 10:00 A.M. Barnardiston made a brief address, read the King's message delivered to the troops in France, and wished everyone well. Then the troops marched ten kilometers to Pu Li over a narrow, congested road. Shortly after their arrival, Pringle reported to Barnardiston with two distasteful pieces of news. Kamio wanted the British contingent in the center near Litsun rather than Barnardiston's desire for a position on the left flank.[46] Moreover, the Japanese planned a major offensive action within the next few days. The British must hurry if they wanted a place in line.

Barnardiston reluctantly decided that his men, and subsequent supplies, must move over a single-track, narrow road filled with Japanese transport. To do so meant putting his men on half rations and marching them very hard. Nonetheless, he decided that he had little choice and ordered the men out the following morning. Departing at 6:00 A.M., they marched some twenty-one kilometers to Chimo. It was not a long march, but it was an incredibly burdensome one. The Japanese idea of march discipline was totally foreign to the Anglo-Saxons, unused to broken columns, individual pauses, and men camped on the road. The road itself was little more than a sea of mud with a few boulder islands scattered about. As the British moved forward, they found that the Japanese often broke into their columns and drove the men into the fields alongside the muddy track. In the fields, the long sweet-potato tendrils impeded progress while increasing tempers. Complaint was useless because of the language barrier. At noon the weary soldiers reached Chimo, but the carts with their equipment and ammunition did not arrive until well into the night.[47]

The next day the marchers reached Liuting, again a mere fourteen kilometers away, but with a repeat performance of the previous day's problems. As they slogged toward their destination, however, they could hear the sound of guns engaging in reciprocal artillery fire, they could observe the Japanese aircraft circling over the battle lines, and they could see the masts of the German vessels. All the sights and sounds excited them once more with the prospect of battle. Barnardiston, equally anxious as his men, hurriedly rode on to Kamio's headquarters, which had just arrived in the area. He wanted to meet his commander, to report on his progress, and to obtain additional data on the operational plans. As he did so he crossed into German territory, the first British commander to do so in the First World War.

Kamio received his ally graciously. He expressed his gratitude for Great Britain's participation and his admiration for their speedy arrival. Throughout the interview Kamio maintained a dignified presence; that is, warm, solicitous, and concerned, but he revealed no military ideas. In fact, Barnardiston left without accomplishing much.

He and his staff found that they could not understand their ally. Even the Japanese headquarters organization was foreign far beyond their anticipation. For the Japanese, any continued appearance of activity or concern resulted in a loss of dignity or personal prestige. Kamio was never busy or preoccupied in public. He spent a good deal of time rambling over the countryside with his adjutants in search of wildflowers. Many staff members tended vegetable or flower gardens. While their certain movement precluded any harvest, they left enlisted men to tend each plot after their departure. Among the large staff conversation was general and continuous, creating a general appearance of intense disorder. There was no place for an individual to do his work among his colleagues.

When orders were required, a staff Colonel held a conference with the concerned persons in an open field. The men gathered around him in a half circle, answered roll call, and listened to the operational instructions. At the end the Colonel asked one officer, selected at random, to repeat the orders. Then the Colonel asked if they had any questions or statements of general interest—which often included articles or animals lost or found. Afterwards, the Colonel would dismiss the group and return to his normal activities.[48] For the British this approach to staff work was incomprehensible and maddening. Nonetheless, Kamio was in charge; on that score there was never any doubt.

On September 28 he ordered Barnardiston's force to Litsun,

where they were to enter the front lines. As they marched out of Liuting, Kamio appeared on the roadside. He expressed his renewed admiration for their participation. At the same time, he found their "shorts" a strange uniform and asked how they kept their knees warm in winter. Then Kamio gave them the welcome news that they could anticipate action within a short time. The British troops, still on half rations and without their equipment, eagerly hurried forward with this anticipation. They were disappointed, however, as the Germans departed before their arrival.[49] The British had moved with enviable promptitude but the situation had changed during the intervening period.

By September 25 events on the frontier had greatly altered military conditions. Both sides understood these developments and prepared for a trial by arms. For the Germans these changes did not augur an optimistic future. They lacked the essential manpower, the sophisticated equipment, the geographic position for a powerful defensive action. Sensing that time was fast running out, Meyer-Waldeck shifted a few men from the redoubts to the forward lines.[50] The Governor also ordered the *S-90* and the *Jaguar* into the bay where they could fire on the advancing Japanese. These latter instructions came at the right moment, since the ships had just completed their preparations for this possible duty. Their crews had laboriously fastened heavy metal plates to the decks and then added coal sacks filled with sand (which quickly brought the descriptive term, "Sack Ships") against enemy artillery fire. Earlier the most important ships' personnel had conducted a careful walking tour of the area and had acquired a detailed knowledge of target zones, range distances, and prominent land features.[51] Despite these final preparations, there was no question that the Japanese alone would decide when, where, and how they would open the campaign.

By September 25, Kamio was ready for action. His efforts to bring the troops, equipment, and other impedimenta of war into place had finally reached fruition. He was confident in his communications, organization, and general preparedness. The Japanese could advance over the frontier.

On this day, Kamio issued his orders for the march against the German positions. These instructions benefitted from his full and precise knowledge of the German situation, which he had gathered

partly from his omnipresent aerial reconnaissance, but mainly, especially the detail, from espionage activities.[52] The espionage, using
both Japanese spies and Chinese recruits, provided him with the
basic positions and movements of the Germans, the locations of their
individual mines, and the general placement of their artillery pieces.
The single error in their estimates was the number of Germans.
Kamio thought that he faced some 2,000 men (the proper figure was
700) on the frontier, which did change his planning.[53] With his
information, Kamio decided that he faced three defensive lines. The
first was merely an outpost system, which might prove a hinderance
to any advance but not provide a serious obstacle. These positions ran
along defensible ground, but they demanded more manpower than
the Germans could commit to them. Behind this general line was a
second—an irregular, fortified position running between the Kouschan and Waldersee Heights. He believed that this area was the
strongest natural one available to the Germans, but, again, beyond
their resources of equipment and men. Behind it were the main
series of fortifications directly in front of the city.

Given these assumptions, Kamio found no reason to alter his
general plans. He wanted a quick resolution of the campaign, but
without a high casualty rate. This latter point was one of great
importance to Kamio, who wanted to coerce his enemy into submission rather than overwhelm him. He thought that a strong attack
would carry through the first two lines with little time loss and few
casualties. His simple orders, issued on September 25, called for an
advance over the Pai scha ho the next day. The crossing should begin
with a general reconnaissance-in-force of the German defenses,
followed by a general deployment. With these broad preliminaries
completed, the major assault would follow the next day with a full-
scale movement into the Litsun valley. He anticipated that September 26 and 27 would be the critical time for breeching the
German first line. By the second day the advance should be stretched
out along the second German position, which would be cut on
September 28.[54] The Japanese would approach the Germans with the
22 Cavalry Regiment, the Twenty-four Brigade (less the Fifty-sixth
Regiment), and assorted other elements on the right flank. In the
center were the Fifty-fifth and Fifty-sixth Infantry Regiments and
several artillery units, together with the normal support forces. On
the left wing was Horiuchi with his Twenty-third Brigade (not includ-

ing the Fifty-fifth Regiment). Kamio's instructions went out to his subordinate commanders that evening.

As Kamio had ordered, the next morning the Japanese crossed over the Pai scha ho in force. A bright morning sun shone on their march, seeming to augur well for their flag's success. The Germans received the first report about 9:00 A.M. Captain Otto Schaumberg, from an observation point on the Tsangouer Heights, reported the long, dark lines of Japanese troops on the march. Immediately the Germans in the area hurried to their various positions and prepared for action. Kuhlo appeared at 10:00 A.M. and, with the men, watched the developing Japanese movement in awestruck admiration. They counted nine infantry companies, six machine guns, and various artillery batteries. It was a powerful body against their meager resources.

From the sea the *S-90* was already in action, and the *Jaguar* soon joined in firing on the Japanese troops. While their fire clearly disturbed the Japanese advance, they did not halt nor seriously impede its progress. The few German artillery batteries, available in the general area, fired at any fleeting target but achieved little success beyond killing some Chinese coolies busy constructing Japanese positions. The guns lacked the range and numbers for an effective opposition. For the defenders the Japanese surge toward the Tsanghou and Lau hou schan Heights implied serious action.

In an effort to observe the movement, von Kessinger and his staff drove to a promontory northwest of Koutsy, where they had a magnificent view of the terrain, positions, and troop movements. What they saw from their grandstand seats encouraged no optimism. The Japanese moved like professionals, presenting few targets. They used the terrain properly, dug in immediately, and avoided any contact with the defenders. Perhaps the greatest shock to von Kessinger was the Japanese ability to move over natural obstacles. The enemy infantry demonstrated a speed and agility in advancing over rough ground which far exceeded German endeavors. German plans had not taken this talent into account.[55]

By 4:00 P.M. the Japanese had reached points near the defending German positions. Kuhlo suggested in orders at that time that he thought the Japanese were satisfied with their advance and that they would do little more that day.[56] Even as he signed these instructions, which also relocated a few reserve people, the Japanese came forward again. The clouds had moved over the sky, darkening the day. There would be no stars that night. There was no contact at dusk, but the Germans could see that the Japanese were still on the move. As the evening turned into night, the attackers laid down a sudden artillery barrage which lasted until the 6:00 P.M. darkness.

As the guns stopped firing, various reports came to Kuhlo about continued Japanese activity. German observers, located along the road between the Lau hou schan and Tung liu Schui Heights, reported Japanese firing on them from both the front and rear while passing them, in force, on both sides. Since the Japanese made no attempt to conceal their movement but did not detonate any mines, and moved easily around the barbed wire obstacles, the defenders blamed the Chinese for betraying them. Hearing these reports, the local commander, Major Kleemann, in great apprehension, ordered a quick retirement. He feared that the fabled Japanese night mobility would cut him off from his comrades. When news of Kleeman's retirement reached Kuhlo, he quickly drove toward the area, meeting Kleemann at a small *Gasthaus* on the road. The neighboring battery had just fired a colored rocket to inform the *Jaguar* and the *S-90* about the retreat. Kuhlo, nonplussed but angry over this hasty decision, ordered an immediate halt. He instructed Kleemann and his troops to take up positions for the night. At the same time, however, he accepted the idea of a further pullback, and told Kleemann to prepare for that eventuality.[57] Should the Japanese attack, there was no reason for needless sacrifice.

In reality the Japanese had, excluding various security patrols, halted for the night. They, too, remained uncertain about the day's events. Their units were still mixed up, confused about German locations, and not entirely clear about the day's developments. In reality, then, the Germans were reacting to their fear of a major Japanese night endeavor. By 8:00 P.M. even Kuhlo fell victim to the same fever and ordered a general retirement.[58] Imagination had proved a greater threat than the enemy.

The men, scattered along the heights, pulled back into Tsangkou, where they stayed the night, sleeping with their rifles on their arms. Even before daylight they pulled out, putting the torch to many buildings and tearing out all the communication links. They moved back along Litsun Creek.

Unfortunately, not everyone received the retirement orders. A

youthful reserve lieutenant, Ludwig Merk, with two machine guns
and an infantry platoon, had his station on a hill near Schykou. He
saw the reflected light of the *Jaguar*'s searchlight beams probing the
darkness, and his men heard the feared night noises heralding a
Japanese assault. For Merk, isolated and alone, the darkness and his
lack of knowledge proved overly confusing. With some trepidation
he ordered the machine guns packed and his men prepared for
departure at daybreak.

As first light increased visibility, Merk's unit received fire from a
hidden Japanese unit some 400 meters away. He quickly ordered the
guns unpacked and prepared for action. Merk's guns raked an
advancing, but totally surprised, Japanese column from the flank and
drove them off the road in precipitate flight. As the Japanese gave
ground, they stumbled into a minefield. The explosions were too
much for them, and they ran off in haste. Other Japanese troops,
uncertain what was happening, did the same.

Merk's platoon, seizing the opportunity, quickly repacked the
guns and left at a run for Litsun. For some distance his flying column
ran along the highway, already crowded with Japanese troops, who
were simply bewildered by the sprinting group. The Germans hit
Litsun Creek at full speed, fortunately near a dry crossing point.
Shortly thereafter they encountered their countrymen, including
Kuhlo, who exclaimed, "I could kiss you, Merk. How did you do it?
We had all counted you among the dead."[59] They had survived their
sudden dash by the barest of margins.

The same chaotic retreat was taking place on the German right
flank. The Japanese, anticipating opposition but finding none, advanced with caution. Their slow pace provided welcome relief for the
defenders. The sole doubters were the men in the Schatsykou who,
despite the lethargic Japanese movement, found themselves cut off
from Tsingtau. They received a short message that night from von
Kessinger, ordering their retirement upon the Waldersee Heights.
The Detachment quickly destroyed the few buildings, blew up two
cannon, and buried two machine guns. At 11:00 P.M. they departed
over a little-used and highly difficult path along the coast. Moving
with stealth behind a knowledgeable guide they slipped around the
Japanese outposts.[60] Their silent departure testified to German fears
of Japanese military superiority—they abandoned an important
defensive point without a shot.

Alfred Meyer—Waldeck

D. Frowein

Japanese poster printed and circulated during the siege

Japanese poster printed and circulated during the siege

Hoover Institution

München, 6. Oktober 1914   Preis 30 Pfg.   19. Jahrgang Nr. 27

SiMPLiCiSSiMUS

Abonnement vierteljährlich 3 Mt. 60 Pfa.   Begründet von Albert Langen und Th. Th. Heine   In Österreich Ungarn vierteljährlich K 4.20

Alle Rechte vorbehalten

Deutsche Wacht in Kiautschau

Cover of *Simplicissimus*, 6 October 1914, "The German Watch in Tsingtau"

Patricia, the Hamburg-Amerika liner, carrying officers and men homebound from Tsingtau, 1914

Adolf Voss

Top left: Ed Leipold. Top right: C. von Wenckstern. Bottom left: Christian Vogelfänger. Bottom right: Paul Kley

Generals Kamio and Barnardiston with staff members in front of the Moltke barracks

Ed Leipold

Japanese supply troops moving forward after the flood

Japanese troops moving through a flooded Chinese village

Ed Leipold

Japanese siege gun
National Archives

The invaluable narrow-gauge railway which served the besiegers so well. In the background one of the large siege pieces

National Archives

The great ditch in front of the German lines as observed from the German lines

Destroyed German casemates on Bismarck Hill

Ed Leipold

Tent of the beachmaster as the British landed

Landing pier with the British troops coming ashore

Public Record Office, London

The Diedrichs stone with the Japanese inscription "7 November 1914" chiseled over it

C. Vogelfänger

On September 26, therefore, the Germans had not succeeded in accomplishing very much. They had created a good deal of noise, and they had impeded Japanese progress, but they had not stopped their enemy at any point. The Japanese advance had suffered more from its own fears and concerns than from any German interference. Kamio made the same observation. He quickly perceived that the Germans, at least in the outlying portion of their territory, did not have the manpower or equipment for a serious defensive effort. They were not fighting as much as they were firing and backing away. His aerial reconnaisance-oreconnaissance made the same observation; i.e., there were no indications of a real battle before the Kouschan-Fuschan line.[61] Kamio's battle orders for the following day reflected this conclusion.

He wanted his troops to move along the entire line early in the morning. If there was any emphasis, he desired it in the center, where the troops could avoid the German naval guns. He also regulated specific troop shifts with even greater care. They were moving into the mouth of a funnel, where overcrowding became both certain and dangerous. Kamio wanted his men close to the German second position by evening.

The Germans, still frightened over their immediately precarious situation, anticipated the Japanese thrust. They began moving back during the early morning hours. As the last troops left Tsangkou, they completed firing the government office buildings and destroyed the water works in Litsun.[62] As fortune would have it, the people responsible for the destruction were those who had either lived in or built the structures which they now sacrificed to the war gods.

Noting the German activity the Japanese reacted in differing fashion. Horiuchi decided against adjusting his starting times because of confusion among his troops. Harada revamped his schedule and hurriedly set his advance for 5:00 A.M. The lingering stars, the soaring flames in Litsun, the *Jaguar*'s sweeping searchlights, and the starting artillery exchange was the eerie backdrop for this advance. Almost immediately after Harada's forces started forward, they began to lose their way in the darkness. In several cases small units ended up behind their neighbors and, when the latter halted for any reason, became entangled to the point of mutual confusion.[63] No one made any progress until dawn allowed the

Japanese an opportunity to sort themselves out and to check on the German locations.

They quickly discovered the German retirement and started cautiously after the defenders. Almost immediately they came under heavy artillery fire from both the land and water sides. On the land side the Germans had some ten guns, most of them around Honan village. They were more effective than their small number might indicate, because of their concealed positions and superb observation posts. From Prinz Heinrich Hill the Germans could see all movement, and they made full use of this opportunity.

From the water side the *S-90* and *Jaguar* welcomed the support of the *Kaiserin Elizabeth*, whose captain, Richard Makoviz, held the helm personally. The three vessels were constantly on the move, firing on the advancing Japanese. The attackers did what they could against this unwanted interruption. At first the Japanese sent their aircraft against them with bombs, but they found that the ships could easily evade bombs. Also the defenders, in this first air-sea engagement in history, gave the aircraft a warm reception. The three bombers had to drop down to 700 meters before loosing their bombs in a hail of fire, and all three aircraft received marks testifying to the defense.[64] Despite the tenacious resistance, the Japanese kept up their bombing during the next few days.

More serious challenges to the naval forces, in the German view, came from the Japanese artillery, which quickly earned everyone's grudging respect. Shortly before noon the Japanese directed several pieces against the Lilliputian fleet. Almost immediately they straddled each one, forcing prompt evasive action. They obtained no hits, but they soon covered the German deck plates with water and iron fragments from near misses. The sound of the near misses reverberating on the ships' plates received the respectful German designation, "the Japanese knock."[65] This exchange of shells provided a good deal of noise and excitement but it was only a minor accompaniment to the cacaphonous roar of the land struggle.

The campaign by the second German defensive line was a loosely conducted affair, with the defenders backing up under cover of their artillery. They made no effort to maintain a continuous defensive front nor to give real battle. For the most part they executed brief, sharp rearguard actions and then retired a short distance for another comparable action. Their greatest fear was still that Kamio would tie them down during the day and then encircle them during the night, cutting their line of retreat. A visibly tired Meyer-Waldeck spent much of the day at a forward observation point, watching without a word. He could do nothing about the pageantry unfolding before him.[66] There was no specific, detailed plan on either side. When they encountered one another, the Japanese deployed, searched for an open flank, fired a few shots, and advanced rapidly. The Germans sought to extract the highest price in blood and to delay the enemy. The artillery kept up an infernal racket, and their impacting shells soon turned the air a dirty, yellow-brown color.[67] The Japanese possessed the initiative, however, and kept up the pressure.

The Germans had fully expected the day's developments. They believed that the Japanese were suffering extraordinarily for their advance, and that the enemy was caught in a difficult position, unable to escape observation from Prinz Heinrich Hill. While the communications link between the "Eagle's Nest" and Tsingtau proved defective at the outset, the occasional telephone connection and the heliographic equipment assisted several successes against the attackers.[68] By evening the Germans believed that they had the best of the day's activities.

Throughout the night the Germans labored to fulfill two incompatible assignments. On the one hand, they strengthened their positions with barbed wire entanglements, laid new land mines, improved the communications system, and relocated artillery pieces.[69] Concurrently, however, the men prepared to move heavy material (artillery, machine guns, ammunition) to the rear, for an orderly retirement into the main city defenses (to avoid the possibility of a Japanese assault at the critical transfer moment), and to properly adjust the command functions (as a way of avoiding all control difficulty).[70] To make certain of this control, von Kessinger undertook the potentially dangerous activity of reorganizing the command structure while shifting troops. He divided the defensive responsibilities into two sections. Major Anders received responsibility for the right flank while Lieutenant Colonel Kuhlo controlled the left side.[71] Kessinger's hope was clearly a more powerful defense against the certain assault the following morning.

Kamio did not share the German opinion that evening that his troops had suffered a setback. In contrast to German reports, his troops had suffered a few insignificant casualties. To be sure, the

German artillery fire had proved highly disturbing, but it had not in any way altered his original plans. Certainly Kamio did not underestimate the advantages of the German position. They could look down on his troops throughout the battle area as though from a balloon. The observation post on Prinz Heinrich Hill precluded free Japanese movement. In the new battle the big German guns on Moltke, Bismarck, and Iltis would play a role. Moreover, Kamio's weather reports indicated another stormy period for Shantung. Rain began falling that evening and continued throughout the night.[72]

He foresaw, despite these developments, no reason to change his original directions. The German fortifications on the Hai po were clearly the important factors. Those in front of the Japanese forces were temporary expedients of little value. His aerial reconnaissance indicated that the position for the second defensive line was naturally strong, but that it lacked sufficient human defenders. The Japanese should get through without difficulty. Nonetheless, he did not want a disaster occasioned by a rash act. Kamio therefore issued orders during the night of September 27 for a detailed reconnaissance of the German positions and a general tightening of the Japanese lines. They would use September 28 in deploying and ordering the units for a general assault the next day, with an aggressive, controlled movement along the entire line. The main event would come a day later.[73] Together with these cautious instructions, he ordered Horiuchi to capture Prinz Heinrich Hill.

That night the Japanese kept up a strong patrol activity which disturbed both the German preparations and their sleep. Starting at midnight, the defenders were at their posts under full alarm conditions. The dark, rainy night made the occasional shots and the sound of moving men eerie and disconcerting. After the strenuous activity of the previous day and the Japanese harrassment during the early night, the Germans found themselves totally exhausted by first light.[74]

At 6:00 A.M. a German battery on Waldersee Heights opened September 28 with a rhythmic fire upon Japanese positions. Their shells fell between Japanese units and did little more than scar the land, but fifteen minutes later the offending battery received heavy Japanese counterfire, losing five men and one gun. Thereafter the

Japanese artillery assumed command of the battlefield and ranged with growing power over the area, driving the Germans from some positions and denying them others with a rain of iron. Not even the German observation post on Prinz Heinrich Mountain could counteract the authority of the Japanese artillery. The Japanese troops started forward.

Even as they did so, the action widened on all sides. Within Kiautschou Bay, the German ships returned to harrass the Japanese flank. While they had had some warning of the attacker's power the previous day, they found the Japanese out in force on September 28. At 7:00 A.M. the Japanese artillery went after the *Jaguar* with a vengeance. As the *S-90* joined the fray, the Japanese gunners tormented her with care. Within minutes both vessels were turning and shifting positions for their very lives. They called in the late-arriving *Kaiserin Elisabeth*, and, collectively went after their tormentors. Using their own visual observation and that of the Prinz Heinrich Hill, they riddled the offending batteries with sharapnel, driving most of them out of action by 9:30 A.M. While the German decks remained wet from the near misses, the Japanese had to move their guns to avoid more bloodshed. The ships had won a clear victory over the hastily committed, poorly concealed land defenses. It was a grand, if short-lived, experience.

As the Japanese infantry flowed toward the German lines, they suddenly encountered, at long last, the defenders' main installations. Bismarck and Iltis both began to fire their first shells against the foe. For the gun crews this opening fire was a major thrill—they were at war! Their exhilaration possessed a short life. After a few salvos, the crews heard the air-denying impact of huge shells. The ear-shattering bangs dumbfounded the crews for a short time until a few experienced observers pointed out that the "blue peas" or "cabin trunks," as the Germans termed them, came from the sea rather than from the land side. At long last the blockading fleet was contributing its noisy rendition to the besieging orchestration. The tempo of the siege changed once more as the Japanese increased their metal pressure upon the defenders.

At a conference on the previous day, Kamio and his staff had decided upon the fleet's participation. While some staff officers had suggested a barrage on September 27, no one in command had seriously thought about the possibility.[75] The bombarding ships, *Suwo, Iwami, Tango*, and *Triumph*, had departed their normal blockade positions in favor of direct intervention.[76] They made two runs, beginning shortly after 9:00 A.M. The Japanese cruiser, *Tone*, assumed station off-shore as a marking ship, observing and correcting the shell fall. During the first run the light was very bad and the *Tone*, along with everyone else, had difficulty following the shells. Also, the lay of the land around Tsingtau was new to the Japanese. The second effort was more satisfying; the shells could be observed striking the defending batteries. In sum the attackers fired some 148 shells. They did encounter some opposition from the defenders' guns on Hui tschuen huk. The battery there straddled the *Suwo* twice, frightening the attackers. The Germans' unusual accuracy forced the attackers to withdraw from the action zone, an hour after their arrival, pleased that they had not received any hits.[77]

While the Japanese had difficulty locating their hits ashore, the Germans had few problems in finding them. As the ships let loose their shells, the defenders closed their apertures and stopped operations. The mood of the gun crews had switched within a few minutes from the excitement of entering the war to the abject terror of perishing in it. The earth quaked as the "boxcar" twelve inch shells came in with an unnerving sound. When the huge shells exploded, the crack of flying metal, hiss of compacted air, and ensuing smoke column gave the general impression of Walpurgis Night.[78] Inside the gun turrets the concussion of the exploding shells precluded all discussion, all activity, all illumination. The frightened crews, listening to the shells, watched for the first signs of cracks in their concrete defenses. There were none, but the sand, rock, and trees tossed around by the barrage clogged the guns' mechanisms and prevented their traversing operations.[79] Throughout the German positions the results of the Japanese fire were memorable. The Germans had not anticipated the incredible force of the large guns.

The survivors' stories quickly circulated among the garrison after the big Japanese ships answered German prayers and departed for a distant station. A cook in the Iltis barracks was so involved with making soup that he did not hear the cannonade until a huge shell came through the wall, tearing the doors off their hinges and passing out the other walls before it exploded in the yard. When the cook finally recovered his senses, he automatically returned to his duties. Commander Sachse, returning from an inspection visit, suddenly appeared at a house door, his horse minus a foreleg, and he in a state of shock. When the local citizens unsaddled the horse, they found a piece of metal weighing ten kilograms under the saddle.[80]

Damage was slight and casualties were few. A pigsty near Bismarck battery, together with its Chinese pig keeper, disappeared in a direct hit. Other shells disinterred the bodies from the Russian cruiser, *Casarewitsch*, which had fled to Tsingtau during the Russo-Japanese War. The cadavers were thrown about as if by a whirlwind. Elsewhere the bombardment damaged walls and smashed windows. The physical damage was not that extensive, but the human shock was extreme. It was a frightening time.

Even as the big ships lobbed their death packages toward Bismarck, the German commanders decided in favor of retreat. They feared a Japanese thrust on their feeble defenses, and they were concerned to get their own troops into the infantry redoubts. By 11:00 A.M. the German troops stretched out along the Fusan-Waldersee Heights received orders to hasten into Tsingtau. They obeyed promptly. But one battery could not extricate itself in time, and the crew blew up the guns. As they did so, a Chinese ammunition column approached them. Just as the guns went up, two Japanese shells exploded among the Chinese, killing several of them. A quick-witted sergeant shouted, "To the rear, march!" and the survivors impassively turned and carried their loads back to the city.[81] It was not their war, but it provided them an existence.

The Japanese followed closely, but without crowding their foe. Kamio still did not want unnecessary casualties. As one group of Germans reached the Haipo bridge, they found that the road-closing obstacles were already in place. The frantic men, screaming profanity, broke through after some effort and, spurred on by Japanese rifle fire, scurried into the city.[82]

By mid-afternoon the Germans were back in Tsingtau. They were tired from their struggle in the protectorate, but they were proud of their accomplishments. Also they were encouraged by the thought that the Eagle's Nest would allow a continued surveillance of the battlefield.

The Japanese, however, assessed the events more objectively. They had moved through the best natural defense line without a major struggle, and they had shut the defenders up in the city. The "Eagle's Nest" was a challenge, but they were already at work on that problem.

In accordance with Kamio's orders, Horiuchi had detailed a reinforced company from the Forty-sixth Regiment and an engineer section (a total of some 200-300 men) to assault the Eagle's Nest. Their colleagues called them "Kesshitai" (men resolved to die). The commander, a Captain Sato, gave an impassioned speech to his men about their difficult assignment and the strength of the German position, and concluded with an emotionally charged cheer for the Emperor.[83] They reached the base of the huge peak after dark on September 27, without opportunity for reconnaissance. In the darkness and rough, unfamiliar terrain, their progress was slow. Dividing his command, Sato sent one group off in search of another path. He also had the men put straw matting on their boots, which cut down the noise.

As the Germans in the Eagle's Nest began their morning activities, a sudden shot extinguished a work lantern and announced the unwelcome intruders. In the murky early dawn the two sides sought each other. Sato fell, mortally wounded, as did his second-in-command. For several hours the two sides engaged in a furious struggle for the peak. The Japanese suffered numerous casualties and could not advance farther. The Germans, sending messages to the city about artillery targets as well as a running commentary on their own battle, could not leave either. At length the second Japanese party appeared behind the Germans, firing a few ineffective shots and waving the Japanese flag. But their interruption proved sufficient, and the Germans began giving way. Boeseler tried a parley with the Japanese, offering them the peak in return for the unfettered retirement of his men. To his discomforted surprise, the Japanese disregarded the flag of truce, seized him, and refused his return to his men. With that the Germans surrendered quickly.[84]

At a cost of twenty-four men the Japanese, using bluff and good fortune, had captured fifty-four prisoners and control of the Eagle's Nest. Henceforth they could see and report virtually all German movements without fear of revealing their own adjustments. The course of the campaign, in that short time, made a major change of direction.

Within the city the news arrived like a lightning bolt in a clear sky that afternoon. The blow was a heavy one, because many Germans had put their hopes for defense in the position on Prinz Heinrich Hill. Now, in a sudden moment, the enemy looked down on them. The Japanese success provided instant food for thought. The sea bombardment's dispiriting influence added to the general depression.

Kamio had no interest in a sudden *coup de main* as the Germans moved back into the city. His men had reached their desired goals by noon. He called a halt and issued orders for holding their positions, strengthening their lateral communications, and beginning their siege preparations.[85] There was no reason to endanger what they had already won. He would wait until his heavy artillery was in place for smashing the defenses. More important than attacking the Germans immediately was consolidating his forces, tidying the battlefield, and creating a new timetable. He had time.

Pursuant to these intentions, Kamio sent part of his cavalry regiment off on a long ride to Kiautschou with orders to seal off all German communications over the Bay. While Kamio had a platoon in the city itself, he knew that they could not control the entire shore line. The movement was very difficult, because the roads were still in a sorry state of repair, and after so many days of hard riding, the horses were in poor condition. There was a shortage of horseshoes and nails, and the general supplies were still far behind them. The troops rode into Kiautschou on September 28 in something less than parade-ground style. But, after setting up their headqurters in a school house, they started patrols along the entire shore line.[86] The Germans would obtain no more men, material, or information by the water route. They were cut off.

Even as the Japanese cavalry rode out on the final leg of the investment, the Germans acknowledged their changed position. Meyer-Waldeck ordered the sinking of several vessels in the harbor. The unfortunate ships could not add to the defensive strength and should not be left as booty. The dockyard personnel quickly assembled the needed explosives and moved the vessels to the deep water near Yunuisan. They chose the old *Cormoran* as the first sacrifice. With the explosion the ship lifted out of the water and then rolled, stern first, into the Bay.[87] For the watchers the sinking of this symbolic ship represented their hopeless status. They might hope for a quick finish to the European War but that was their sole choice for relief. The ultimate decision was clear. For the more symbolically minded, the demise of the *Cormoran*, with her long association with Tsingtau and Asia, meant that Germany's position in Asia was in jeopardy.

On September 28 Sergeant Eugen Rudiger marched a platoon to Moltke hill. The men, tired from their exertions against the Japanese, looked out at the scenic splendor. Rudiger allowed them a few moments thought and then moved them a few steps to a square, deep, freshly cut pit. He put the men on the dirt pile, jumped into the pit, and spoke up to them:

> What you see here is no house construction or garbage pit, but an anticipated mass grave. It is surely for me, for you, for all of us. Drive the thoughts of seeing Father and Mother out of your heads. We cannot obtain victory here; only die. Still, before it reaches that point, take as many of the yellow Apes with you as you can. A last thought for home: Hipp, Hipp, Hurra!

Thereafter a quiet group of men started back to their quarters. Rudiger ordered them to sing. When no one complied, he repeated the order. A muted rendering of "O Deutschland hoch in Ehren" followed, trailing off into silence. During the rest of the march only the sound of the boots accompanied the men's thoughts.[88] They were alone.

V

A Desperate Position

Der dammernde Morgen, in schimmerndem Rot,
Lasst bluhendes Leben erahnen.
Ein fernes Verklingen "Getreu bis zum Tod"
Verwehend, als wollt' es uns mahnen

Friedr ch Blaschke "Das Falklandsgrab"

Meyer-Waldeck, with his men clearly in their final defensive positions, had no time for idle thought. His role was that of a duelist who possesses a small-caliber, simple revolver against a large, more complex cannon. He must get off an effective first shot before his opponent can bring his cannon into action. The disproportionate strength of the Japanese was an extreme challenge to German ingenuity.

On September 28 even as the troops settled down in the infantry redoubts, the Governor held a lengthy conference. He wanted all troops properly informed about the organization and conduct of the defenses. Their losses in the previous few days had been only 107 men. They had all of the available manpower and had a good opportunity to make the Japanese pay a heavy price for their conquest. The tactical arrangements were, unhappily, self-evident; the fire and maneuver ideas employed in the protectorate would not work in the new battle.

The conferees quickly organized the command structure: the right wing, running from the sea through Redoubt 2, came under Major Anders, with 400 men. Major Kleemann would control Redoubts 3 and 4 as the defensive center. Eventually he would have the troops already in the two installations, an Austrian landing detachment from the *Kaiserin Elisabeth*, and men combed out of other units (about 350 men). The left flank, going on through Redoubt 5, went to Lieutenant Colonel Kuhlo. He had his East Asiatic Detachment, some men released from the city's needs, and the assigned force—in total, over 800 men.

There were no doubts about the strengths and weaknesses of the defenses. They knew that the entire line was highly effective against a Chinese assault, but not against a Japanese operation. The weakest point was the center, which was, given the terrain, vulnerable to artillery fire and to infantry attack. There were too many hidden ravines and dead angles for an effective defense. In view of these known weaknesses, the staff members did not anticipate a formal siege. There was no need for such care; the Japanese could conquer by a sudden, resolute thrust with the resources at hand.[1]

With reference to the defense itself, the staff could not reach agreement. Meyer-Waldeck pointed out the untenability of their position in the long run. They possessed no general observation over the enemy lines. Their artillery was largely unprotected and vulnerable to massed enemy artillery fire. The great shortage of howitzers would allow the Japanese to move in close to the defenses, where they would be safe from German artillery. Moreover, the artillery munitions were in short supply. Given all of these considerations, Meyer-Waldeck predicted a prompt assault. He thought that the Japanese would either come that night or attempt a measured assault within a short time. For the latter eventuality, he envisaged a careful artillery barrage against the German guns, followed by drum fire against the redoubts, and terminating with the final storm. At no time did he consider a lengthy siege as a possibility.

Not all of his staff agreed with his assumptions. They divided along service lines. Those with land experience found the Governor's premises logical, authoritative, and acceptable, but the sailors did not agree. They believed that the Japanese would mount a longer, methodical siege operation. It would demand more preparation time, but it proffered a certain end. There was no way for either group to win the argument since the answer was in Kamio's hands. Nonetheless, they needed to decide how to arrange the defensive system. The sailors recommended waiting until the Japanese began the assault and then throwing their full force against it. The soldiers favored disrupting the enemy's preparations. They believed that they could not alter the outcome of the siege, but they could postpone it, and time might bring miraculous relief.

Meyer-Waldeck, after careful thought, accepted the soldiers' proposals. A key factor was the limited munitions supply, which he did not want to fall into enemy hands. Since he believed in an early attack, he wanted all the shells expended before the end. Even though he made this critical decision, his staff never really accepted it. They fought the issue daily in their meetings and discussions.

After the staff conference the Governor published instructions implementing his view. He wanted every effort against the enemy's artillery movements, against all the approach roads and communications, against the organization and preparation of enemy manpower. The foe must have no respite, no repose. Each day and night, at constantly changing times, the Germans should fire upon different areas. They knew the terrain and could outwit the attackers through a sudden, overwhelming rain of shrapnel and explosives. Since their observation was limited to Plüschow's aircraft, they must outwit the Japanese. They should fire blind but with the goal of destroying the enemy's timing, preparation, and rest.[2] Meyer-Waldeck wanted a methodical and powerful attempt to keep the Japanese off balance. The latter would never know when, where, or how much would be fired at them.

With this tacky issue resolved Meyer-Waldeck turned to other needs, beginning with orders for new improvements in the defenses. While he believed that the earlier efforts had accomplished a good deal, he wanted adjustments in light of the recent combat experience and the improved understanding of their needs. In particular he wanted screened paths between the redoubts to allow the movement of men without revealing anything to the besiegers. The Governor also required new artillery positions, new protective shields, and new forward depots. Concerned over an immediate assault, he levied these requirements with the shortest possible time limits.

At the same time Meyer-Waldeck decided against forming any reserves. The small space and meager resources did not allow more. When the Japanese started their last assault, the men in Tsingtau (from the ships, dockyards, bureaucracy, etc.) would be gathered up for service as a final reserve. Meyer-Waldeck also decreed that all movement, vehicular or human, would take place at night. The

Japanese should have no idea about the defender's strength or intended activity.[3]

That night the artillery began its disruptive mission, firing at predetermined points at different times. Certainly the guns disturbed everyone's sleep in Tsingtau. In particular the guns from the sea defenses, firing over the city, left the citizens in no doubt about their precarious situation. As the big shells rushed overhead, they rocked the houses, rattled the windows, and changed the air pressure. It was the first of many like events, since Meyer-Waldeck kept up the din with approximately 1500 shells per day.

For this assignment the artillery men needed targets when possible. Imagination provided insufficient data for professional artillerymen. They had only four information sources: (1) the *Jaguar*, (2) aerial observation, (3) observation posts on high points within the city, and (4) Chinese agents. The *Jaguar* was of limited intelligence value since she could not move beyond the flank position.[4] She did have the singular advantage, however, that she could move along the coast behind the enemy, fire on targets of opportunity, and coordinate her fire with the land guns.[5] The artillerymen worked out a direct communications system together with an abbreviation code for speedy exchange. This expedient worked very well, and the *Jaguar* became a central nerve in the general artillery plan. On September 30, the first experimental trip, she moved inshore and opened fire and communication with the land batteries. The Japanese responded quickly, and they traded shells at a fierce rate.

Shortly afterward the *S-90* and the *Kaiserin Elisabeth* joined the engagement. They steamed back and forth, firing away at the stubborn Japanese. When the Austrian cruiser received a heavy shelling from a particular battery, the *Jaguar* intervened and, after a brief time, the offender went silent. Bodecker brought his ship close to the *Kaiserin Elisabeth* and called to Makovz, "Captain, I have taken our revenge and destroyed the battery." No sooner had he uttered the words than a towering water spout, spattering water over both ships, announced his error. The *Jaguar* left in haste.[6]

For the ships these days were filled with intense but successful activity. They confirmed the British presence, called attention to many targets, and surprised the Japanese on several occasions.[7] The Japanese found these accomplishments irritating in the extreme and decided to take remedial action. On October 4 they went hunting for the *Jaguar*.

Even as the morning broke, the ship found herself the day's quarry. Initially four Japanese aircraft dropped their bombs, forcing her into evasive action. Shortly afterward the *Jaguar* reached her normal position and started looking for targets. About 11:00 A.M. four big howitzers began a carefully programmed search for the ship. As soon as they ranged her, they fired as fast as they could load the shells. Observers lost sight of the ship behind the huge water columns. Twisting and turning in a mad swirl, von Bodecker retreated as fast as he could. Once free of the steel storm, he reported the locations of his tormentors to the land batteries. As they entered the fray, he took the *Jaguar* back to the Tsankouer area. All was quiet until he reached his firing zone when the Japanese went at him again. Bodecker fled once more.

He refused, however, to accept the idea that the enemy could deny him any area, and ordered the ship back a third time. The Japanese let him return once more and, on a common signal, reopened fire. Aboard the ship the results were immediate. While the guncrews fired the *Jaguar*'s three guns, everyone else dropped behind the nearest protection from the steel rain on the deck. At last a shell hit the bow, making a large hole just above the water line and filling the superstructure with holes.[8] Bodecker ordered hasty repairs and instant retreat. The Japanese had won and he knew it.

That afternoon Bodecker reported directly to Meyer-Waldeck about the encounter. He described the exchange in detail, concluding with the unhappy sentence, "I can no longer remain in the Tsangkau area." There was no way he could sustain the ship as an observation or gun platform. That portion of the garrison's information sources was no longer pertinent.[9] The *Jaguar* could show herself but not for extended periods. The Japanese had made such demonstrations risky affairs.

For aerial observation the Germans possessed equally limited resources—one balloon and the single airplane. The balloon, which had arrived in February on the *Patricia*, was a huge yellow affair, termed "the yellow sausage" by the troops. Lieutenant Freiherr von Soldern was in charge of the balloon. He went up several times in early October but found that his line of vision was obscured by the mountains. The crew then shifted the balloon to the front line, and on October 5 another observer, Lieutenant Hans Weihe, climbed in and ordered the ascent. Scarcely had the tie line grown taut than the Japanese artillery put four shrapnel shells in an almost perfect white ring around the big bag. Weihe did not need to signal his desires to the ground crew; they were busy reeling him back. An ashen, shaking observer was helped from the gondola, fully aware of the seventy or eighty holes in his balloon. Shortly afterwards he agreed with the suggestion that the balloon not be used again.[10]

Soldern, then decided to use a decoy to draw and to locate Japanese artillery fire. He had a meteorologic balloon, and he supervised the construction of a gondola and a strawman (with a clean uniform, wine-bottle binoculars, and a false rifle). All the observers in Tsingtau received instructions about its ascent. When everything was ready on October 7, Soldern started the decoy up. At 320 meters the whimsical wind ripped the balloon from its lines and blew it toward Japan. The ground crew shouted a few choice phrases from the sailor's lexicon, and finished with "Best greetings to the little women in the land of the rising sun from their lovers and us."[11] The failure of the balloon put all of the pressure for visual reconnaissance upon Plüschow.

His single airplane was a key factor in the German defensive scheme, for Plüschow could gather reliable information in a brief time and relay it to the interested parties. The Japanese fully understood his importance and did everything possible against him. Since he was limited to his single runway, they set an artillery battery against him. Whenever his Taube appeared over the hills, they immediately fired at him. The exploding shells, with their beautiful white smoke rings, tossed the aircraft around in curious gyrations. Once through this layer of danger, Plüschow took his aircraft up to 1500 to 1800 meters and glided over the enemy's positions. He could not carry an observer, because of the weight problem, so he was forced to steer with his feet while making notes.

Once the Japanese learned of Plüschow's takeoff, they sent their aircraft after him. They came armed and hostile. As they circled each other, they often fired their pistols at one another. It was the first aerial combat in history. While a thrilling byplay for the ground troops, the exchanges provided some harrowing experiences for Plüschow. He was not a coward, but he was fully aware of his important mission and of the fact that a single lucky shot could destroy the aircraft. Whenever possible, he fled as soon as the Japanese aircraft gathered around him and returned home.

As he started down, the Japanese battery resumed its attack. Buffeted about once more, Plüschow dropped through the layer of explosions and hurriedly landed his craft. Immediately he frantically ran for a safe haven since the following Japanese aircraft often chased him down and dropped bombs. Then Plüschow sent his sketches and notes to Meyer-Waldeck's headquarters.[11] Certainly he did well, and, despite the constant need for repairs on his airplane, Plüschow's activities provided the only reliable information for the defenders.

The observation posts within the city were not high enough for proper vision. They could see into the Litsun area, but little else. Moreover, the Japanese quickly proved their reputation as camouflage artists. In German parlance, the Japanese used the principle of "the empty battlefield." A few isolated efforts to coordinate the observation posts with deep patrols proved abortive. There were too many Japanese troops, and they were vigilant in turning back patrols.[12] In sum, observation from the defenders' positions proved useless.

Only the espionage service remained as a possible source for information. Since its earlier formation, the organization had improved a great deal in its structure, trustworthiness, and ability. As the organization had improved its talents, however, the requirements had changed considerably. Before the Japanese closed the encirclement, Vollerthun had a constant flow of reports. Using large numbers of informants, he could stitch together an accurate mosaic of Japanese movements. But with the enclosing ring snapped shut, he could no longer do so.

Nonetheless, Vollerthun maintained his efforts. From the many Chinese volunteers (usually policemen or soldiers) his staff selected those men who had some reputation for integrity and intellect. After some limited training, they crossed into no man's land with a patrol. Following a previously arranged schedule, normally eight days, they returned to the same point, where a contact man steered them through the barbed wire. This activity, the guidance instructions for the spies, and the first interpretation of their reports all came under an experienced policeman, Fritz Patitz. He worked out a definite pattern for these activities. After one agent departed, another followed one or two days after him with the same general assignment. Patitz made certain that the two agents' routes did not allow their meeting and preparing together a fictional report. If the two repots confirmed one another, each man received one dollar.

The agents earned their rewards by risking constant danger. Even as they entered the front area, they faced the numerous Japanese patrols. After passing the first line, they were in danger from their own countrymen, who knew whenever a foreign person entered a village and who also knew the Japanese rewards for betrayal. Once they had reached the designated search area, they had to keep their eyes and ears open while serving as cigarette sellers, construction workers, or impressed laborers. After completing the assignment, they had the dangerous return trip (the Germans were eternally mistrustful of the Chinese trading sides).[13]

Under such circumstances, their data were often out of date, very often exaggerated, and equally often beyond confirmation. The agents had constant difficulty with maps and numbers. In the end the Germans relied upon their own sense of reality in accepting or rejecting information.[14] Unfortunately for the Germans, these agents were the only basic source of continuous, visual details of the territory held by the enemy.

Throughout this activity, many Germans found the entire search for information degrading and unprofessional. Resenting the Japanese initiative and power, they called for a more aggressive policy to keep the Japanese off balance, aware of German authority, and wary of the future. In so doing the defenders would not need the information for harassing artillery fire; they would do the job themselves by mounting local attacks.

On October 2 this attitude brought the desired solution and the Germans decided to take the initiative. The lack of Japanese aggressive efforts bothered everyone on the German staff. The quietude was against all Japanese tactical doctrine, opposed to the realities of the defenders' desperate situation, and posed a severe strain upon German morale. During the day Kuhlo and von Kessinger agreed on a sortie against the Japanese right flank, which they believed was the more dangerous portion of the enemy line. After some rigorous discussion, they decided on a night assault on Schuang Schan, a small hill where they believed the Japanese had stationed some sixty men. By attacking at night, they would be able to surprise the enemy and return before morning light exposed them to the Japanese artillery.[15]

The plan, quickly evolved, provided for a simple sally in force. Starting at 8:00 P.M., the German artillery would fire a shrapnel barrage for an hour. This would disrupt the Japanese, while unobtrusively sealing off the enemy position from possible reinforcement. Three companies, under Kuhlo's command, would then cross the Hai po and move on the target area. One company would move on the enemy right; one company, starting a little later, on the enemy left; and the remaining company, located in the middle, would remain in reserve. The purpose of the attack was to determine Japanese strength, to show German aggressiveness, and to capture a few prisoners.[16] While the night was dark, there was some moonlight filtering through the clouds. The Germans were also confident that they could travel more easily than the Japanese because of their superior terrain knowledge.

As the artillery fire lifted, the companies marched into the darkness. Unfortunately their march discipline was, inexplicably, most lax. The men talked freely with one another, and some used lights when they lost their way. Some officers drove their automobiles close to the front for convenience and for removing casualties. They made sufficient noise to alert the Japanese almost immediately after their departure. Twenty minutes later the right-hand column, already in some disarray because of the rough ground, received rifle fire. The Germans, totally lost in the dark, had only the sketchiest details of the Japanese positions, and they had stumbled into a Japanese reconnaissance unit which was ready for them.

Shortly thereafter came the frightening "tack, tack" of Japanese machine guns. The defenders had had time to get several into position. Severely surprised, the Germans halted, uncertain what to do next. As they did so, the German searchlights in Tsingtau, seeking to help their comrades, switched on, illuminating the battle area and silhouetting the attackers for Japanese marksmen. Following light flares from both sides helped keep a temporary version of daylight over the area. The small 3.7-cm German cannon in the redoubts sought to help the beleagured assault, but made matters worse by firing into the men they needed to help. The assault force looked for hiding places on the front, flank, and rear, but did not find many. The total chaos terminated their advance as the Germans lost contact with each other and fired at any movement.

The left-hand column had precisely the opposite reception. They advanced over unoccupied trenches without meeting anyone. The Japanese occupants had shifted over toward the other side, leaving the area clear for a brief moment. As they neared their goal, the quiet, contrasted with the noisy reception of their colleagues, disturbed the commander, Captain Schaumburg. The mixed "Hurrahs" and "Banzais" reflected a savage engagement at close quarters to the untrained German ears. Fearful of a trap, he called for a subordinate who spoke fluent Japanese and ordered him, "Shout some abuse at them so that we finally get the rascals in front of our eyes and shoot them!" The man thundered out, like a modern Götz von Berlichingen, "Come finally out of the bushes, you eternal cowards, and show yourselves when you want to behave like men!"[17] Scarcely had he uttered the words than the Japanese opened a withering fire. They were clearly confused by the unfamiliar terrain and the uncertain circumstances of night movement, for the fire was ragged, uncontrolled, and inaccurate. At the same time there was no doubt about their presence.

The cracking rifle fire, chattering machine guns, and the bright sheets of flame springing from impacting shells, together with the searchlights and dazzling light flares created a genuine pyrotechnical display. Under these circumstances Kuhlo decided, with no more than sight and sound as his sources, that the Japanese were out in force, and ordered a prompt retirement. With a heavy artillery barrage to cover the return, by 1:00 A.M. the three companies were back behind their barbed wire.

During the next few days, various individuals returned from the engagements. The reconnaissance cost the Germans twenty-nine dead and six prisoners, a high price for no return.[18] Instead of teaching the Japanese respect, the Germans came back with a new attitude toward their opponents. That they were good soldiers was never a question, but that they could mount an investment so quickly was impressive evidence of their professionalism. For the Germans the blow brought a short-lived morale boost in that it did reflect an offensive commitment. The casualties gave pause for thought, however, and the men could only take consolation in the much repeated phrase, "It really doesn't matter when everything goes well at home."[19] The defenders had suffered a loss well beyond the short casualty list for the Japanese had blunted the sortie, turned the defenders back, and kept the initiative. They were in charge of the battlefield.

For the attackers the days after September 28 were also important. Under the circumstances, Kamio had two choices: immediate assault or lengthy siege. He did not, however, consider the option anticipated by Meyer-Waldeck, i.e., immediate attack. The Japanese commander thought that adventure was risky, costly, and unnecessary. Having decided to besiege the city at his own pace, he was forced to pause again for reorganization. He had to improve his communications system (in particular the road and the Decauville railroad), to build up a secondary landing area at Schatsykou Bay, to bring up his heavy siege artillery, and to make a detailed ground reconnaissance.[20] All of these operations demanded time, but Kamio remained a patient man.

The Japanese possessed a mass of information concerning the city, its main defenses, and its position on the Shantung Peninsula. They were not, however, as well informed about the immediate terrain. Their initial endeavors, therefore, were to collect data on the combat zone. There was no reason to hurry their movements, since the enemy was trapped. The Germans could neither escape nor obtain reinforcement. Kamio wanted a full and complete terrain analysis while maintaining proper security against a possible sortie. As the information from ground and aerial reports came into his headquarters, Kamio soon learned that he had no real problems with the siege.

He quickly received a terrain analysis. While the Hai po was, in theory, a natural obstacle along the northeast boundary of the city, it was dry for the most part and fordable where there was some water. The river moved southwesterly to Hsi-wei-tschio-tsun, where it made a right bend into the bay. The south side of the river bed was a bit higher than the north, providing the defenders some observation. On the whole, however, the Japanese found several agreeable surprises. The hills were cut by small rivelets and gullies and local farmers had terraced the inclines for cultivation. There were, as a result, many dead areas where the besiegers could hide sizable groups of men and equipment without fear of detection.

Trenching was difficult because of the high water table and the hard ground. On the other hand, the extensive ravines (three to four meters deep) ran diagonally to the Germans, allowing the attackers some unexpected advantages in moving forward.[21] The Japanese found the physical area ideally suited to their purposes.

More important than this discovery, for Kamio, was getting his forces together, organized, and prepared for the final action. While the previous weeks had provided useful field experience and some combat activity, the Japanese now confronted the last, all-out battle, which must be more complex in resolution. In the forefront of Kamio's concerns were the timely arrival of the siege artillery, the integration of new troops, and the construction of communication lines. Once all of these diverse activities were in motion, he could develop his assault plan.

Since Kamio had decided on siege rather than attack, the heavy artillery played a significant role. The Tokyo authorities had anticipated this requirement from the onset of hostilities. As early as August 24 they had assigned Major General Kishinos Watanabe as commander for the big guns. In the weeks thereafter, his superiors on the General Staff gave him many directions concerning the employment of the big guns in conjunction with land troops; the general difficulties of landing, transportation, and operations of the siege pieces; and broad instructions on the organization and supply of weapons and material. After receiving all of his directions and instructions (they were much more detailed than those provided Kamio), Watanabe completed his operational preparations and moved on to Lau schan Bay, where he landed on September 23. Following his obligatory duty call on Kamio, Watanabe started his assignment.

His fundamental concern was getting his units forward. He would have somewhat more than 100 guns and howitzers, varying in size from 12-cm to 28-cm (including 10-cm and 15-cm naval guns). For them he would have ammunition for fifteen days, based on eighty rounds per piece, per day.[22] To move this monstrous assemblage of men, guns, and supplies, Watanabe had to depend upon the tiny railway. He learned that it would become functional by October 5 as the line from Lau schan reached Litsun.[23] With this link complete, the troops and their Chinese laborers could muscle the guns and supplies toward Tsingtau without interruption. In addition to the railway, Watanabe had some 800 Chinese carts (narrow, two-wheeled, pony-drawn vehicles), whose carrying power was limited to light loads, but whose mobility over rough terrain was remarkable for the time. He had an unknown number of the efficient Chinese wheelbarrows, seized from their owners. These wheelbarrows, drawn by one man and pushed by another, carried up to 350 pounds and could move at a rapid rate over almost any fairly level grade.[24]

Watanabe chose a single installation as an observation post for the siege artillery. Situated some 900 feet high on a spur of Prinz Heinrich Hill, it provided a panoramic view of Tsingtau. The construction crews added some five telephone lines, all radiating in different directions, as a precaution against German destruction, and a wireless station for communication with the fleet units. The station had two minor drawbacks, the distance to Tsingtau and its right-angled location to the battlelines. Nonetheless, it was the best available location.

Watanabe reported to Kamio on October 2 that the artillery operations would go well. The big siege pieces would be emplaced without strain, would be efficiently controlled, and would be able to clear a path for the infantry. A delighted Kamio congratulated his subordinate for his dispatch and his success.

At the same time Kamio did not want to rely too much upon the artillery for the siege itself. The final Japanese victory must come through the proper mixture of guns, material, and manpower. The manpower factor had already occasioned various second thoughts to both Kamio and to his Tokyo superiors. The reason for their concern, ostensibly, was the maintenance of the Shantung Railroad. The confusing diplomatic situation with China had created some uncertain moments and Kamio had sought additional troops to protect his rear. Already on September 22 the General Staff had accepted his plea and ordered the Twenty-ninth Brigade from Japan as a general reinforcement. It would be understrength, with a single regiment (67) and portions of another for the operation but should provide the desired additional support. The men loaded in Japan in late September and started landing in Lau schan Bay early in October. Since they were not in the original plans, the landing authorities filtered them through the siege units, which were still going ashore.[25] Once ashore, the units began moving toward the rail line, which they could use for their own advance. It was slow going because of their piecemeal commitment. They provided Kamio with extensive additional manpower, which he clearly appreciated and intended to use in his own fashion.[26] He needed only shift these forces to Tsingtau whenever he felt that they might prove necessary for the siege operations.

Along with his troop movements, Kamio maintained a steady pressure on the Germans. No day went by without some rifle fire between colliding patrols or some defensive artillery fire on the Japanese. These activities gained the Japanese good information on the terrain, a few prisoners, and the continued control of the battle area.

As the results of these investigations, preparations, and activities arrived in Kamio's headquarters, he and his staff studied them. With his normally deliberate manner, he then issued the general operational instructions on October 7. He was in no hurry.

Kamio indicated that the main effort would be against the German center, defended by their redoubts 3 and 4. For the assault Kamio divided his forces into four parts. On the right flank would be the recently arrived Sixty-seventh Regiment, which would be redirected from its assignment with the Shantung Railroad. Adjacent to them would be the South Wales Borderers, with Barnardiston in command. Next to the British would be the main assault force of Yamada's Twenty-fourth Brigade. Horiuchi would maintain his left flank supportive role. The siege artillery would remain under Watanabe's direction for massed fire against the German positions, but with some emphasis on the designated attack points.

In the actual movement to assault, Kamio demanded a measured drawing up of the forces. There would be no reckless spirit of adventure. When the siege artillery was in position, the infantry would establish an advanced investment line (running Hsiau tsun tsch, Tung wu tschia tsun, Tien tschia tsun, Hsin tschia tsch) which must, under all conditions, be held against any German sortie. As the infantry occupied this position, the assault artillery would advance into their prepared positions.

Once every man and artillery piece was ready for action, the siege would begin on a given signal. As the bombardment guns opened the battle, they should obliterate the enemy batteries in the assault zone, drive the German naval vessels away from any participation, and inhibit any response from the German defensive installations. These massed fires must be coordinated with the naval forces, which would employ their guns against the German forts and sea batteries. Under the protection of this overwhelming steel cover, the infantry would advance from their investment trenches to the first parallel line, dig in, and hold it against possible German attack. From here, and under continuous artillery fire, the infantry would shift forward, using normal siege techniques of sapping and mining, to successive parallels. At a given point they would breach the enemy's lines and launch the final assault.[27] In preparation for this undertaking Kamio shifted his headquarters again, this time to Tunglitsun.

Along with his general instructions for the assault, Kamio provided directions to his other units. The cavalry should continue and improve its efforts to seal off the city. Kamio suspected that the Germans were still obtaining men and materials, as well as valuable information, over the Bay. He wanted the air force moved forward from Chimo and their aircraft employed in preparing a detailed map of the German defenses. Kamio insisted on a proper report, giving precise locations of installations, exact armaments, and estimated troop strengths.[28]

At the same time he asked that they continue their bombing efforts. The pilots had improved their aim a good deal and had increased their bomb weights correspondingly. Nonetheless, this first use of aerial bombardment did not achieve very much. They did damage some buildings, frighten many civilians, and wound one soldier.[29]

For the engineers Kamio also had instructions. In addition to their road building, railway construction, and position digging, they received supervision over the siege lines. Kamio required explicitly that the trenches be at least two meters wide, built in a wavy pattern, and protected with a splinter-proof covering. Kamio also set down a general timetable for the early approach construction. His extraordinarily precise instructions left nothing to doubt or to interpretation.[30]

With these directions clearly set down, Kamio could turn to their implementation. Almost immediately he encountered irritations, the first of which involved his British ally. On September 29 came reports of serious difficulties—a series of incidents between the two forces. The Japanese could not always differentiate between their Caucasian friends and foes, and Japanese infantrymen had mistreated some British officers, fired at others, and wounded one enlisted man.[31] In view of these incidents, the two parties agreed that the British should wear a white patch on top of their helmets as a distinguishing mark.[32]

That same evening the Germans, alerted by Plüschow's report of tents with different shapes than the Japanese version, fired upon the British with great vigor. The headquarters staff, bracketed by shrapnel, spent a miserable night in a ditch. With Kamio's approval, Barnardiston shifted his men the next day to the reverse slope of a nearby hill.[33]

These human considerations were only a minor part of the difficulties between the two allies. On October 4 Kamio reported his intention of sending the Germans a plea for the removal of noncombatants. He sent a complimentary copy of the note, signed by himself and Kato, to Barnardiston. The latter filed a prompt rejoinder. Since they were allies acting in conjunction with each other, he wanted his signature on the note. Kamio, visibly shocked by this proposal, then accepted Barnardiston's further proposal that they delay the dispatch of the note and consult with their respective governments.[34] The British War Office replied promptly, quoting Barnardiston's earlier instructions, "You will be subject to the control of the Japanese commander and will cooperate with him as a complete formation. . . British troops are engaged merely to show that England does not refuse to join Japan in this enterprise."[35] The answer, however, did not move rapidly through the command channels, and the uncertainty did no good to the strained human relations in the field.[36]

Finally, on October 12, Kamio and Barnardiston received some clarification. A terse note from the British Embassy in Tokyo indicated that the latter should be a signatory to any declaration only when Kamio desired it. In this case the Japanese commander did not desire his colleague's signature. Nonetheless, he did change his own title to "Commander in Chief of the Army Besieging Tsingtao."[37]

The contents of the long-prepared message were simple. Kamio and Kato suggested to Meyer-Waldeck that their Emperor wanted to avoid the needless sacrifice of human life. They offered to let the Germans remove their noncombatants.[38]

Glad for this opportunity, Meyer-Waldeck sent out his adjutant, Major Georg von Kayser to discuss the removal of the noncombatants. Kayser, wearing all his medals (which included a Japanese order), led a party with a translator, a trumpeter, a horse holder, and a white flag carrier. He was met by a Japanese Colonel Isomura, equipped with a comparable group and wearing his medals (also including a German one). They met in the village Tung wu tschia tsun, saluted, shook hands, and read the Japanese proposals. They quickly agreed to a transfer at Taputou, a point on the other side of Kiautschou Bay. Kayser gave Isomura the last effects of a Japanese officer. They briefly discussed the war; the Japanese indicating their sorrow over the conflict. One of them, a Captain Yamada, asked von Kayser to pass on his best wishes to his friend Captain Walther Stecher, for whose life he prayed each day. Then they shook hands, mounted, and rode off.[39]

The Governor immediately issued a brief public announcement of the departure opportunity for noncombatants. Among the Germans, two nurses, Sophie Herlin and a Mrs. Mathes, reported their desire to leave. The American Consul, Willys Peck, also accepted the offer.[40] The departees left on the small steamer *Tsimo*, which took them to Taputu. As the crew unloaded the baggage, under close Japanese supervision, a band aboard the ship played several songs. Then, as the ship moved off, everyone on board waved a hat or handkerchief.[41] When the ship returned to Tsingtau, hostilities resumed in full force.[42]

An additional concern for Kamio was the lack of naval participation. The German fortress guns were a distinct nuisance, forcing the continual displacement of his men and artillery. Kato, on the other hand, was not eager to attack the German batteries. He believed that the final barrage would allow the effective coordination of all Japanese artillery and assure the suppression of all the German batteries. Meanwhile, his healthy respect for German gunnery made him wary of being overly adventuresome without land support. Besides he was highly reluctant to risk crossing the German mine fields. The minesweepers turned up a mine here and a mine there, but they did not locate very many.[43] This fear of mines was intensified on September 30, when the seaplane tender, *Wakamiya Maru*, struck a mine, blowing a gaping hole (4.5 x 6.7 meters) in her hull and disabling her engine. The crew just managed to beach the ship. Fortunately the explosion did not damage any aircraft, and the Japanese simply shifted the seaplane operations to the army shore base.[44] An hour later a trawler coming to help the tender hit another mine and went down in ten minutes, losing three men. Another trawler, with four men, sank from another mine the following day.[45]

As further harrassment, Plüschow flew over the repair ship, *Kwanto Maru*, and dropped two bombs. They exploded as they hit

the water, just missing the ship. While the German pilot did not
return again, his explosive calling cards provided a chilling memory
for everyone aboard ship.[46]

Kato, whose fleet units were undergoing some reorganization,
finally ordered a brief bombardment of the Iltis Hill forts on October
6.[47] The *Suwo* and *Triumph* started firing about 1:00 P.M., but they
were well out-of-range and their shells fell some 270 meters short.
Rather than move in closer, they broke off action. On October 10, in
deference to a direct request from Kamio, the *Suwo* went after Iltis
again, but broke off action once more. Kato's respect for Hui tschuen
Huk precluded a direct confrontation.[48]

With Kamio's growing pressure Kato ordered a major attack for
October 14.[49] This time he increased his safety factor by ordering the
Suwo listed sharply to increase her range.[50] The *Suwo* started firing
on Hui tschuen Huk at 9:00 A.M. at a range of 15750 meters.
Immediately The German fort replied, but this time her shells fell
900 meters short. At 9:40 the Germans shifted their fire to the
Tango, which was a bit closer inshore. This ship, which had moved in
closer for better results against Iltis, was promptly enveloped in a
maelstrom of water fountains. She quickly broke off action and
withdrew precipitously.

The *Triumph*, again last in line, slipped into a firing position
somewhat removed from the other two ships. Fitzmaurice believed
that he had found a dead area, shielded from German fire. His gun
crews fired some thirty shells at Iltis from a stationary position.
Shortly after ten o'clock, he ordered the ship prepared for
withdrawal. As he did so, observers reported a smoke puff on Hui
tschuen Huk, and forty-five seconds later a 24-cm shell hit the
mainmast, miraculously killing only one sailor and wounding two
others. It holed the mainmast, seriously damaged the ship's secondary control system, and destroyed several communication lines.
Splinters riddled other installations. The *Triumph* quickly filled the
yard arms with colorful flags informing Kato of the hit and moved
seaward. As she did so, a second shell hurled a towering water spout
into the air at the old location.[51]

Fitzmaurice's crew quickly rigged a temporary reinforcement for
the mast and moved alongside the Japanese repair ship, *Kwanto*.
The Japanese workers had her ready for sea in twenty-four hours.[52]

Certainly the blockading squadron fully understood the German message.[53] Kato had buoys put down beyond the range of Hui tschuen Huk. There would be no more disasters.

Almost immediately Kato received other ominous news. A Japanese signal station near Formosa reported the sighting of the *Scharnhorst, Gneisenau,* and *Nurnberg,* moving north. Kato ordered his ships, including the injured *Triumph,* to sea on October 15. He treated the warning with much greater respect than did Fitzmaurice, who discredited it from the outset. Kato issued careful orders for any engagement and assigned detailed patrol stations for each unit. The weather was very bad, with strong winds, driving rains, and a high-running sea obscuring all vision. After two days at sea, the squadron gave up the search.[54]

Nonetheless, the results of all this naval activity were decisive. Kato would wait until the general bombardment before endangering his naval units again. Even Kamio realized the sense of this decision and stopped asking for naval support

By this time he had other worries. His troops were not fully in place, and the roads, despite extensive repairs, were still badly cut up by overuse. He needed the units sorted out, in line, and semiprepared before opening the operation. On October 10 the mass of Johoji's Twenty-ninth Brigade started ashore at Lau schan, where the advance units were already strung out along the road. As the Sixty-seventh Regiment headquarters reached shore, it received Kamio's orders to move into position along the right flank. It did so by October 15, with a minimum of difficulty.[55]

Next to the newly arrived Sixty-seventh Regiment were the British. On October 10 Barnardiston received the operational instructions for his men. The Borderers, delighted with the prospect of activity soon discovered that the actual work was strenuous. The area was clay, with a high water table. Since they lacked the essential picks and shovels, the men found the digging hard work.

At the same time the British discovered that their allies had a shocking lack of concern for sanitation. While the Japanese soldier was meticulous in his individual cleanliness, he was not concerned about the sanitation of his camp or the adjacent water sources. They simply dropped their refuse at the most convenient moment. Also, at night the Japanese fired first and then investigated suspicous movements, so the British soon learned to be wary of night activities.[56] However, by October 15, the British were well dug in and ready for the next steps.

The Japanese Forty-eighth Regiment simply leapfrogged sideways from their old positions, circling around the British positions and into their new assault location. Yamada's men had no difficulties whatever in making the change. On occasion the random German artillery fire required some rapid local adjustments of the route but that was all. On October 13 Yamada established his headquarters and started his preparations for the attack. These efforts must begin by October 15 in order to conform with Kamio's deadlines.

On the left side Horiuchi simply maintained his state of preparedness. His basic mission for the time included flank protection, artillery position construction, and general security. Horiuchi reallocated his resources, and, with a narrow front, quickly resolved his requirements for the attack. The major challenge was developing the road network for the big guns and organizing the base investment position. By October 15 he, too, was ready for the start of the final attack preparations.[57]

The siege artillery units moved into three general areas—Kushan, Pauerl, and Fouschan. Watanabe had his instructions a bit earlier than his infantry colleagues, and as a result, he had a slight advantage in his timing. He was to carefully reconnoitre both firing positions and targets, submit detailed sketch maps, and coordinate lists of ammunition requirements. His staff labored with the construction of siege gun platforms, the timetable for their occupation, and the testing of the essential firing tables.[58] Watanabe was confident that the artillery would be prepared and in place by October 18. His optimistic prediction did not prove correct, albeit not through his error.

On October 15 an unseasonal rain storm swept over Shantung. It started about 7:00 A.M., rained throughout the day, halted briefly that evening, and then poured continuously through October 17. The sodden men assumed that heaven's sluices had opened up and poured their contents on the earth. All work came to a prompt halt. The torrents roared down off the hills and the streams flooded over their banks. Since the besiegers had already started their trenching and had erected their camps without concern for the weather, the rain did extensive damage. The ravines and trenches quickly filled with water and mud, the loose soil washed away, and the manmade structures simply collapsed in a heap. The shelters and dugouts, as they gave way, often buried their unwary occupants alive or carried them away to an unhappy fate. Flood waters destroyed food depots, clothing supplies, and material stores. The roads turned into ill-defined quagmires, eliminating all movement. Every step had to be taken with care, since one could not tell whether he was putting his foot in a hole, a mud sump, or on the tenuous road bed. Many roads had a series of naval-like buoys marking the center of the road.

The Japanese had erected an extensive supply and ammunition depot in a dry portion of Litsun Creek, which they could not evacuate in time. Everything washed away—packs, supplies, first aid packages, all floated into the Bay. At first the Germans thought that the boxes and crates were floating mines and fired on all of them. There were many angry recriminations when the men discovered that some of the floating objects were beer casks. At Chimo a wall of water ten feet high overwhelmed another supply base, with similarly castrophic results.

In Lau schan Bay the storm washed the pontoon landing wharf away, wrecked some 100 sampans, and drowned 25 soldiers. While practically everything of importance was ashore, replacements would now be less easy to obtain. The Decauville railway, finally completed on October 14, failed on October 15. The fast-moving water eroded the supports for the tracks, often carrying them some distance away.[59] For two full days the investment procedures came to a complete halt.

When the rain finally disappeared again, each Japanese soldier went hunting for his belongings, often in knee-high mud. The entire area was a beehive of men poking through the muck in search of various military and personal effects. They exercised caution, because the Germans, although also seriously hurt by the rain, remained vigilant and renewed their harrassing artillery fire. There was no question, that the scheduled attack must be put off until the troops could remedy the storm damage.

Kamio did so grudgingly, growing somewhat impatient over the delays. Accordingly, he assembled all of the senior commanders on October 18. After explaining his concern for the strains brought on by the rain, he showed them his outline for the forthcoming operation (the printed copies arrived the next day). His instructions were very simple, little more than restatements of the general principles already on record. Clearly the discussion was as much a pep talk after a setback as it was militarily informative.

The recently occupied investment line, the officers learned, was to be the base line of departure. Shortly before the siege artillery opened fire, the siege troops would advance to the line Hsiau tsun tsch, Tung wu tschu tsun, Hsi un tschia tsch. At the same time the frontline infantry and engineer troops should prepare for the subsequent advance, expanding their communication trenches and observing their immediate frontage.

The next step would begin during the night of the second bombardment day. At that time the infantry would occupy the high ground west of Han-Chia Chung, south of Tung Wu-Chia-Tsun, and north of Tou-Schan-So. Under the cover of the continuous land-sea-air bombardment, the troops would repeat their previous procedures, i.e., dig in, establish communications, and prepare to advance forward.

At Kamio's orders the line would move to the next position, which would run Pump Station, Hsi-Wu-Chia-Tsun, Kang-Chia-Chuang, and Fou-Shan-So. Once lodged in this area, they should prepare the final assault by constructing trench lines, destroying obstacles, and advancing assault weapons.

The artillery, in close conjunction with the blockade squares, would destroy the enemy's artillery, drive the German warships away, and fire against the defensive installations.[60] Kamio did not elaborate on the focal point of the final assault. He did indicate his desire for a continuous, coordinated general advance so that he could keep all of his options open. Should an opportunity appear unexpectedly, they could take advantage of it quickly.[61]

Concurrently the unit requested by Barnardiston, a half battalion of the Thirty-sixth Sikhs (450 men), began arriving after a long trip from Taku. They anchored off Lau schan on October 22, but another storm at sea made their landing a difficult one. The rough sea rudely tossed the boats about. While the tall, full-bearded, turbanned Indians ordinarily made an impressive sight, they arrived on shore a bedraggled, frightened group of men.[62] Their movement overland was also a genuine trial, comparable to that of their compatriots in the

Borderers. The mules and carts brought from Tientsin proved unreliable, the road was a sea of mud, and the local authorities remained behind schedule in repairing it.

The next morning the officers discovered that the best harness, which they had purchased the previous day, had been retrieved by the sellers during the night. The remainder required a good deal of hastily collected string—not the best equipment for raw mules unused to harness. While the Sikhs struggled manfully against their predicament, the first leg of the trip to Litsun was a nightmare. In an eleven-hour march they made nine kilometers! They were soon exhausted from pulling mules out of the mud, digging carts out of the same substance, and unloading overturned vehicles. The next day they covered eighteen kilometers in equally difficult circumstances. Thereafter, they improved their pace somewhat, and, following a brief rest and visit from Kamio, they reached a front-line position on October 30.[63]

With all troops and material moving forward at last, Kamio decided that he could begin the final assault preparations—mainly specialized training exercises. Specialists dispatched from Tokyo trained carefully selected men with rifle grenades, explosive tubes (for barbed wire destruction), night signaling, and assault team coordination. The searchlight crews received their final orientation and directions. A special survey section moved out into the field to record the precise location of all Japanese and German installations.

Satisfied, that everything was moving well, Kamio ordered the occupation of the advanced investment line on October 29. He wanted the artillery bombardment two days later, the Emperor's official birthday.[64] He and his men were ready and confident about their preparations, their situation, and their future. The Germans had greater concerns.

Within Tsingtau the Germans had made some changes, for their sortie on October 2 had taught them a lesson: the Japanese were alert to all movement and to all surprise. The Germans could not engage in any aggressive activity. In the following days, Plüschow and the Chinese spies reported that the Japanese were not preparing an immediate assault. The enemy was clearly interested in a ponderous siege operation.[65] This Japanese decision was not agreeable to Meyer-Waldeck. In a direct engagement his men could give the

Japanese a bloody nose, but in a lengthy siege they could anticipate only frustrated defeat. The Japanese would choose his time and place for terminating the siege.

To make the enemy pay the highest possible cost, Meyer-Waldeck continued his preparations for the Japanese attack. Within the redoubts every commander used all possible methods to strengthen his defenses. The men were constantly at work with additional trenches, sand bags, and barbed wire entanglements. Their major interest was in expanding the defensive links between the strong points and the redoubts. While this work had started much earlier, there had not been time to finish it satisfactorily. For von Kessinger the construction of a single, wellprotected line was of the utmost importance.

Working steadily, the men advanced the work. The Chinese poured concrete forms, cut wood, and repaired equipment by day, while the Germans did the digging and emplacement by night. In such fashion the troops finished their assignment in two weeks' time.[66] Additionally, the troops improved their own living situation by excavating areas around the forts for expanded quarters, better drainage, and additional facilities (electric generators, water storage, etc.). Within a short time observers termed the area "cellar city" since it was honeycombed with excavations.

Concurrent with this construction activity, Meyer-Waldeck sought a major review concerning the availability of every able-bodied man in Tsingtau. He had reversed his position on the need for a reserve force, but he had no additional source of manpower. Combing through the available people, his staff did find some 600 extra men among the German dock personnel, the ships' crews, government officials, and men who, according to regulations, were either too old or too young for war.[67] Meyer-Waldeck intended this composite force for commitment against any Japanese break-through.[68] As time progressed, however, the newly created positions gradually absorbed these men. While the German front was not very wide, their human resources were not sufficient for covering every place.

With the endeavor to strengthen all installations, the employment of men in unfamiliar situations, and the strain of waiting, the siege brought many changes in human life styles. Surprisingly, there was only one serious accident. Shortly after dark on October 16, a sailor in

Redoubt V dropped a heavy box cover on a magnesium light flare, and the impact set the flare off. It quickly ignited other flares, creating an enormous fire. Because of the intense heat, the men could not get to the fire; some three hours later, it reached the ammunition stores. For two hours the explosives went off in all directions, forcing everyone into precipite flight. In the course of the night some 200,000 bullets, 1500 light flares, several hundred hand grenades and other explosives disappeared in an impressive fireworks display.[69] The troops scattered along the defensive line, anticipating an immediate Japanese assault, stood to arms throughout the night, but the attackers did not oblige them with any sign of interest.

In point of fact, throughout October, the Japanese did not disturb the defenders from the land side. They carefully observed the Germans working on their defenses and made notes on the location, purpose, and strength of such installations. Throughout these preparations they were content with the information and saw no reason to reveal their own strength, location, or intentions.[70] This caution bothered the Germans, but they could do nothing about it. Whenever the defenders advanced their patrols or their warships too far, the Japanese contained the Germans with relative ease.

More disruptive to German preparations were the October shellings from the sea. The "fat steamers," as the defenders termed them, reminded them unpleasantly about their hopeless position. In particular the October 14 bombardment was most harsh upon morale. As the day began, the troops on Iltis Hill started their usual activities. One of them, Jakob Neumaier, remarked to a friend, "Another glorious morning," only to receive the pessimistic response, "Yes, but we can still lose some sleep." At the same moment Lieutenant von Wenckstern, just out of the hospital, reported to First Lieutenant Falkenhagen on top of the same battery. Just as the latter saluted, a dull, roaring sound, followed by a heavy, earth-rocking thud, jarred the men. They stood rigidly still, their arms at a stiff salute for several seconds. Neumaier and his friend heard the shell coming in and its heavy explosion. They also heard a cry about, "heavy travel trunks coming in from the sea." A startled officer screamed at the four men, galvanizing them into action.[71] They reached cover just in time, since the Japanese aim was very accurate.

The shelling grew in intensity as the enemy ships found the correct range. In the battery the men sat on benches and listened to the thunder of shells exploding nearby. The concussion soon jarred the chalk paint off the walls, stirred the dust into a choking storm, and filled the observation points with muck. Caught in the trap, the men retreated into witticisms and small talk, but one huge shell—the last one, it turned out—opened several fissures in the roof and terminated the conversation. It also placed a scar on a gun tube, without permanent disability, as a reminder of the Japanese accuracy.

Afterwards the still ashen men observed the result of the barrage. Their grass cover was cratered every place, the cement was pitted with shell splinters, and the surrounding sand was piled up in regular mountain ranges.[72] The ships had not accomplished very much in terms of their destructive purposes but they had made their impression on the Iltis defenders.

They did just as well in Redoubt 1, where *Suwo* dropped several shells. Five of them hit the fortifications, but two were duds and the others, because of the vertical impact, did little damage. They knocked over some barbed wire, chipped some concrete, and taught the German infantry respect. The huge shells, which the men called "blue peas" or "sugar boxes," made a memorable noise and created unpleasant earthquakes.[73]

For the defenders the bombardment, despite its lack of military success, underscored their plight. They were caught in a trap, unable to move about freely, and ignorant of Japanese intentions. On the day of the sea bombardment, the dockyard personnel sank the steamers *Durrendart* and *Ellen Rickmers* in the harbor entrance. They settled in different ways, but their masts remained above water, constant reminders of the German's grim situation.

To counteract the effects of this depression and the Japanese silence, Captain Saxer proposed a foray by the *S-90*.[74] Meyer-Waldeck accepted the idea immediately, as did the *S-90*'s Captain Brunner. At darkness on October 17 the ship headed for the open sea, with the simple orders to attack all enemy warships. Thereafter he would be on his own as to the next step, i.e., return to harbor, self-destruction, etc.

Outside the harbor Brunner slipped past the Japanese without detection. After cruising back and forth for several hours, he started back for Tsingtau. Shortly after midnight Brunner observed a shadow moving in the opposite direction. Instantly he decided in favor of attack. He brought the *S-90* in at full speed on the starboard side of what he assumed was a Japanese cruiser (it proved to be the old cruiser, *Takaschio*). At 500 meters Brunner ordered the first torpedo fired, following it with two others at brief intervals.

The flash of the torpedo leaving its tube awakened the Japanese, who rang an alarm horn—too late. Apparently two of the three torpedoes hit the *Takaschio*. The first caused a brief explosion, while the second blew the ship apart. She was carrying 120 mines, and they apparently went off simultaneously, shooting a tower of fire 100 feet into the air. Within seconds the *S-90*, which had drifted within some 300 meters of the enemy ship, received a rain of ship's parts. The crew took hasty cover as the metal pieces hailed down on them.

Brunner felt certain that the explosion must bring the Japanese out in force, and he would not be able to get the *S-90* home. Therefore he took the ship south, and, after slipping past a Japanese cruiser, sank the *S-90* on the China coast.[75]

Behind him the Japanese were in complete disarray. The *Takaschio* went down without time for any safety measures. As relieving vessels arrived on the scene, they could hear a few survivors singing the Japanese national hymn, "Kimagayo." Only 3 men lived through the inferno, while 253 perished (10 men had left the ship before the attack). More serious to the Japanese than the mortification over the disaster was their uncertainty about the *S-90*'s whereabouts.[76] The only available aircraft was undergoing overhaul, and the land observers filed conflicting reports about the ship's presence in Tsingtau. Until someone found the *S-90*, Kato broke off all supply shipments, redirected merchantmen, and sent off fleet units in frenzied search.[77]

After a continuous effort, the searchers found the beached *S-90* on October 20. Troops from the cavalry regiment hurried to the spot. They found several papers, some flags, and a chart showing the German minefields. This chart, a totally unexpected reward, helped pay for the loss of the treasured ship.[78] Nonetheless, the Japanese recognized the deed as a valiant one and increased their vigilance a great deal thereafter.[79]

The Germans' success helped restore some measure of their confidence and pride, and decided them on a more aggressive land endeavor as well. Kessinger sent out stronger patrols, seeking information and combat. The strongest attempt was made on October 21, when a patrol indicated a weak place in the besieger's line. Kessinger ordered an eighty-man group from Redoubts 2 and 3 into the area. At 5:30 A.M. the next morning, after another sudden artillery barrage, they set out. The leader, First Lieutenant Ernst von Ramin, divided his group into four sections, hoping that they could thereby avoid detection during the approach. They planned to concentrate at the designated point and attack. No sooner had they moved into no man's land then they all received strong rifle fire. The alert Japanese quickly drove the Germans back to their starting point.[80] The Germans learned nothing beyond the Japanese strength and alertness.

Certainly the failure of this patrol precluded a repetition. Kessinger shifted back to smaller patrols intended only to report on the Japanese movement.[81] On October 22 a small patrol left for Fouschan, their mission was general reconnaissance and the removal of a marking buoy about 150 meters offshore. They quickly fulfilled the latter task, one man returning with the trophy. As the other two advanced inland, they came under Japanese fire and Sergeant Wilhelm Diehl fell, shot through both legs. He ordered his colleague back, since the Japanese were still firing. When the man returned later with a Red Cross team, they found that Diehl had tried to bind his wounds, but he had not succeeded in time.[82] Next to his dead body was a notebook in which he had written, in a wavering hand, "I have a difficult death, but I die gladly for my Emperor."[83]

Even these patrols became less and less useful as the Japanese advanced their troops. The Chinese agents generally found it impossible to get through the Japanese lines. Furthermore, Plüschow could no longer penetrate the air-space over the besiegers' positions. By the end of October the Germans could not even obtain information about Japanese progress.

As time ran out Meyer-Waldeck received a message from the Kaiser, "With me the entire Germanic nation looks with pride on the heroes of Tsingtau, whom, true to the word of the governor, are fulfilling their duties. You should all know of my appreciation."[84] While the message indicated that they were not forgotten, it also reflected the reality of their situation. The siege could not go on indefinitely nor would the Japanese prolong their preparations. Sending this message on to his staff, Meyer-Waldeck added a few encouraging lines of his own and ended with a cheer for the Kaiser. After the officers read the missives to their men, they led them in three cheers. In every recorded case they were loud ones, for the Germans would have few opportunities to cheer anything in the future.

VI

Tsingtau Falls

Im Jenseits, da druben, seh'n bald wir euch wieder,
Ihr jungen, ihr tapferen deutschen Soldaten,
Heut grussen euch noch uns're Worte und Lieder,
Als Bestes: "Ich hatt' einen Kameraden!"

Friedrich Blaschke "Unsere Toten
im fernen Osten"

By the last week of October the suspense had reached the maximum
bearable levels. For Kamio the final days were more important than
they were for the defenders. His troops had reached their departure
lines and his artillery had moved into their firing positions. Certainly
his instructions left little room for interpreatation. He had set them
up on October 25 and had not made any alterations.

The Japanese headquarters provided a detailed outline for each
step in the investment. The responsible engineer officers would
begin by outlining the proposed trench lines on the ground. Since
much of the slope was open to German observation, all the heavy
construction work would take place at night. Just before dark the
troops would assemble in predetermined positions and crawl out to
the tracings—over open ground in the beginning, through wide
communication trenches later. Beginning immediately, they should
throw all dirt forward to serve as partial protection until there was
sufficient protection for a man in a kneeling position. There must also
be proper cover for a strong outpost guard the following morning.
Shortly before dawn the diggers would retire for rest and the preparation for the next night's labor. All of the parallel and communica-

tion trenches must follow the construction directions in the Manual on Field Fortifications.[1]

The work was not easy, in part because of the uneven terrain. The troops could never be certain about the texture of the subsoil, nor could they know the water table. Often they encountered an extensive water stream just below the surface, impeding all progress. The development of drainage ditches required time and study as well as extra work. While the troops quickly learned to use vines and stalks as matting and sandbags for the forward walls, they never satisfactorily solved the water problem.[2] The hard soil quickly dulled and broke the equipment, which was in limited supply. The rains continued intermittently, and, while they did not again flood any areas, they did soak the soil and the men and test the tenacity of their earth works.

The defenders, fully aware of the continuous Japanese activity, utilized every available device against the besiegers. They illuminated the entire area with light rockets, star shells, and searchlights. The latter, periodically "washing" over the work parties, proved a particularly effective harrassment. As a searchlight lit up a given area, the Japanese dropped into the muck, listened to the inevitable flight of bullets overhead, and then resumed their activities. The nights generally turned into a marvelous fireworks and light show as the brilliant lights appeared and faded away, the searchlights sent out shafts of light and went dark, and guns fired sudden, short-lived, colorful sparks. In peacetime everyone would have marveled at the colors, technology, and splendor which now they simply cursed.

In the confusion of these activities the advancing Japanese often heard, or imagined, suspicious noises. Immediately they fired upon them. The Germans hearing the rattle of machine guns or rifles, then joined the melee. Throughout the night periods of war alternated with periods of peace. For a period everything would be peaceful and incredibly still, only to be interrupted by a carnivallike demonstration.[3]

Despite all these distractions and difficulties, the Japanese labored on to establish a base operational siege line. Once it was in place, the formal attack could begin. As the infantry labored with this assignment, the artillerymen followed closely behind them under Watanabe's constant and dominating leadership. His instructions were always explicit and fulsomely detailed. By October 25 his concerns were fourfold—supply, communication, firing missions, and gun locations.

His supply problems hinged on the railway, of which the mid-October rains had destroyed a goodly portion. Later rains, while not nearly as heavy, eroded the roadbed and made necessary constant repairs. While seeing to it that repairs were prompt, Watanabe also demanded new branch lines. These additional tracks went to artillery positions, where the guns could have greater access to their ammunition.[4] By October 25 he had the required ammunition in place, the railway running, and the artillery supply functioning without mishap.

Communications involved the careful establishment of sufficient telephone lines between the various batteries, the command sections, and the observation post on Prinz Heinrich Hill. This requirement forced the wire-laying signalmen into great haste. Stretching their wire above ground, they suffered many breaks, both man-made and natural, because of it. Nonetheless, they did make Watanabe's deadline of October 29.

By October 27 Watanabe believed that his units had reached a state of readiness sufficient for formal assignments. At 11:00 A.M. that day he convened a meeting of his senior commanders, showing them the fire plan for the siege artillery. There were no real surprises. The first-priority targets were the German artillery and naval units. Both must be destroyed or silenced before the major assault could take place. Once the enemy's guns ceased to be a menace, they could focus their full attention on the defensive fortifications. After the attackers had occupied this line, the guns would shift to the German rear areas, ranging at will over the area, without real concern for the defenders' response. Watanabe, unlike Kamio, added a time projection for the operation. He anticipated a week-long engagement, ending in certain victory.[5]

The final artillery requirement was preparing the gun positions and establishing a firm ground base for them. This demand was somewhat more complex than the normal field manual description, for Kamio had ordered that the guns could not fire on the enemy, other than his shipping, until the final attack. This understandable reticence over providing information to the enemy had the serious disadvantage that the artillerymen could not test their positions, range assumptions, or field difficulties until the final barrage.

Moreover, the big guns continued to be difficult to move over the roads, which were, even in the best conditions, totally inadequate for such heavy equipment. The men had no choice beyond manhandling the guns themselves. Since this activity often blocked the roads, the artillerymen had many unpleasant discussions with their own associates as well as with other advancing troop formations.

The Germans posed only a minor inconvenience to the Japanese artillery. Although they based their entire fire plan upon stopping this deployment, their intensive effort accomplished very little. They did force the redeployment of several batteries, but they managed only a single direct hit (October 24, with eight Japanese fatalities).[6]

On October 26 Watanabe, satisfied with progress, started the preparations for the employment of the huge 28-cm howitzers, the ultimate in siege artillery. These huge pieces of metal, without their breechblocks, and plugged at both ends, looked like giant bottles; in fact, the British quickly dubbed them the "Ginger Beer Bottles." They demanded enormous labor investments and careful supervision, because their weight often divided the rail tracks. By October 29 they too were in position.[7] By pushing his men to great exertions, Watanabe had every other gun in place by the same date, together with proper communications and sufficient ammunition. The artillery were ready for action.

By October 29 Kamio had ordered the advance of the investment line from the base line to the scheduled first position, 1,200 to 2,000 meters from the German lines. He also shifted his headquarters to Fouschanhou, where he would control the final operation.[8] That same day, October 26, he met with General Johoji who had arrived at the front area with a battalion from his Regiment. It would take part in the final operation, while other Regimental units would serve in the general reserve. Johoji assumed command of the right flank force on October 29, relieving Colonel Takano who, together with his Sixty-seventh Regiment, came under Johoji's command. The fact that the transfer took place without difficulty was a demonstration of Japanese military sophistication. The troops slipped quickly into the siege line as the former occupants slid to the left.[9] Both groups were in their assigned positions by the night of October 29, a remarkable achievement.

The British were also involved with troop adjustments, although not on the same scale. On October 28 the Sikh unit joined Barnardiston's force, attracting attention from everyone with their unusual dress, especially their turbans. Coincidently they came under German shrapnel fire that same night, which made the Borderers somewhat suspicious of them. Also there was an acrimonious exchange over the distribution of space along the front. The Japanese, having already set out the total frontage, let the two parties fight it out among themselves. Within a day, however, they had resolved their concerns, and the Sikhs could start their formal participation. The addition of a Japanese engineer platoon helped their progress, albeit the language barrier forced both sides into sign language.[10] However, an increased allocation of Japanese liaison personnel improved communication, if not results.

Otherwise Kamio had few challenges. The other troops moved into place without difficulty. Both Yamada and Horiuchi issued the simplest of orders: they wanted all troops in place by October 31.[11] They possessed a direct challenge, but both commanders had no serious adjustments in meeting their assignments.

Elsewhere Kamio increased his pressures upon the Germans. His air force carried on reconnaissance activities, bombing missions, and counteractions against Plüschow. They moved continuously over the city and its defenses, seeking the latest information concerning German positions, adjustments, and strengths. They also added a new type of activity—the first night bombing operations in history. While the defenders offered a much more sophisticated aerial defense than they had presented earlier, they could do no more than damage aircraft.

The first night operation came on October 28, with a romantic full moon. Taking advantage of this light, the Japanese flyers took to the air. For the Germans located at the proper angulation, the Japanese aircraft seemed to appear suddenly in front of the moon, moving back and forth like oversized bats. Ground observers could readily see the small pellet-like objects drop suddenly from the aircraft. During a lull in the ground fire, those unable to see the aircraft would hear a hum like that of an automobile nearby. Just when they anticipated the honk of a horn, a bomb explosion shattered the illusion.[12]

Concurrently the Japanese launched a specific offensive against Plüschow, for, under no circumstances, did they want him over their positions. Plüschow adapted to the resulting game of hide and seek with ease and quickly developed new tactics—spiraling down, approaching from different directions, or hopping over hills at low altitudes. The Japanese never let up their pressure, mounting numerous attacks upon him. While they could not bring him down, they could, and largely did, keep him away from their troops.[13] He would not locate their dispositions, intentions, or secrets.[14]

As they moved forward on land, the besiegers did not neglect their sea power. For unclear reasons, Kato reversed his former opinions against early involvement and, on October 25, started sending various ships against the German forts. Normally one or two vessels went out and fired at Iltis, Hui tschuen huk, and Redoubt 1. They did so by listing their ships, firing at high angles, and staying outside the range of the German guns. Under such circumstances, their chances of hitting the target were highly uncertain. The resultant observers' reports all indicated a growing weakness in the city. They suggested that Iltis and Hui tschuen huk were disabled, that the Germans were firing practice shells filled with sand as a last resort, and that the defenders were on the verge of surrender. Kato accepted all of these assertions, but, out of respect for Hui tschuen huk, stayed well out to sea.[15]

By October 29 Kato clearly believed that his units were sufficiently experienced and the Germans properly weakened for a full-scale bombardment. Starting at 9:30 A.M., *Suwo*, *Tango*, *Okinoshima*, and *Triumph* took turns lobbing shells on the Germans until 4:30 P.M. They chose a firing position very close to their marking buoys. Hui tschuen huk fired sporadic responses, but never did more than displace water. For the first time the spotting station located on Prinz Heinrich Hill coordinated the firing program. It worked to perfection. The Japanese were confident that the 197 shells fired during the day had done extensive damage.[16]

The next day the Japanese returned to action and spent the day from 9:00 A.M. until 4:20 P.M. firing 240 shells. In doing so they accomplished two key assignments. They finally established, with confidence, the precise range (14,130 meters) of Hui tschuen huk. Shifting their buoys to that distance, they then fired from that point with impunity. The second success was the perfection of their communications with the Prinz Heinrich Hill station. The professional exchange and reporting throughout the day indicated that the fleet was fully prepared for the assault.[17]

On October 30 Kamio proclaimed everything in order for the assault. Having met all of his deadlines, the troops could now provide their Emperor a birthday present. Kamio renewed his orders. The troops would continue their advance that night, while the massed fire of land and sea guns would open the last act at dawn.

For the Germans time had also worn thin. Their preparations, limited by their resources, were complete. On October 25 Meyer-Waldeck informed his key officers that the attack must come at the month's end.[18] With this assumption, founded upon the reports of Chinese agents, the Governor started the preparations for the last rites of the city. On October 28 he ordered the dock personnel to sink the steamer *Michael Jepsen* in the gap between the vessels sunk on October 14, closing the harbor's mouth. The, by now, accomplished destruction crews sank the *Michael Jepsen* that night.[19]

The next day they moved the old, disarmed gunboat, *Tiger*, out to a buoy in the Bay, preparatory to sinking her. After the crew left, the Japanese started firing at her. The range was a bit long for their guns, but they persevered in their efforts. They had observed some movement aboard the ship and feared an escape attempt, but what they saw was really a Chinese thief who had paddled his small boat out to the *Tiger* in search of loot. Since the ship lay parallel to the Japanese guns, it was not a simple target, and their shells made a grand display as they dropped all around the ship. Finally they hit her three times in a row and called it a day. After undergoing a barrage of 200 shells, the terrified Chinese who had brought it on staggered out and left the ship.[20] Fearing that the Japanese might somehow disable the ship, the Germans moved her to deeper water and sank her that night.

The following morning Plüschow managed an early-morning flight just at sunrise. Catching his tormentors off guard, he made a lengthy run over the Japanese positions. The Japanese aircraft drove him back, but not until he had completed his mission. His report indicated the advanced state of preparations, the continuing supply movements, and the obvious masses of troop. While German artillery fired on some of Plüschow's reported targets, they lacked sufficient ammunition to attack all of them. The Japanese were clearly ready for the final movement. That night a solitary Japanese aircraft circled the city, dropping bombs. In the silence the unpleasantly dull sound of detonating explosives seemed like a starting signal.[21]

That night was very cold, but the following sunrise provided hope of a warm new day. For the Germans it was just another Saturday, but it was crisp and clear, a spectacular dawn.[22] The men in the batteries had just completed their morning exercises and had lined up for a much-anticipated cup of coffee. Some men were taking an early morning stroll, others were involved with their toilet, and a handful were busily fishing in the harbor. Everything was peacefully calm.

On the Japanese side, after a ceremony honoring the Emperor's birthday, each man moved to his assigned position. High on the Prinz Heinrich Hill, the men in the observation post barely had time to marvel at the glorious rising sun. At 6:10 A.M. General Watanabe ordered the firing of the signal gun, and the subsequent collective roar provided an entirely new dimension in sound.

As the hundred guns suddenly blossomed into life, the meaning of war changed immediately for everyone in Tsingtau. Within seconds the huge shells rained down on the defenders, and thoughts of coffee, walks, cleanliness, or fish disappeared in a frantic search for a hiding place.[23] The experienced men on Iltis paid little attention at first until their commander, Falkenhagen, observed, "Children, that is the opening of the dance. The Land Concert has begun," and ordered them into the casemates. Within seconds of their compliance the first shells began moving the sand around their haven. Falkenhagen's observation had noisy confirmation from all sides.

The Japanese fired their guns for two hours with a steady hammer-like barrage. Their initial endeavors were direct and simple: the guns fired without extensive integration, but each gun had its allocated mission and sector. Within these zones the guns fired, increased their range fifty meters, and fired again. Whenever they learned about a target of opportunity, they adjusted their fire against it and then returned to their earlier fire plan. This approach gave them every advantage through their numbers and superior observation. After two hours the guns received independent assignments, which Watanabe's staff coordinated with care, against the German artillery.[24] These firing plans proceeded without a single interruption. The sole worry was the rate of fire; various artillery men used up their allotments too quickly, causing some delays in the course of the day. Otherwise everything functioned according to plan.

Within the German defenses there was no doubt concerning the Japanese intentions or their ability to carry them out. The end was at hand. One of the most frightening aspects of the attack was the reaffirmation of the Japanese reputation for accuracy and efficiency in artillery fire. While the earlier naval bombardment had created a good deal of noise, it had not proven overly accurate, or, after the first adjustments, particularly awesome. The Japanese land batteries, however, quickly established their sovereignty over the battle area. The damage reports flooded into Meyer-Waldeck's headquarters. The famed Austrian battery took two direct hits. For the "LifeInsurance" battery time had run out; the thirteen casualties reflected their changed status.[25] They were not the last losses of the day as the cannonade swept ponderously over the defenses.

Shortly after the opening of the barrage, the Japanese gunners hit the huge Standard Oil storage tank and, an hour later, the tank of the Asiatic Petroleum Company. They went up in huge sheets of flame, oily smoke roaring skyward and forming a huge umbrella-shaped cover over the city. In the cloudless sky, without any significant wind, the two black columns provided an impressive show. It proved too much for the Chinese in the area, who fled in disorder as the flaming oil poured throughout the adjacent streets, fires quickly breaking out in its wake. The flames spread to the lumber yard, the coal storage area, the wharves. All of them burned fiercely; only the most extensive efforts saved the wharves from total destruction. The firemen labored as best they could but found the oil-fed fires beyond their control abilities.[26]

Even as the second oil tank ignited, the roar of the bombardment increased in volume. The fleet had moved into line and, shortly after 9:00 A.M. had started their heavy-throated contribution to the general confusion. They quickly went after their favorite targets, Iltis and Hui tschuen huk. In the course of the day they fired 126 big shells.[27] Their contribution was more noise than destruction, more psychological than physical. In the general confusion, however, no one could identify the source for a particular explosion.

The total barrage "walked" over the German area looking for guns, positions, and, in fact, anything alive. It missed very little. The Japanese aim was superb, and only the fact that many shells did not explode saved the Germans from genuine disaster. Within the casements the oil lamps went out, the cement cracked, and the air fouled. What German response there was came through the hours of training which allowed the men to function in the dark or by flashlight. The Japanese efficiency, however, precluded most answers. In all of the major German batteries there were losses. While some guns kept quiet in the hope of avoiding detection, the others could accomplish very little. The Japanese knew most of the locations, and the Germans could not move their guns so quickly. In the fixed positions they could do nothing. These positions soon filled with the remains of buildings, pieces of concrete and iron, pockmarks of innumerable explosions, and rubbish and earth tossed up in surrealistic display. The exploding shells also cut all telephone contact beyond repair.[28]

As the Japanese fired at everything, many shells went wild and carried on into the city. For the first time Tsingtau suffered appreciable harm.[29] The Chinese quarter received the greatest damage; at least a hundred Chinese perished in the barrage. In the city the citizens quickly learned the various sounds which differentiated Japanese and German shells, as well as the noises heralding an approaching shell. They soon made up something of a macabre game. If one heard the relatively regular humming sound of a German shell, the expected comment was, "Don't worry, it is only an export." At the less regular humming of a Japanese shell or the sound of an explosion, the more urgent shout was, "Import, import, down!"[30]

The Japanese barrage obscured the landscape, overwhelming the Germans with the smoke, fire, and sound. The Japanese prevented any response until noon, when their fire slowed in favor of a less rhythmic effort.[31] As the Japanese fire lessened, the Germans immediately began clearing their guns for a fulsome response. They soon discovered the value of their antique weapons in such difficult times. Unless an enemy shell had made a direct hit, the old guns were almost immediately ready for action. They did not have the complex control systems, the sensitive firing systems, or the scientifically machined parts of their more modern neighbors. One needed to do little more than hastily shovel away the debris tossed up by the Japanese barrages and quickly swab the bore, while the more modern guns could not be made serviceable without far more extensive service.

Even as the gun crews cleaned up and fired a weak response, they could see the damage wrought by the Japanese within a short time. Around them the trenches were smashed beyond recognition, the ironwork twisted into grotesque shapes, and the communication lines destroyed without hope of repair. The devastated landscape provided no pleasant walkways. The "Port Arthur Crackers," as the Germans termed the 28-cm howitzers, left their "crumbs" (as the defenders called their shells) everywhere. For the defenders the first response, beyond elementary survival, was shoveling dirt, sand, and trees. It was heavy labor.[32] Afterwards they started a slow response against their tormentors. Since the Japanese had also used the pause to prepare for a new barrage, the two sides exchanged a heavy fire, although the Japanese were clearly ahead in both quality and quantity.[33]

By day's end the entire German position was in chaos. With a dozen guns out of action, communications gone, human movement precluded, the trench line destroyed, the wire entanglements smashed, the Germans could only gloomily and fearfully admire the forceful celebrations of the Emperor's birthday. That night the still-burning fires luridly outlined the city and the mountains for Japanese naval observers.

With nightfall the defenders hoped for some relief in order to repair some of the destruction. While the Japanese did slow their fire, they shifted from high-explosive shells to shrapnel, which they burst over the German positions. This interdiction proved highly effective and denied the defenders sufficient opportunity for repairs.[34] Nonetheless, the Germans managed to take stock and began their preparations for the next day. They shifted every possible man into the combat line, and all the commanders moved into their field headquarters. They made yet another search through the unit rosters, looking for additional manpower.

Concurrently, and in accordance with direct orders from Meyer-Waldeck, they began the systematic destruction of excess equipment, machinery, and some weapons. Since ammunition was in limited supply, various gun crews blew up their guns as they expended their final shells, and marched off to the front lines.[35] In the dock area the officers supervised the destruction of the huge crane, the dry dock, the tug boats, and all of the reserve naval equipment. They also laid the explosive charges to destroy the entire area, to avoid leaving anything for the conquerors.[36] The men freed from their jobs through this destruction also joined the infantry.

Elsewhere the Germans remained on full alert, anticipating a sudden Japanese thrust in the dark. They repaired some damage and dug new holes against the renewal of the bombardment the following morning. Progress was slow, but the men were busy most of the night.

On the other side the besiegers also welcomed nightfall, albeit for other reasons. The artillerymen could review their day's activities, reconstitute their ammunition supplies, and begin the preparations for the next morning. They maintained the harassing fire throughout the night, but with understrength gun crews. The others had a good night's rest.

During the day the infantrymen had listened to the barrage, carried building materials, or rested while awaiting nightfall. With the arrival of sunset, they resumed their entrenching activities. They advanced to the first parallel line in accordance with Kamio's schedule, their molelike traces springing up at a fast rate despite the hard ground. They retired at daybreak with the assurance that they could finish entrenching the night night.

Kamio, after reviewing all of the reports during the night issued new instructions on November 1. He pointed out the successful digging on the first investment line, the weak German response, and the visible damage wrought by the artillery. He ordered the first line occupied that night and the communication trenches begun toward the second line, which should be ready for occupation during the night of November 3. The assault artillery would move forward with the infantry, while the siege guns would continue their normal assignments.

Kamio's confidence appeared in a corollary order of the same date, in which he discussed the appearance of a truce flag. Should the defenders show such a flag (or the normal red cross symbol), he wanted it accorded every respect. Kamio laid down minute instructions on the handling of such incidents and on Japanese behavior after the breakthrough into the city.[37]

With dawn the Japanese reopened their furious and "earth shaking Sunday musical concert." The Germans did not hold church services, although most of them did some praying during the day. While the volume of fire was little different than the previous day, the Japanese gunners had improved with experience, and they were far more efficient and deadly. For November 1 their main mission again included the German artillery (where they were running out of targets). They also began shifting some guns against the German fortifications, in particular the Redoubts 4 and 5.[38] The Germans, however, did not appreciate this subtle change; to them it seemed that the Japanese had simply discarded any organized fire plan in favor of general obliteration.

All morning the Japanese poured shells upon the German line engulfing it in spiraling dirt, choking fumes, and flying metal. They received ample support from the fleet units, which fired 112 huge shells against targets within their range.[39] Their combined efforts wrought havoc in the German defense.

While the damage to the defensive artillery was much less than that of the previous day, the redoubts suffered horrendous destruction. All of the infantry works bore the scars of exploding shells, the intervening laboriously built trenches simply disappeared, and the communication paths lost all identity marks. No one dared cross the open ground between the positions. Messengers, who had no choice, but to make the trip, spent hours jumping from one shell hole into another. Within the works the men tried counting the impacting shells but gave up the effort; there were too many.[40] Redoubts 4 and 5 suffered their first real trial. They had holes in the roofs, scars on all the walls, and enough metal around them for a scrapyard. Miraculously the human losses were small, and the physical damage was not serious to the vital areas, thanks in part to the totally unexpected strength of the fortifications. The concrete survived far more stress than anyone had anticipated in the construction specifications. Moreover, an incredible number of duds, caused by poor fuses, marred the superb Japanese marksmanship. Every German position was littered with a collection of unexploded shells.[41]

After midday the Japanese began adjusting their artillery fire. While they maintained their steady barrage on the fortifications, they shifted several guns to other targets, such as the signal station.

Within a short time the signal crew ran for a new haven. The Japanese, landing four 15-cm shells on the building within the space of one half hour, demolished most of the building as well as a goodly portion of the extensive wireless antennae. The station looked like a sieve. The last shell shredded the halyards holding the battle flag, the symbol of German sovereignty, which drifted off into the Bay. An observant sailor quickly put up a replacement flag, but the incident served as yet another reminder of the hapless German position.[42]

By the day's end Meyer-Waldeck believed that the final assault was at hand. He issued a strong statement encouraging his men for the final stand, recalling the messages from the Kaiser, the honor of German arms, and the German position in the Far East. The eyes of all were upon them, and they must maintain their military obligations and honor until death.[43] His following instructions for the night were that the troops must remain in the front line throughout the night rather than repair damage or rest in nearby areas. This was unpleasant news, since the positions were in complete disarray and often filled with water. No relief from the Japanese pounding could be expected either, since that would unquestionably go on.

Shortly after nightfall the attackers returned to their digging. They quickly occupied the positions prepared during the previous night and began pushing the wide communication trenches forward, expediting their progress with sandbags. Since the shortage of sandbags continued, they often moved those from the rearmost positions to the new areas. At the same time, they sent out patrols searching for new details concerning the defenses.

One of these patrols, under Lieutenant A. Fukakusa, reconnoitered along the bank of the Haipo. As they neared Redoubt 4, they noted that the German outposts had not detected them. Impetuously, Fukakusa advanced along the defensive wire and ditch. When the defenders still gave no sign of life, he advanced a demolition party of four men. They soon found an iron ladder into the big ditch, and, descending it, began cutting their way through the wire. Only after they had made good progress did the Germans finally hear them and opened a furious machine gun fire on them, killing one man. The other three climbed out of the ditch, rejoined their group, and returned to their lines. After they reported their success, another patrol moved directly to the same point and finished cutting the wire. The new group reached as far as the fort before the defenders drove them off with a hail of bullets. Once back in the lines the second patrol leader also reported his successful activity.[44]

For the Germans this encounter assumed immense dimensions. The redoubt commander, Captain Lancelle, called for immediate artillery support and all available reserves. On Iltis a battery opened fire against this reported breakthrough attempt. Sachse, with the naval reserves, hurried toward Lancelle. En route he reported to Kuhlo, who quietly suggested that the Japanese were not interested in any assault at that time. There was not enough noise to support such notions. However, the subsequent report from Lancelle of a successful defense which had "thrown back" a Japanese probe was good for morale, despite its falseness.[45] Apparently no one investigated or questioned the defensive laxness, the erroneous reporting, or the overreaction to the weak Japanese probe.

Neither side suffered major losses, but the Japanese gained several advantages from Fukakusa's daring. They had their first precise information concerning the German redoubts and their defenses. Concurrently, they received an eye-opening insight into the German lack of readiness. The defenders had been in their redoubt (despite contrary orders) and did not have sufficient outposts for early warning. While the Japanese decided against any immediate assault, they did have more confidence about their ability to succeed at the proper moment. Moreover the German battery of Iltis, responding to Lancelle's message that the storm was at hand, had revealed its location to the observant Japanese. Early the next morning the Japanese destroyed the two offending guns with a pinpoint barrage.[46]

Elsewhere the Germans spent the night destroying more property. The *Kaiserin Elisabeth* fired her last shells in a random barrage against the Japanese positions. In the darkness the besiegers could not locate the moving ship. After the last shell was gone, Makoviz shifted the ship to deep water and prepared to scuttle her. Obtaining the needed permission from Meyer-Waldeck, he ordered all but ten men off the ship. They went ashore and joined infantry units. Shortly after midnight the remaining men wired four torpedoes in strategic places, raised full steam in the boilers, and opened all the sea valves. When the circuit closed, firing the explosives, the ship was illuminated for a brief moment before she disappeared from sight. Markoviz said quietly, "Addio 'Lisa,'" and all the men shed tears over the inglorious end of their ship.[47] The action clearly depressed the Austrians because of their emotional attachment to the ship and because of the stress brought on by its destruction. They could no longer avoid the full grim realization that, if they did somehow survive the siege, they would be prisoners of war.[48]

Equally somber events took place in the dock area. There the last of the work crews completed the destruction of the last equipment, installations, and ships. Only the *Jaguar* survived the night. By dawn there was nothing left, and the men marched off to the front.[49]

By the early light the Germans found the Japanese movements much closer than they had thought possible in the short time. The sandbags, trenches, and spoil thrown up by the besiegers were clearly visible. They saw little human movement, but the product of Japanese industry kept them aware of the enemy's activity. A young German officer spent each morning on Iltis Hill, carefully noting the changed positions. He then hurried to Meyer-Waldeck with a map marked with the latest developments.[50] By November 2 the Japanese had advanced their lines up to the Hai po. They were particularly close to the German lines in the center and toward the Bay, where they were almost on the Water Works.

For the defenders the pressures of these advancing trenches, the continuing artillery fire, and the widespread destruction was increasingly hard to bear, but on November 2 they confessed to their inability to fight back. During the day the Germans began destroying their artillery. There was no more ammunition, and that which did remain must be saved for the last assault. All but a few of the gun crews redistributed the last shells, destroyed their guns, and joined the men in the trenches.[51] They could no longer answer the Japanese bombardment.

Each day for the next two days the Japanese guns maintained their withering bombardment, and each night they kept up their inexorable land advance. A steady drizzle on November 2 somewhat slowed the Japanese efforts. Many parapets, arduously set up, simply collapsed into the mire, forcing the reconstruction of several trenches.[52] The closeness of the river also made drainage a very serious challenge.

The artillery kept up its activity, although the Japanese withdrew their huge 28-cm siege guns from action. They could not stand the strain imposed by the constant firing and required extensive modification.[54] The other guns, during the afternoon of November 2, began running out of effective targets. They started firing on the barbed wire, the wall, and other lesser obstacles, in order to blow lanes through the defenses rather than expend lives on the job.

That same night the Japanese finally hit the electric works, toppled its huge stack, and turned off the city's electricity. Thereafter the inhabitants were forced to use candles and oil lamps. In the hospital this brought some discomfort to the wounded. The wireless station, while it could continue receiving messages through the *Sikiang*, could no longer send any reports to the outside world. The redoubts had their own power which allowed them to carry on, but they were alone in that regard. There could be no optimism in the city as the damp darkness anticipated the end.[54]

During the day of November 4 the besiegers continued their bombardment. There were few interesting or useful targets left among the defenses. The entire area had lost any identity, and the defenders no longer bothered with repairs. They could not match the Japanese destructive powers. During the day the Japanese disengaged several batteries and shifted them forward into new positions, demonstrating impressively the advanced sophistication of the Japanese artillery.[55] They shifted their positions, relocated all of their equipment, and quickly adjusted their fire with the speed, precision, and accuracy of true professionals.

With this advanced fire power and the infantry available, Joholji ordered a prompt assault on the pump station. Lieutenant Hayashi Yoshi in command of this operation, quickly assembled a task force of infantry and engineers. As the company-sized group left for the assault, a small German patrol arrived at the pump station with food supplies. The patrol also brought to Sergeant Hamann, the commander, the conflicting instructions that he should hold on to the position as long as possible, but that he should not allow needless sacrifice. The patrol departed only a few minutes ahead of the Japanese.

Hayashi's assault force quietly surrounded the station as artillery shells isolated it from relief. They detonated two mines in accomplishing their mission, but the oblivious defenders, too interested in their new supplies, did not take any notice. The engineers quickly exploded their long, destructive tubes in the barbed wire, and the infantry hurried through the holes. For the defenders, there was only a single possible action beyond death and they fled into their installation, slamming the iron doors shut behind them. The Japanese immediately started pounding upon the door, and one cried out dire threats in broken German. Hamann, who could not understand these threats, decided promptly that honor was satisfied and surrendered. A group of twenty-one prisoners marched away. The Japanese movements had been so quick that the defenders were unable to warn their colleagues by flare signals of the coup de main, and the garrison's first inkling of the captured pump station came from the suddenly dry waterpipes.[56] A hurriedly assembled relief effort could not, because of the Japanese artillery fire, even move forward, much less attempt a breakthrough operation.

The struggle at the pump station, however, was one of many continuous small actions along the entire line. The trench lines were too close for comfort and the Germans fought hard everywhere.

The British spent the night of November 4 laying out their final assault position, directly in front of the German wall and just over the river bed. Unfortunately for them the position came under German flanking fire. Captain Douglas G. Johnson, in charge of the local advance, started out on his stomach, laying out the traverses with little white pegs. As the men, pushing sandbags in front of them for protection, advanced to the designated location, the vigilant defenders loosed a heavy small-arms fire on them. When men began falling, Johnson stopped all digging and ordered the men back. He supervised the retirement of both the dead and the wounded men. This action, while of short duration, was the most serious one for the British contingent. They lost eight dead and had eighteen wounded within a few minutes.[57]

On November 5 the Japanese opened the day with a new approach. Instead of the usual artillery sounds, the Germans heard only the throb of airplane engines. Three airplanes dropped low over the German positions and dropped leaflets. Most of the packages did not burst upon impact, thereby facilitating their collection. Meyer-Waldeck, nonetheless, did not have the propaganda destroyed, but

encouraged their distribution as curiosities and souvenirs. The leaflets carried the message (unaccountably dated October 30):

To the Respected Officers and Men of the Fortress!

It would act against the will of God as well as against humanity if
one were to destroy the still useful weapons, ships, and other
structures without tactical justification and only because of the
envious view that they might fall into the hands of the enemy.

Although we are certain in the belief that, in the case of the
chivalrous officers and men, they would not put into effect such
thoughtlessness, we nevertheless would like to emphasize the
above as our point of view.

Siege Command.[58]

Even as the Germans found some humor in the choice of words (as
God's will, chivalry, thoughtlessness). They also heard new battle
sounds. On November 5 the *Mishima, Tango, Okinoshina,* and
Iwami moved into Hai hsi Bay behind Cape Jaeschke for an entirely
new bombardment on Tsingtau. They fired, in conjunction with the
land batteries, a heavy barrage—some seventy-seven shells—on the
city itself. At the very outset one of the shells, apparently an ill-aimed
one, hit Hui tschuen huk, killing seven men and wounding three.
The crew and the destroyed gun had been responsible for the earlier
hit on the *Triumph.*[59]

Within the city the bombardment created more damage than all of
the previous ones. The huge shells smashed buildings as though they
were paper mache, cut down entire walls, carved house-sized holes
in the streets, and shook the earth in a continuous earthquake. The
city dwellers lacked the ready water supply and the essential manpower for a serious defense against fire. As a result, many homes
burned to the ground without the slightest rescue attempt. Only a
few buildings escaped some scars from the shelling. The distance
between structures spared the city a horrendous fire. In the Chinese
settlement the same problems were magnified through crowded
conditions and less substantial construction. The fire proved less of a
threat, however, since the shells just collapsed the buildings. With
the streets pitted from fragments, the houses defaced or burned, and

the citizenry hiding in cellars, Tsingtau was truly a city under siege. The Japanese had, at last, moved to a position where they could easily level the city, should the struggle go on.

The Japanese, however, had no interest in doing so. Throughout November 5 they evidenced their intention of storming the city. They were up against the German wall now, close enough for the defenders to hear them talking and digging. Throughout the day they kept up their work, albeit on a reduced scale, without fear of interruption. The artillery also maintained its continuous fire on the defenders.

For the Germans there were few possible preparations for defense. They collected the last few men from around the city, blew up the main sea defenses, and awaited the end.[60] The men in the front line, weary from the continuous pounding, had few illusions concerning the future. A report from Redoubt 3 to Meyer-Waldeck reflected the universal condition: "The entire work is shot to pieces, a hill of fragments, without any defenses. The entire trench system is knocked out; the redoubt still holds together, but everything else, including the explosives storage room, is destroyed. Only a single observation post is in use. I shall hold the redoubt as long as possible."[61] They no longer even pretended that they could make good the damage.

Meyer-Waldeck realized that the final assault must come momentarily. The artillery ammunition was exhausted, the last human reserves were committed, the defensive works were ruined, and the Japanese were in their final assault positions. His own men were exhausted from their October trials, the constant pounding by enemy artillery, their own impotence, and the continuous activity of watch posts, patrol, and alarm. They could not go on for long. Even the password for the next day, "For Emperor and Country" reflected the growing desperation and dispondency.

On November 6 the Germans saw Plüschow's lonely aircraft rise from his landing area. Even as he started upward, the observent Japanese battery went after him. A single shell exploded very close, and the craft dropped heavily. With his normal iron-fisted control Plüschow mastered his craft, made a quick turn over the city, waved goodbye, and turned toward China.[62] As he left, his ground crew burned the remaining documents and diaries, the two hangers, and the decoy aircraft.

The Japanese aircraft ranged over the city throughout the day, dropping bombs everywhere, in their first collective endeavor for some days. The turbulent air currents made flight difficult and bombing more psychologically symbolic than physically threatening, but the bombs did add to the general din and confirmed Meyer-Waldeck's decision that the Japanese were about to make their final thrust. He ordered a general alert for everyone that afternoon. Satisfying his requirement was no easy. For the men to move out of their shelters into the barely discernible trench line was extremely dangerous, for the Japanese gunners knew the precise location of everything and fired at the slightest movement.[63] Conditions within the redoubts were not that pleasant either, but they did allow a sense of collective security, as well as greater safety.

For Kamio the long-awaited time for decision was at hand. His troops, with the exception of the struggling British, had reached their final departure line; his artillery had completed the anticipated position shifts; and his men had brought up all of their assault equipment. He could not decide whether to order a general assault for that night or the following one. As a result, he hedged his orders. His instructions called for a constant probing of the enemy's resistance with numerous patrols, a powerful artillery barrage, and a search for a breakthrough opportunity. He said nothing about the assault time.[64] The instructions were general and flexible, since Kamio did not want undue risks or a large-scale failure. At the same time, he knew the German military training manual's dictum that the enemy normally attacked at dawn. Since the defenders remained dormant at night, he concluded that they accepted this aphorism about the Japanese as well. A night attack preferred greater possibilities for surprise and success.[65]

That night a splendid moon illuminated the darkness, allowing better observation and movement for both sides. The Japanese moved boldly into the big ditch. They dug quickly to the big wall, broke through, and then pushed the dirt and concrete onto the wire. In some places they filled the trench full enough to lay matting or boards on the waste and walk over the wire. As their troops moved forward, the Japanese fired a heavy artillery barrage. Concurrently they mounted numerous patrols, which quickly developed paths through the German defenses.

The first serious engagement began at 11:00 P.M. around Redoubt

4. As the Japanese moved around the fort, they quickly encountered the alert German defenders. Having learned from their earlier experience, the Germans met the probe head on. While the resultant struggle was a brief one, it was fiercely fought with rifle butts, bayonets, and fists. The defenders succeeded, and the Japanese retired back into the wire and the darkness. Even as they did so the Japanese artillery, obviously in close contact with the advanced troops, reopened its fire on the area. The Japanese made no progress here.[66] Afterward the artillery fire quieted down to an occasional mortar or artillery shell.

As the activity quieted here, the attackers shifted their probing efforts toward Redoubt 3. Their artillery had pounded the area repeatedly throughout the day. At the same time the Japanese force assigned here was better prepared than the probe against Redoubt 4. During the day Lieutenant Jekizo Nakamura had received orders to mount a strong patrol that night to test the German defenses. He had informed his men that they should prepare themselves for a powerful effort. The men had carefully prepared their equipment, the officers had put on their *Shirotasuki* (a white band across the breast, as a sign of willingness to die in battle), and the men had prepared their *Kokki* (the self-made national flags). The group had assembled along the bank of the Hai po. The waterway held some water at this point, and the men were thrilled both at the prospect of action and at leaving the misery-creating waterway. Various officers made brief talks to the men, exhorting them forward to victory with the need for sacrifice, for dedication, for success. At the end everyone faced toward the Imperial palace and presented arms, an action symbolizing taking leave from the Emperor.

Nakamura's group, about company size, left around midnight. Using assault ladders, they descended the wall, moved through the holes cut by the artillery in the barbed wire, and reached the outer boundary of Redoubt 3 without difficulty. They advanced in a column, almost as if they were on parade.

The defenders, harassed by artillery fire and tired by the siege, were not on guard. They had retired inside the work, and the attackers slipped by the few scattered outposts without discovery.

Amazed at the ease with which they had advanced to this point, Nakamura's men quickly spread out, searching for the flanks of the defense. By chance they saw a door open, and the escaping light helped pinpoint the installation for them. The German voices discussing the siege added confirmation. As the Japanese began their final advance, a single sentry noted their presence and tried to fire on them. At this critical moment, his rifle malfunctioned and failed to fire. He became a prisoner.[67] By this time the Japanese noise finally alerted the defenders, who opened fire—too late!

Nakamura's men quickly surrounded the redoubt and loosed a heavy fire on its sole exit. The defenders could not get out; they were shut up inside the installation. At this crucial moment Japanese reinforcements arrived, assuring the victory. Another infantry company under a Captain Okazaki began augmenting the rifle fire and vocal noise. Okazaki, sword in hand, advanced into the shelter. As he did so a German shouted in Japanese, "We give up! We give up!" Okazaki started immediate discussions with Lieutenant Ramin on the German side. Using English, which neither of them spoke fluently, they took several moments to agree on the surrender terms. The entire struggle had lasted one half hour, and some 200 Germans surrendered their positions.[68]

Okazaki reported his totally unexpected success to Kamio, who promptly informed a wide range of people—all the unit commanders, the Military Attaché in Peking, and the Chief of the General Staff—about the breakthrough. There was no question about the continuance of the attack.[69]

Meyer-Waldeck understood the danger and ordered an immediate counterattack, together with the concentrated fire of all available artillery pieces. His instructions were militarily correct, but his resources were insufficient for their implementation. The few available guns fired their last shells in haste. It was their last sound. In their anxiety, the gunners often misdirected their aim and fired on their own positions, thereby increasing the general confusion. In any event, they could not really accomplish much beyond firing all of their shells and then destroying the guns. Among the bright flashes of impacting shells came the briglter lights of exploding guns to light the battlefield.

In the front line the Governor's instructions brought the same inadequate result, for there were insufficient men for any counteraction. A few engineers, some Austrian sailors, and a handful of displaced artillerymen commandeered for the undertaking strove to seal off the penetration, too few and too late. As they hurriedly scrambled toward the Japanese, they screamed, "With God for Emperor and Country."

They first stumbled onto a Japanese group of fourteen men, which they overwhelmed in furious hand-to-hand combat. A German artilleryman, his legs cut off by an artillery shell, tried to charge on the stumps; a Japanese sergeant fell with eleven bayonet wounds. While the Germans lost men, they annihilated the Japanese group. Almost immediately afterwards, the attackers encountered a more extensive Japanese formation and came to a complete halt. They fell or surrendered within minutes.

The Japanese spread out quickly, their many-throated "Banzai" roared over the front line as they poured all their reserves into the gap. The Germans in Redoubt 4 could hear the sounds, but they did not interpret them properly. After their own engagement they assumed that the front line had held the attackers off. One of the flank guards, Paul Kley, watching towards his front, suddenly received a bayonet thrust in the arm. Turning instinctively and firing at the same time, he shot three Japanese soldiers in the next shell hole—the enemy was on the flank.[70] Immediately everyone turned to a general defense but they did not have the manpower for their needs. With some assistance from the *Jaguar's* final shells, they managed to fight back the assault for three hours before they gave way. After a curious and brief exchange between a German speaking flawless Japanese and a Japanese using flawless German, the fort surrendered to the enemy.[71]

The same outcome was recorded at Redoubt 2, where the Japanese encircled the fort and drove the defenders inside. Meyer-Waldeck managed to get a message to the surrounded men, ordering them to hold out but not to suffer a needless sacrifice. That was sufficient inducement for the defenders, who decided that they had done enough and gave up quickly.

Their surrender assured the Japanese victory. They had a wide gap in the enemy lines, general momentum, and no serious obstacles. With such advantages, they simply rolled sideways against the two remaining forts. The troops in the center kept up their advance and moved toward the dominating hills of Moltke, Iltis, and Bismarck.

On Iltis were three positions, all on the alert when the Japanese arrived at the foot of the hill. The first was a hastily assembled artillery position with four small ship's guns and observation responsibilities for Bismarck, commanded by Lieutenant Julius Aye. Without any communications, he assumed that the assault would come at dawn. He ordered his men to rest while he took the guard duty. When he heard a strange noise, he alerted one man and started his investigation. Aye quickly found a Japanese officer with drawn sword. The German, neglecting both his warning whistle and his pistol, drew his own sword and attacked his foe. His subordinate alerted the twenty resting men, who watched the incredible display. The Japanese soldiers did likewise. Their officer was faster and, in quick succession, sliced Aye's hip and his right hand, before killing him with a slash to the neck. Each of his men thrust a bayonet into the dead lieutenant before assaulting the others. Only one German survived the uneven struggle.[72]

With that position secure, the Japanese turned on the other two gun positions, where the defenders were awake and cognizant of Aye's fate. A Japanese officer approached the lower installation with a white flag and asked, in German, for the surrender. From out of the dark came a shot, killing him. The attackers then began boring holes and preparing explosive charges, rather than attempting a direct assault. Before they could explode the charges, wild Japanese cheers informed everyone that the other position had given up. Dispirited, the remaining Germans surrendered quickly.[73]

On Bismarck Hill the gun crews fired off their last shells and, at 5:00 A.M., started the preparations for destruction. They deployed dynamite charges and mines throughout the position and then ran the detonating wire to the bottom of the hill. The first firing attempt failed, because a Japanese shell cut the line. After a volunteer repaired the break, the charges went off with a huge roar, littering the area with fragments. Among those injured by the fall of debris were several Japanese, who arrived just a little late.[74]

The struggle continued in a whirling melee of sound and action, but the results were clear. At 6:00 A.M. Meyer-Waldeck held a brief staff meeting and reviewed the most recent information and their possible options. The Japanese had broken through the defenses and opened the way into the city. The defenders could try a house-to-house, last-ditch defense, or they could surrender. Several staff members wanted a final defense, but the Governor decided against it. Ordering the colorless surrender flag hoisted at prominent points, he signed a message to General Kamio reading:

Your Excellency!

Since my defensive means are exhausted, I am
now ready to enter into surrender negotiations for
the now open city.

If your Excellency agrees to this proposal, I
request you to appoint plenipotentiaries to the
discussions, as well as to set time and place for
the meeting of the respective plenipotentiaries.
For my part I will appoint as chief negotiator
the Chief of Staff, Captain Saxer.

The Imperial Governor
Meyer-Waldeck[75]

Major von Kayser delivered the message, taking with him a
trumpeter, a white flag carrier, and a horse holder. The small party
set out through the continuing battle, searching for a path through
the chaos. Kayser finally found a path through the city and directed
his party toward Tai tung schen, but they soon found themselves in a
crossfire between the lines. The first Japanese would not allow them
passage. All the German started waving and shouting, while the
trumpeter played the call for cease fire. Stray shots killed one man
and von Kayser's horse.

After a lengthy wait they received Japanese permission to proceed.
Eventually they reached the same place where von Kayser had
negotiated on October 13. Shortly afterwards various Japanese officers arrived, including the concerned Yamada who was delighted to
learn about his friend's survival.

In a hurried exchange they agreed to a general armistice and to
open the formal surrender discussions that afternoon. The Japanese
asked that the Germans stop their destruction, but von Kayser
replied that they had already completed it. Thereafter the Germans
rode back to their lines. On his way back, von Kayser found the
British already located in a former factory building, nearby was a long
column of German prisoners. As he neared the prisoners, someone
called "Attention!" Kayser saluted, called out a greeting, and rode
on. Shortly thereafter, he passed three indolent British soldiers. One
of them, without shifting his informal position called out in German,
"What now, Herr Baron?" Tsingtau had fallen.[76]

VII

A Turning Point

Das Land versinkt am Horizont,
Ein lichter Streifen, hell besonnt
Der Lauting fern und ferner gluht.
Leb wohl, du schones Kiautschougebiet

Friedrich Blaschke, "Abschied
von Tsingtau"

Despite von Kayser's agreement with the Japanese, the battle raged
on. The lack of wind left the white flags, like limp rags, uncertain
symbols of surrender, and in the heat of the engagement many men
could not see them. Meyer-Waldeck sent out five motorcycle riders
with the message, but they were all captured and detained by the
Japanese. In some desperation the Governor dispatched his staff
members to the major battle points. They did get through the Japanese to the resistance areas, in particular Redoubts 1 and 5, which had
refused to give up. The staff messengers briefly explained the general surrender and advised everyone to comply with the agreement.[1]

At last the war sounds died out as the news circulated among the
troops. The final sound was a German light artillery shell, which
killed two British soldiers who had gone out for a walk, assuming that
the campaign was long over.[2] After the week-long, interminable
bombardment, the silence was a disturbing contrast.

Everywhere men were in movement. For the confused and fearful
Germans it was a time of contemplation and thought. While they had
not had to endure a prolonged siege, they had lost the campaign. In
addition they faced the uncertain future of all war prisoners. For

182

most of them the final activity was singing the national anthem and then quietly awaiting Japanese arrival. The Japanese often waited patiently until the Germans had finished this final song. They then broke into a victory dance, waving their rifles festooned with the small, homemade national flags, and screaming "Banzai." Afterward the Japanese hustled the captives off at a brisk trot, without any comraderie or general exchange.[3]

In the confusion there were, of course, many unplanned incidents, although Kamio tried very hard to avoid any difficulty. Even as the battle ended, he issued strict instructions that there would be no looting, no disorder, no trouble. In fact, he did not want any Japanese troops in the city. The transfer of ownership should be an orderly one, without the slightest damage to the Japanese reputation.[4]

Nonetheless, small groups of Japanese soldiers appeared in the city streets, followed shortly after by groups of cavalrymen riding aimlessly about the city. They quickly rounded up the hundred or so old reservists who had controlled the city's security. Lodging no protest, these elderly men quickly surrendered their weapons to the grim, still grimy, victors. Without any symbol of authority, the soldiers began entering homes and looting those items they could carry with them, particularly money. The most serious loss was in the house of Pastor Winter, who had received a good deal of money for safe keeping.[5] In this search some Japanese found caches of alcohol, and, thereafter, began manhandling civilians. These incidents, despite their relatively small number, caused numerous wild rumors throughout Tsingtau. Most individuals stayed inside their houses but soldiers gathered in small, quiet groups on the street. As on the front line, the uncertainty, fear, and general apprehension pervaded everyone.

The combat troops suffered this same uncertain anticipation. As the Japanese occupied the German installations, they generally chose one of three means in dealing with their captives. The first, for people who were neither in the front lines nor in organized units on november 7, was simply to allow the individuals to go about their business without interruption. They circulated in the city, visiting old haunts, fraternizinv qith hhs Japanese soldiers. For them the following days were not unpleasant diversions.[6]

A second group were the men taken prisoner in the redoubts. The Japanese moved them quickly to the Moltke Hill area, where they assembled a goodly crowd under a loose guard. The captors were just as tired as the captives, and both sides rested most of the day.[7] For a few reservists this loose control provided a good opportunity to check on their property in the city, and they quietly departed for their city houses.

The Japanese counted 2,300 prisoners that day. In the late afternoon, apparently fearing sabotage, the Japanese marched the men inland. They allowed the prisoners a blanket or coat and whatever they could carry of their personal possessions. The older men and officers could use rickshas for their belongings. While the Japanese allowed such privileges and a loose march order as well, they did not permit delay. Once outside the defenses, the guards lodged their charges in the closest Chinese villages, unceremoniously turning the inhabitants out to sleep in the open. German morale remained high, since they firmly believed that the European campaign would be resolved quickly. In fact, the majority of the prisoners believed that they would not leave Shantung except for home.[8]

The third group consisted of officials, individuals needed for the surrender activities, and persons required for maintaining the city's essential services. For them the Japanese kept a loose control, allowing them a maximum of freedom, but never leaving their fate in doubt. Once the surrender festivities were completed, they would be incarcerated with the others.

In this chaotic situation, the official ceremonies for the transfer of power remained highly uncertain. The surrender caught Kamio by surprise, for the first and only time throughout the war. He did not have all of the preparations at hand. The British made the first organized movement to take over the city. Since they did not participate in the battle, they were better organized than the Japanese. By 7:30 A.M. Barnardiston ordered his men into Tsingtau. Following a brief delay, they marched off at 8:30 A.M.[9] As they marched toward the city, four men abreast, all whistling, "Everybody's Doing It," the former vice-consul Eckford joined them. A German prisoner column was on the road. When the Germans learned that the advancing column was British, they quickly turned their backs and, as the column passed, bent over, showing their buttocks. It was a tense moment, embarrassing for Eckford and the British, but the Japanese guards simply laughed at it. When the British reached the old artillery depot, they quickly set up their flag before it.[10] The building marked the high point of the British advance.

That afternoon, at four o'clock, the official surrender deliberations opened in the Moltke barracks. The German representatives, including von Kayser, came under the Chief-of-Staff, Captain Ludwig Saxer. The Japanese Chief-of-Staff, Generalmajor Yamanaschi, was in charge with several aides, including the faithful Yamada and Lieutenant-Colonel Calthrop for the British.[11] Yamanaschi made a brief presentation about the capitulation terms and gave two copies to the Germans. He then proposed an hour's recess for the translation and consideration of the terms. Saxer accepted the proposed delay, but added his hope that something could be done about the Japanese soldiers loose in the city, since security of German property and lives was an immediate concern. His remarks clearly shocked Yamanaschi, who reported Kamio's order against such activity. The Japanese evidenced the same surprise when informed of the British movement. Saxer proposed that the Japanese employ the recess for a reconnaissance in his automobile, and Yamanaschi accepted the proposal.

The two parties then divided, the Germans simply moving into a neighboring room. They quickly discovered that the terms, simple and direct, closely resembled those set down at Port Arthur in 1905, terminating the Russo-Japanese war. All German military personnel would become prisoners, all equipment would become Japanese property, all destructive acts would be promptly and severely punished. A set of addenda set up various commissions to oversee the transfer of the protectorate, which would take place on November 10. Nothing was said about discussion, German rights, or possible alteration.

The second part of the discussion began at 7:00 P.M. Much of the prolonged delay came from Yamanaschi's visit to the city. He had, much to the Germans' pleasure and surprise, promptly ordered his soldiers out of the city. By darkness there were no Japanese soldiers in Tsingtau who did not have special permission.[12] Yamanaschi also set up a demarcation line running along the Iltis, Bismarck, and Moltke Hills. One side would be manned by Japanese military police, the other by armed Germans. Saxer interposed his appreciation for such decisive response, adding a quick plea that the German officers be allowed to keep their swords. Yamanaschi refused, on the ground that his authority did not go that far.

Saxer then accepted the terms of surrender document. Yamanaschi signed first, followed by the representative of the Naval squadron, Commander Takakashi. Saxer put his name last. No one consulted the British representative, nor did anyone propose his signature on the document.[13] The signing made the capitulation final and terminated hostilities.

With the official end of the campaign Kamio allowed Meyer-Waldeck two final messages. The first was a brief announcement to his soldiers, thanking them for their service and wishing them courage and good fortune as prisoners-of-war. He also added a severe injunction against any new destruction of property.[14]

The second, dispatched by the Japanese wireless, was to the Kaiser. In it he reported that they had surrendered after exhausting their ammunition, suffering the long Japanese bombardment, and losing their major defenses.[15] The two messages marked the end of Meyer-Waldeck's service as governor.

Throughout the following days the Germans collected their dead. They learned very little about the battle from the enemy dead, because the Japanese had taken care of their own casualties with impressive dispatch. On November 9 the Germans had a collective afternoon burial service, with those civilians and soldiers still in the city in attendance. The most moving memory for all was a widow with three children mourning her reservist husband. The two clergymen from the campaign, Pastor Winter and Father Schoppelrey, made brief statements, and an honor guard fired three salvoes. They were most careful, since they employed live ammunition. The graves were covered with greens and marked with pieces of paper with the man's name in pencil. Afterwards the bell in the Christ Church tolled the last goodbye. The unreal atmosphere continued as the Japanese guards signaled the end of the ceremony with a wave of their rifles.[16]

The following day, in response to Meyer-Waldeck's request, Kamio met the Governor in the Moltke Barracks. As he approached the conference, the defeated Governor passed by a Japanese honor guard at rigid attention. Kamio arrived on horseback almost immediately, and they sat down to champagne and cigars. The Japanese commander, through two interpreters, carefully explained his sorrow over the conflict. Only political circumstances, he said, had necessitated Japanese-German hostilities. Kamio underscored the debt of the Japanese military leaders to their German tutors, in particular to his own teacher, General Meckel. Finally, Kamio expressed his own hope that the two armies, which had worked together so closely in the past, would be able to do so again.

A somber Meyer-Waldeck, pleased with this reception, replied warmly with his own regrets over the conflict. He then complimented the professional excellence of the besiegers, in particular the artillerymen. Afterwards the two men exchanged a few personal observations involving the operations.

Kamio concluded the discussion with his personal sorrow that circumstances precluded Meyer-Waldeck's departure for Japan until November 14. It was a pleasant three-quarter hour conversation made even sweeter for the Germans by the patent Japanese inattention to Calthrop, who was present as the British observer.[17] Certainly the exchange was an honorable end to the campaign; the Germans believed that they had served with distinction, and the Japanese were happy that they had the protectorate. After the conference the Japanese assumed official control of the city. As they did so, they proclaimed an official end to both the blockade and to the protectorate.

That same afternoon the Japanese started the departure of the prisoners-of-war still in the city. They assembled the Germans in the Bismarck Barracks, and, after a long roll call, turned the 1300 men over to von Kessinger, who would lead the group. He shouted a few words at the large assembly, praising their brave service, recognizing their surrender to a superior force, and exhorting their proper behavior in the prison camp. Finishing with three cheers for the Kaisers of Germany and Austria-Hungary, he then reported the men ready for movement. They marched past Meyer-Waldeck in parade formation, executing each step with proficiency, without either officers or commands. It was a sad but proud and memorable moment.[18]

Shortly afterwards the Germans marched past a small platform, on which the several foreign military attachés, still struggling to learn about the Japanese tactics, observed the prisoners' march. The latter immediately began voicing crude remarks about the "garrison heroes," as they termed the attachés. Some were crude, others merely rude; i.e., "Monsieur, could you tell us where our Kaiser currently resides in Paris?," "Russians, Pashas, Hindenburg is coming!" Finally, an impetous German broke ranks, ran in front of the platform, and squatted in a manifestly insulting fashion. Taken aback by the permissiveness of the Japanese guards and the verbal insults of the men, the attachés deserted their platform.[19]

The column followed the footsteps of their predecessors, captured in the front positions, which led them to Schatzykou Bay, where the Japanese loaded their prisoners for Japan. Along the road crowded the Japanese and Chinese onlookers, but they made no comments, giving column itself was a motley one. There were several rickshas loaded with personal effects, as well as some coolies, hired by the more affluent as carriers. The officers carried their swords and made a professional appearance, but their men, clad in an odd mixture of clothing, did not look professional at all. All of them noted the detailed Japanese siege efforts,—the rail line, the munitions dumps, the carts, and, above all, the masses of infantrymen still moving forward.[20]

In Schatzykou they found another surprise, small but meaningful—their old friend, Jacob, the retired pirate turned custom's policeman who had earlier enlightened them with his memorable stories. He reported how the Japanese had uncovered the buried weapons and how they had punished him for his knowledge. Moreover, the victors had dispossessed him and had put him to heavy field work. Since he did not enjoy this labor he intended a resumption of his old career until the Germans returned to Tsingtau.[21]

Wasting little time with the prisoners, the Japanese moved them aboard several elderly vessels for the trip to Japan. For the Germans the trip would be a long one. In part they suffered psychological depression, since few had counted upon eventual imprisonment in Japan. In part they suffered from the poor accommodations aboard the ships—poor food, limited space, and no honors.[22]

On November 14 Meyer-Waldeck followed his men into the prison camp. As he drove along the road to Schatzykou Bay, he carefully surveyed the Japanese siege lines with professional curiosity. He finally boarded an old coal steamer, *Satsuma Maru*, for the trip to Japan. Like his troops, the Governor did not receive the treatment one might have expected for a prominent person.[23] As he boarded the ship, Meyer-Waldeck remarked to his colleagues about the Japanese sense of history. He left Tsingtau seventeen years to the day after the Germans had moved ashore for its conquest. In the Bay, the old

Cormoran, which had participated in the earlier German takeover, rested on the bottom. Meyer-Waldeck fully understood the significance of both his position and the *Cormorans*. The Germans were out of Tsingtau, out of Kiauchou, out of Asia.[24]

Meanwhile, the British confronted some challenges to their victor's role. To be sure, they had marched forward well ahead of the Japanese and had taken up their quarters. There they remained, however, without any visitation privileges for the city and without any role in its occupation. They had emerged victorious, but had entered a confinement camp.

Officially there were only the most cordial relations between the British and the Japanese. The commanders competed with one another in exchanging messages of praise, uniformly felicitously written, generously phrased, and textually brief. Barnardiston also received a wide range of congratulatory messages from Japan, from the Emperor, military leaders, civic officials, and ordinary citizens.

Beyond this curious role-playing game, the British confronted two other dilemmas reflecting their ambivalent position. The first was the military issue of redeploying the troops. Barnardiston was never in the slightest doubt that his troops should be redeployed elsewhere. Anticipating serious problems from the limited water supply and the lack of military purpose in Tsingtau, he requested authority to return his force to Tientsin. There the Borderers could reorganize their equipment for active commitment elsewhere, while the Sikhs could assume their old duties. The London authorities, after a lengthy exchange with their Ambassador in China, decided against this request. There was some danger, they believed, that the Chinese, using the precedent of the German *S-90* crew, might intern any combatants entering their territory. They decided in favor of shipping the Borderers directly from Tsingtau to Hong Kong.[25]

More significant, and a point the military men, British or Japanese, did not discuss, was the need for political presence. The Chinese sensed very quickly that the fate of their territory depended upon the British remaining in the city. They sent off a note to Jordan on November 11, calling for the British military authorities to respect Chinese property and rights pending Shantung's return to China.[26] In passing the note on to London, Jordan drew attention to the tacky nature of the problem; i.e., China's future was important to Great Britain, but control of that future largely belonged to the Japanese.

In London the Foreign Office people likewise understood the dilemma between breaking faith with the Chinese and satisfying the Japanese. They decided on the latter course as the lesser evil.[27] The decision was a fortunate one, since the Japanese clearly had no intention of sharing Tsingtau with their allies. The Japanese Minister of Foreign Affairs, Takaaki Kato, passed a brief note to the British Ambassador in Tokyo on November 20, and Greene quickly sent it on to London. The simple message proclaimed that the Japanese would leave a garrison in the protectorate and that they thought, ". . . it would be more convenient for practical purposes if [the] task were left in the hands of the Japanese Military Authorities."[28] The issue was closed.

For the British contingent at Tsingtau, life was much less exciting than it was for their diplomats. Beyond discussing the inevitable rumors concerning their next station, the men wandered about the German fortifications and the hills beyond, but they could not go into the city proper. On November 15 they received a visit from an emissary of the Japanese Emperor. They paraded before the messenger, whose sartorial splendor staggered them. He wore a bowler hat, an evening dress jacket with tails, knickerbockers, colored stockings, and yellow shoes! Certainly, given the circumstances, he provided an unusual attraction. Instead of the anticipated medals, however, his attaché case contained only a parchment scroll describing the Emperor's pleasure over the British participation. The aide read the message and announced a gift for the battalion of cigarettes and cakes, all bearing the imperial chrysanthemum crest.[29] Despite their disappointment over the rewards, the British found the entire affair a curious incident in their generally curious involvement in the campaign.

The next day a representative group of the British contingent marched off for the triumphful victory parade and concurrent service for the spirits of the dead. The British group had the best uniforms which the entire British force could provide them. The parade, in which Barnardiston led his troops, had representations from all the Japanese and British participating units. Barnardiston's group was well back in the line of march, lost among the Japanese units.

The impressive parade wound through the city to the Iltis assembly ground, where a wooden monument, shaped like Cleopatra's Needle, stood alone. It was surrounded by many bamboo stakes, which, via an intricate series of ropes, held it erect. Around it were piled the traditional straw-wrapped casks of sake, an Imperial gift to the departed souls of the dead. On the casks were other containers with tobacco, rice, and chrysanthemums.

After the participants had assembled in ordered ranks, Kamio approached the monument. Everyone removed his headgear. He, too, removed his cap, bowed, and moved to the foot of the memorial. There was no sound from the thousands of men massed in the area. Slowly Kamio unrolled a scroll and read a brief address indicting Germany for forcing the conflict, praising the army's tenacity, and closing with a plea to the fallen for understanding. As he finished, reading an aide stepped forward with a pine branch—the Japanese symbol for life. Kamio accepted it, placed it on the monument, and then walked slowly back to his original position. He bowed again and terminated the ceremony.[30]

Afterwards the troops returned to their various locations, while their officers attended a massive banquet hosted by Kamio. Although the British participants enjoyed the meal, they were even more appreciative to learn that from that time on they would be allowed to visit the city. To be sure, they could do so only in parties commanded by an officer and only between 1:00 and 6:00 P.M., but they could see the object of these restrictions.[31]

Equally unpleasant for many men was the short duration of their visiting time in Tsingtau. After the long, arduous activities getting to the city, they anticipated a chance to sample its pleasures. Two days after the grand ceremony the Borderers left Tsingtau for Schatzykou Bay, marching along a road lined with Japanese troops. Both sides were soon hoarse from cheering each other.[32] They reached the Bay that afternoon and quickly boarded the hired transport, *Delta*. The accommodations were not the best, but they did assure a change of scenery, which was enough to prevent complaint. They sailed the following morning, stopping briefly in Lau schan Bay for some British details working in that area and then continuing to Hong Kong. The Japanese naval vessels formed a double line with their sailors on deck, cheering and waving. In response the British bawled out numerous collective "hurrahs," albeit they often interspersed them with individual witticisms or, more often, bitter ejaculations about their allies. They were leaving and few of the British were depressed by the departure.[33]

General Barnardiston received permission for a quick side visit to Tokyo. He arrived, together with three staff officers, on December 9 in Miyajima. Thousands of school children lined his route, shouting "Banzai!" and waving little flags. His party reached Tokyo on December 12, where they had a memorable reception. Representatives of all the government ministries, all of the foreign military attachés, and a vast throng of the general polulace were present as Barnardiston emerged from the railway station. Over the exit were the crossed flags of Great Britain and Japan. The ride through the city streets was an exhilarating one for the visitors as the crowds went wild with cheering, flag waving, and flower throwing.[34] Following several receptions Barnardiston received a medal, The Order of the Rising Sun, second class.[35]

On December 15 Barnardiston visited the Emperor, who appeared in his Field Marshal's uniform. The British commander made a pleasant speech concerning the distinction of serving with the Japanese, the generosity of his Japanese reception, and the honor of receiving the medal. Following a ceremonial visit with the Empress, Barnardiston, together with the British Ambassador, had dinner with the Imperial couple.

In the next few days Barnardiston attended many formal dinners, theater performances, and speech-making parties. It was a dizzying experience in adulation. When Barnardiston left on December 19, he carried with him several valuable presents for his family, and left behind him his sense of pique over the campaign.[36] His departure terminated the British participation in the campaign, finished the strange military association, and removed any European influence over Shantung.

Among the Japanese the events of the victory day, November 7, brought few changes. They did not celebrate particularly, seeming content with the event itself. Having assumed victory from the beginning of the campaign, they had already anticipated many requirements concerning the German protectorate. They had a fully organized, carefully designated military administration for the city already in being. Within two weeks the Japanese had all of their desired administrators in Tsingtau. Among Kamio's railway troops were suffient personnel for operating the Shantung railway, and they soon had it running once more. The Germans had accomplished some damage to the rolling stock and had destroyed portions of several bridges, but in most cases, they simply blew up the supports of the middle span, allowing it to fall into the river bed. With the end of the rains the waterways went dry, and the industrious Japanese engineers simply jacked the fallen span back into place. The trains were, as a result, back in service soon after the city's fall.

With this advantage the Japanese turned to clearing the debris of war. Their first priority was removing the explosive charges put down by the defenders. For the sea mines they possessed both the chart from the S-90 and various diagrams provided by the Germans after the surrender. Despite these precise aids, the combination of shifting tides, inaccurate locations, and Japanese impatience brought disaster. On November 10 a torpedo boat hit a mine and sank with a loss of eight crewmen. Kato, who officially ended the blockade that same day, moved his ships back to Lau schan Bay and forbade free movement until the mines were cleared up.

The land mines posed the same problems. Again, the Japanese demolition experts used the Germans as sources for locating the mines. Unfortunately the German maps and memories were not overly precise. Again Japanese curiosity brought difficulties. On November 11 a mine near Redoubt 4 exploded, killing nine and wounding fifty-seven. The following day another explosion killed three men. Instructions for greater care followed immediately.[37] After two weeks of searching and of clearing, the engineer officers responsible for mine clearing, declared the area safe and allowed free movement.

Once they completed this clearance project, the Japanese turned toward organizing their new acquisition and restoring the required services. Again, they were prepared for this activity. Japanese stonemasons quickly chiseled a new imprint on the German Diedrich's stone. It carefully obscured the German eagle with the date, November 7, 1914. They replaced the German street names with Japanese designations and created Japanese names for all Chinese villages in the district. Along with these adjustments, they introduced a war currency to replace that used by the Germans.

With these changes and adjustments the Japanese authorities could begin the transfer from military occupation to civilian control. An initial troop contingent left for home on November 28, and the final group departed on December 25. A garrison force remained behind both for occupation duties and as a reminder of Japanese authority. Kamio, who had received a title of nobility for his accomplishments, became the first garrison commander. In December he too made a quick trip home for a victory reception. It was not as grandly organized as that for Barnardiston, but it was more sincere. The campaign was over, but the general, historical impact of the struggle had really barely begun to take effect. The struggle for Tsingtau could not be numbered among the grandiose battles of history. Some 60,000 men had challenged 4,000 men, scarcely a serious test of strength. The casualty lists did not reflect a huge, bloody engagement. The Germans lost 199 dead and 294 wounded, the Japanese suffered some 415 dead and 1451 wounded, and the British had 13 dead and 61 wounded during the struggle. It was in no way comparable to the bloody losses of the European war. Yet in many ways the Tsingtau siege was more historically significant than the savage battles in the trenches of France.

The Tsingtau campaign provided the first indication of a profound adjustment among international powers. In 1914 most nations recognized Japan's political growth and economic vigor but no one granted much recognition to her military power.[38] The eruption of the European war involved all of the major powers except Japan and the United States. Then, because of their initial panic, the British sought the active participation of Japan. The British, rather tremulously, had struggled with their decision; they desperately wanted Japanese aid but only on a highly restrictive base. They were reluctant to bring the Japanese in as a full partner but impotent to do otherwise. Their request for help reflected a basic shift from the earlier British paternalism toward the Japanese alliance. After August 1914 the alliance directorship moved to Tokyo—the Japanese were in charge, the British were the supplicants. In their haste for imagined relief, the British put short-term goals above future strategy, speed above thought, and success above understanding. Their anxiety would have a much higher price than that envisaged by any British diplomat.

The Japanese welcomed this timely opportunity to widen their Asian horizons. They could move onto the mainland, set up power bases, and generally do as they pleased without the frustration or fear of foreign interference. Their conquest of Tsingtau provided them with a major base for mainland propaganda, enhanced trade possibilities, expanded raw material sources, and, above all, gave them the chance to meddle in Chinese politics. All of these advantages came from a single, limited, inexpensive campaign. They could now consolidate their fortune, absorb it, and study future moves in detail while their chief competitors, Great Britain and the United States, involved themselves in the European mess. Surely there was, despite the memory of 1894, no particular animosity toward Germany. The attack on the leasehold was essential for the continued growth of Japanese power. Strangely the Japanese success provided the first genuine victory of the war.

Kiauchou itself, despite the extensive destruction, was a splendid prize. By 1913 the German government had invested somewhat more than 200 million marks in the protectorate. The harbor still was the finest in the Orient. Its appeal to international shipping, its climatic advantages, and its rail access to China guaranteed a sure return.[39] This cornucopia of riches came at a bargain price.

For Germany the loss did irreparable damage in several ways. As much as anything else, the defeat was the last phase in a totally inadequate colonial and international policy. The naval authorities had built the port, the defenses, and the commercial position of the protectorate with rigor, discipline, and enthusiasm. They had accomplished a great within a short time. Unfortunately, the naval authorities and their countrymen in the Foreign Office did not coordinate or properly direct their mutual interests. The result was neither office considered the needs of the other and the chancellors allowed their naval colleagues total freedom. If Germany could have isolated either Great Britain or Japan, there could have been a possible stand-off. When they joined together, the entire German position in Asia could not last for long.[40] The Berlin diplomats had paid little heed to the implications of the Anglo-Japanese alliance, and their oversight proved a costly one.

As severe as the geographic loss was the human price. The Germans took great pride in the number of reservists who joined the colors in Tsingtau. These reservists represented a major portion of the German economic community in Asia. Few of them died in battle, but the rest suffered six years as prisoners of war, in Japan. This loss in motivation, youth, organization, knowledge, and position could not be made good. Meyer-Waldeck's effort to save something of this power by releasing reservists back to the business community before the end did not fool the Japanese, nor did it succeed. Within a few months the conquerors owned the key economic properties.[41]

The Germans surrendered a great deal more than their economic investment. They gave up economic vitality, political position, and physical presence.

Great Britain suffered a similar loss. In Asia the British had played a powerful role until 1914. Their incredible confusion over the Japanese entry, their ineffective efforts to limit its extent, and their inability to control Japanese activities created an obvious power vacuum. Then the token force at Tsingtau provided ample evidence for any observer that the British were no longer a major Pacific power. The subsequent exchanges over the ultimate disposition of the German colonial holdings merely confirmed the power shift. [42] Great Britain could not play the dominant role in the Japanese alliance or in Asia. They had managed to save their trade from German raiders and to close off German bases, but in doing so, they had helped to power a far more formidable force.

Equally damaging to the British reputation was their military performance. They had contributed a ridiculously small force, had served ingloriously under Japanese command, and had departed like fugitives. The weak military contribution provided a public proclamation concerning British weakness in every area of national endeavor and at every level of military competence. The British would never intimidate other countries again. [43] Their position in Asia was irretrievably lost.

This international military power adjustment received greater force through the military victory itself. The Japanese advance was as predictable as the mating dance of the praying mantis or as a stylized problem in geometry. They moved with the artistic grace, simple determination, and deadly certainty of the European master, Sebastian le Prestre de Vauban. When his axioms had proved much too efficient for the time, Louis XIV, in the interests of military economy, had changed the rules of siege warfare to allow a commander's honorable surrender. After the besiegers made a small breech in a defender's walls and had been repulsed once, the defense could give up with dignity. War had now become more scientific and less gentlemanly. The Japanese clearly understood Vauban's principles but they neglected Louis XIV's etiquette. They made the breech and went on to conquer the city.

The Japanese had entered battle with a first-rate European military power. They had a token force from another European country of equal stature under their command. For the first time an Asiatic had exercised command over a Western force. One could raise many explanations about distance, about strength relationships, about military fair play, but one could not doubt the Japanese authority. They did their job in enviable fashion—efficiently, quickly, and without great fanfare. The Germans surrendered with honor and departed pridefully from Tsingtau, but at no time was there any doubt about the outcome. Kamio might suggest his sorrow over the battle against the land of his teacher, but he conquered on his terms at his convenience. The Japanese Army, and, to a somewhat lesser extent, its Navy, could compete favorably with any other military force on equal terms. As Lieutenant Colonel Casson of the Borderers replied to a question about Japanese efficiency, "My one wish is that I may never have to fight them."[44]

His reply was a profound one. As the Japanese army marched through Tsingtau, they heralded the new power relations for a new era. The old European centered world with its imperialistic pretensions, historical pride, and traditional structure was leaving history's stage. A new set of actors was in motion. The United States, soon to rescue Europe from itself, was undergoing its metamorphic emergence as an international colossus. With its Pacific commitments, collective aspirations, and growing power the Americans would play a leading role in any drama. The Japanese would obviously be another actor in the play. By 1918 the older actors were gone, leaving the only two competitors for power.

The military lessons to be learned from this siege were innumerable, although the Western observers did not always profit from them. Among the more obvious developments was the military use of aircraft. In bombing, aerial combat, and, above all else, reconnaissance, the aircraft had proved its reliability without question. The sophistication of Japanese aircraft employment—i.e., coordination with land forces, bombing equipment, and general mobility—was well ahead of any other country. Also the first use of airpower against naval vessels sketched out the future of such combat in a limited, but accurate, fashion.[45]

A second basic lesson was the declining role of sea power. An eager First Sea Lord, Winston Churchill, at the height of the great bombardment, sent an imperative request to Fitzmaurice for data on the naval effectiveness. The response was more direct than he may have wished. Fitzmaurice, on the *Triumph*, reported that it was most difficult to hit enemy guns without unduly endangering the ships.[46] In his final report the British observer, Captain Neville Brand, provided more damaging evidence that naval vessels were ineffective. He pointed out that the ships could not do serious damage to modern, permanent forts; the fleet had fired some 1118 shells to put two guns out of service. He did suggest that the presence of the big guns affected troop morale favorably, but that was the best rationale he could provide for the sea bombardment.[47]

The third major lesson was the impact of technology on artillery. Unquestionably, the growth of artillery's awesome power came as a general surprise to the participants and the military observers. Once they started the final barrage, the Japanese artillerymen ruled supreme. Given their advantages of observation, of limitless supplies, and of fire control, they demolished the German defenses, halted all movement, and drove the defenders into their casemates. Once the artillery had effectively smashed the defenses, the final assault was not an overly dangerous undertaking.[48] The machine gun proved its efficiency in modern warfare. The Germans, employing them with some skill, did inhibit the besiegers' activities with them.

Finally, the Western appreciation of the Japanese soldier changed a great deal. To be sure, the Germans and the British both passed defamatory remarks about the Orientals, but they did so quietly and with respect. The British, despite their disgruntlement, admired Japanese equipment, much of it superior to their own; their physical stamina; and their mastery of combined arms warfare. The Germans learned memorable lessons from the Japanese patience, organization, and general professionalism. The foreign military observers made many reports on the Japanese transport system, supply depots, communication control, and general organization.[49]

Certainly the siege of Tsingtau, usually treated as a minor campaign, shaped a new world far beyond the hard soil of Shantung. The world's newspapers took note of the siege of Tsingtau, but lost interest as other events overwhelmed it. At the end of 1914 the balance of power in the Asian portion of the world was far different than it had been at the beginning of the year. The Germans were out of the Pacific, the British were losing influence, and the Japanese were on the march.

A singular incident summed up this shift in international power. As a German column passed a British group, shortly after the surrender, a German called out in English, "Well, chaps, where will we see you in London?" A British soldier quickly responded, "Standing outside your cell in the Tower of London." His neat riposte elicited a quiet comment from a neighboring Japanese soldier in uncertain English, "Only after he leaves our prison camp." There was truth in each thought.[50]

Notes

CHAPTER I: Tsingtau: A *Casus Belli*

1. The leitmotiv for this, and subsequent chapters, comes from the songs and poems of Friedrich Blaschke, who served with the III Sea Battalon in Tsingtau.

2. Much earlier the island had contained a small fishing village. In the spring its steep cliffs and hills were covered with green grass. The neighboring islands, either because of climatic reasons or because of the natives' need of fuel, did not possess the same hue. As a result, the fishermen termed their home the green island.

3. The German naval authorities responsible for Tsingtau had long since made a decision allowing the Chinese customs officials. They disliked the symbolism of Chinese sovereignty but they needed a customs system to expedite trade within the city and to facilitate the movement of goods to China. For an excellent account see John E. Schrecker, *Imperialism and Chinese Nationalism; Germany in Shantung* (Cambridge: Harvard University, 1971), pp. 73-78.

4. This description comes from many reports written by the participants. The most useful came from Ed Leipold, Paul Kley, Gustav Müller, Walter Hermann, Georg Puls, Otto Stegemann, and Fred Bischof.

5. The murders followed closely upon another incident in Hankow where some Chinese malcontents had mishandled a few sailors from the *Cormoran*. Again the responsibility for the action remains highly uncertain. It did create the proper emotional state, both in Berlin and among the German naval crews, for the subsequent event. For brief descriptions of the incident see Jonathan Steinberg, *Tirpitz and the Birth of the German Battle Fleet: Yesterday's Deterrent* (London: Macdonald, 1965), pp. 154-156; Schrecker, Imperialism and Chinese Nationalism, pp. 33-36.

6. Shortly afterward the Kaiser had created the III Sea Battalion and the Naval Artillery Detachment Kiautschou as the units serving in the area. A colorful history with numerous photographs is C. Huguenin, *Geschichte des III. See Bataillons* (Tsingtau: Verlag Adolf Haupt, 1912).

7. They did so singing a locally created traditional song:

Und wen der da di Dampfer kommt, dann wissen wir,
was wir tun:
halli! halloh! dann nehmen wir unsern Kleidersack
und Ziehen nach Mole zwo!
Holderie! jetzt gehts zur Heimat, holderie!
jetzt gehts nach haust!
Holderie! jetzt gehts nach De-qui, holderie,
jetzt gehts nach haus!

("da-di" connoted large while "De-qui" meant Germany in the local pigeon-like dialect.)

8. The Governor's personal staff included a chief-of-staff (normally a colonel), a staff officer, an adjutant, and an intelligence officer (who was also in charge of the signal and wireless station). There were a lieutenant and ten enlisted men attached to this staff. The Fortification Department (ten officers and men) maintained and planned the use of naval mines. The Ordnance Department (twenty-five officers and men) had responsibility for all armaments. The lieutenant in charge of the Wireless and Telegraph Station had four signalmen. The Observatory had a chief with three men for its obvious purpose, while the chief of the generally oriented Naval Bureau directed ten men.

9. Until 1911 the unit had mustered twenty men as consulate guards. With the Chinese uprising that year which led to the overthrow of the Manchu dynasty, the foreign powers, mindful of the sudden eruption by the Boxers, increased their garrisons. While the German force was not as large nor as powerful as other nations' contingents, it did possess the capabilities of a more extensive unit; that is, cavalry, engineers, artillery, transportation, and infantry. They could serve under all conditions.

In addition to their prospective assignment, they guarded the Peking wall, which divided the foreigners from the Chinese populace, and mounted various patrols along the railway lines.

10. Useful descriptions of the area are in F. Behme and M. Krieger,

Guide to Tsingtau and Its Surroundings (Wolfenbuttel: H. Wessel, 1905);
F. W. Mohr, *Handbuch für das Schutzgebiet Kiautschou* (Tsingtau:
Deutsch-Chinesischen Druckerei, 1911); *Kiaochow and Weihaiwei*. Hand-
book prepared under the direction of the Historical Section of the Foreign
Office, No. 71 (London: H. M. Stationery Office, 1920). A very useful guide
for the early years of the protectorate is Schrecker, *Imperialism and Chinese
Nationalism.*

11.   The plan's generalized direction reflected the Germans' unwilling-
ness to seriously consider the possible foes. After the formation of the
Anglo-Japanese alliance in 1902 and the termination of the Russo-Japanese
War, Tsingtau confronted several potential enemies with military power.
Apparently such thoughts did not enter into the plans for defense. See
Gouverement Kiautschou, "Grundzuge fur die Bearbeitung des Armierung-
sentwurfe," Tsingtau, 2. Dezember 1908. The papers which accompany the
report further underscore the official unwillingness to do much more than
construct fortifications with the Chinese as the practical opponent and a
hypothetical, unnamed foe of little consequence as a possible attacker.

Unless otherwise indicated, the documentary sources cited hereafter
come from the Bundesarchiv-Militararchiv in Freiburg, Germany. While
the United States National Archives possesses microfilm of these records,
the copies are not always legible, the frames are not always numbered, and
the order is not always clear.

12.   The best analysis of the defenses is in Klehmet, *Tsingtau Rückblick
auf d. Geschichte, bes. d. Belagerung u.d. Falles d. Festung* (Berlin: Bath,
1931). Useful information is in Captain R. H. Silman, "Report of Japanese-
German Engagement at Tsingtau-China," December 12, 1914; Captain H.
L. Landers, "The Capture of Tsing-Tao by the Japanese," report for War
College Division, General Staff, December 1915; Captain Philip Yost,
"Monograph on Kiaochow," War Department, Office of the Chief of Staff,
War College Division No. 1842-13 (n.d.). All of these studies are in the
United States Army Research Collection, Carlisle Barracks. A brief observa-
tion is in "Notes from Tsingtau," *Journal of the US Artillery (Antiaircraft
Journal)* (May/June 1916), pp. 374-375. Some excellent photographs are in
Emil B. Perry "The Siege of Tsingtao" *United States Naval Proceedings* (Vol
55 June 1935) pp. 562f.

13.   For a delightful description of the *Patricia's* arrival ceremonies see
the account of Captain Hans Pochhammer, *Before Jutland; Admiral von
Spee's Last Voyage, Coronel and the Battle of the Falklands*. Trans. H. J.
Stenning (London: Jarrolds, 1931), pp. 13-16. For the *Patricia* this voyage
provided her last success. She played no role in the First World War and
went to the United States as a prize in the peace agreement. Shortly thereafter the Americans delivered her to the British. They used her until 1921
when the owners wrecked her. Letter from Hapag-Lloyd Aktiengesellschaft,
April 11, 1972.

14.   Spee's understandable question of the motivation behind the
British visit has no answer in the surviving records. The documents for the
entire

affair are not, apparently, in the archives. Letter from D. Lawson, Naval History Branch, Ministry of Defence, Great Britain, January 27, 1972; letter from Mary Flower, July 6, 1971. An intriguing possibility, and one which entered von Spee's mind, was a British search for new intelligence on the German colony. He may well have been correct. In 1913 the British War Office called for the development of an offensive plan against Tsingtau. The staff planners in Hong Kong did not have sufficient information at hand for developing this scheme and asked for an espionage mission. They wanted to locate the best coastal landing positions for guns and stores. See "Plans of offence against Tsingtau (Kiochow)" [January-March 1913] in War Office records deposited in the Public Record Office, London (hereafter cited as WO), 106/660. An interesting view of the general period, drawn from the Jerram papers, is I. H. Nish, "Admiral Jerram and the German Pacific Fleet 1913-15" *Mariner's Mirror*, 56 (November, 1970), 441-421.

15. Letter from Walter Hermann, May 1, 1971. Hermann was the Governor's gardener and personal servant. He overheard the comment during a subsequent meeting between von Spee and Meyer-Waldeck. Spee made a like observation over the tug-of-war contest. The *Scharnhorst's* sailors, clearly outclassed by their burly opponents, had started their first hard pull just as the British paused for breath. They did not let up and walked away with their foes still gasping for air. Spee suggested that, in the event of a war, Germany must strike hard and quickly. A long war could only end in German defeat.

16. Bernard Smith, "The Siege of Tsingtau" *The Coast Artillery Journal* (November-December 1934), p. 13. They could also engage in a favorite hobby of the time; the collection of seaman's caps from other navies. The exchange provided a much-desired opportunity for talk and comradeship. Letters from many individuals, especially Ed Leipold, whose report, "Bei der Besatzung in Tsingtau im deutschen Pachtgebiet Kiautschou in China 1914," has been highly enlightening.

17. It also provided the basis for an enduring story, which, true or not, made a great impression upon the Germans. One of the senior British officers, somewhat in his cups, purportedly observed, "Very nice place indeed! Two years more, we have it!." The episode received prompt, widespread attention throughout the German community.

18. Gouvernement Kiautschou, G.B. Nr. 796 A. Ia, Besuch des englischen Geschwaderchefs in Tsingtau, 19. June 1914. Mr. J. D. Lawson kindly provided a copy of this report from his files.

19. Alfred Meyer-Waldeck, "Bericht über die Armierung und Belagerung Tsingtaus," pp. 2-3 (hereafter cited as Meyer-Waldeck, "Bericht").

20. The crew had long since changed the meaning of S.M.S. from Seiner Majestats Schiff to *sempre manca soldi* (the money is always missing).

21. The reception in Hong Kong had been a most warm one, far exceeding normal protocol requirements. Abschrift des Berichtes des k.u.k. osterr. ungar. Konsulates in Hongkong Nr 811 A Res. vom 23. Februar 1914 an das k.u.k. Ministerium des Auessern," Kriegsarchiv Wien, file OK 2171-

16. Karl Christl, "Memoiren," pp. 1-2. Mr. C. Casapiccola kindly gave these papers to the writer.

22. The news made an immediate impression upon the crew and dignified the pessimistic oracles who had predicted trouble when the ship had departed Europe. Some men had drawn attention to a paradox in the ship's history. Francis Ferdinand had traveled aboard his beloved "Lisl" in 1892-1893 during her most successful voyage. When the ship had left the harbor at Pola for Asia, however, she did so without the slightest fanfare and late at night, somewhat like a fugitive fleeing a crime. The more superstitious crew members now predicted serious difficulties for their ship in the months ahead of them. C. Casapiccola, "S.M.S. Kaiserin Elisabeth 1914 in fernen Osten" (unpublished manuscript in the author's possession); letter from Emil Schrott, 7 August 1971; letter from Sepp Winkler, 14 August 1971.

23. S. M. Schiff "Kaiserin Elisabeth" Res No 132, "Vorfallenheits-bericht fur die Zeit vom 16.31.Juli," in Kriegsarchiv Wien, file OK 2176-16; Hans Sokol *Osterreich-Ungarns Seekrieg 1914-18* (Zurich: Amaltha-Verlag, c1933), p. 753; Karl Christl, "Memoiren" p.3.

CHAPTER II: War Is Declared

1. This verse from the song, "Die D. U. - Kompagnie" was the product of many men. In the parlance of the time "DU" meant *Dienstun-taugliche*.

2. Kriegstagebuch [hereafter cited in all cases as KTB] des Etats-Department, 27 Juli 1914; letters from Walter Herrmann, 1 May 1971, 14 June 1972; letter from Jakob Neumeier, 21 June 1972; letter from Dagmar Frowein, nee Meyer-Waldeck, 13 January 1972.

3. At the time the Detachment had two companies in Tienstin and one in Peking. Meyer-Waldeck's orders simply told Kuhlo to assemble his scattered soldiers and to await further orders. Paul Kuhlo, "Kleine Beschreibung der Tatigkeit des Ostastiatisches Marine-Detachments wahrend der Belagerung von Tsingtau 1914," pp 1-2. This report, one of many similar ones, came from the loss of many records during the siege. After the war the German naval historians asked various commanders for a narrative account of their activities, and Kuhlo's long reply was one of the most valuable responses.

4. In the course of their prison stay in Japan, several officers undertook a history of the campaign. Lieutenant Colonel Friedrich von Kessinger

was the general leader of this group which included several staff officers. The ameateur historians put a tremendous amount of energy into their pursuits. They questioned their colleagues in detail and assembled their responses into a rough-hewn, topical narrative. It is the best German account of the siege, despite a cumbersome format, uneven discussions, and officious patriotism. For reasons which remain mysterious, this version was not published, despite its obvious superiority to the official history. Kessinger "Geschichte," p. 187.

5. KTB des Etats-Department, 28 Juli 1914.

6. Kessinger "Geschichte," pp. 187, 197. Meyer-Waldeck refused his permission for any mobilization measures which might embarrass his visitor. Fukuschima had been a pleasant guest. He had served as an attaché in Berlin from 1887 to 1892 and knew the German language and culture. When he left Germany he traveled home by horseback across Russia, a trip lasting over a year, which earned him the Germans' respect.

7. The horses in use were really Mongolian ponies. Despite their ragged appearance, the soldiers respected them for their toughness and durability. Because their mottled coloration made them possible targets, their riders found a potassium permangate compound with which they painted the ponies a uniform khaki color. Soon afterward the mounted company of the III Sea Battalion received orders to paint their ponies in the same fashion. The paint was not always long lasting, and soon many of the ponies had a dilapidated appearance. No one paid any attention to the naval staff Veterinarian, Hans Pfeiffer, the only one in German military service, who protested the possible damage to the animals. Letter from Dr. Otto Stegemann, July 29, 1971; Kessinger, "Geschichte," p. 234.

8. KTB des Ettape-Department, 3-5 August 1914; letter from Korvet-tenkapitan a.D. Otto Fliegelskamp August 10, 1972. Waldemar Vollerthun, *Der Kampf um Tsingtau. Eine Episode aus dem Weltkrieg 1914/1918 nach Tagebuchblattern* (Leipzig: S. Hirzel, 1920), p. 20. Despite his participation in the prison camp history, Vollerthun's book is filled with nationalistic rhetoric and calculated factual omission. There are few textual errors, but there are many details which he, who as a high-level participant had to know about, neglects completely. Other details are given a highly unfortunate coloring which appreciably distorts the events.

9. Kuhlo knew as much about conditions in China as anyone in the area. In addition to his own observations, he had the experiences from the international maneuvers around Tientsin in November 1913. See H. F. Walters, "International Manoeuvres at Tientsin, North China, November 12th, 1913," *Army Review*, VI (April 1914), 498-507. He also had his own research in the area. In 1912 he had surveyed a possible land route for shifting his troops to Tsingtau. His associate in this investigation was the local railway engineer, Julius Dorpmuller. The latter had pointed out an unused rail line which the original rail construction crews had built for shifting building materials. After some exchange, the two men had worked out a code system which would alert Dorpmuller, under the guise of an accident on the

line, of the mobilization. The latter would bring a train to the unused line, load the troops, cut the telegraph lines, destroy a few key bridges, and head for Tsingtau. On July 29 Kuhlo sent off the designated code words, which Dorpmuller remembered despite the passage of time. The latter brought the train to the rail spur with the cover story that he wanted to test it. Paul Kuhlo, "Bericht uber die Abfahrt des Ostas. Mar. Det. von Tientsin und Peking nach Tsingtau am 31.7. und 1.8. 1914," pp. 4-5.

10. The major portions of the French and Russian troops were already gone. They had departed with full honors, which included a brass band, several honor guards, and a German delegation at present arms. Letter from Major a.D. Tschenscher to Hans Ehlers, n.d. (c1959). Photographs of these departure ceremonies are in the Carl Bormann papers in the Historische Sammlung, Marineschul Mürwik.

11. Interview with Hans Ehlers, November 14, 1972.

12. Kuhlo, "Bericht uber die Abfahrt. . . ." pp. 5-7. They were the largest single contingent, but not the last one. The remaining company of the East Asiatic Naval Detachment from Peking arrived shortly after the main force. Also a troop of thirty-six reservists left Tientsin on August 1 under their own authority. As they boarded their train, a large group of Englishmen, awaiting their own departure the next morning, gathered to say good-bye. As the train started out the Germans sang a verse of "Deutschland über Alles" which ended with the waving Englishmen shouting "Hip, hip, hooray!" No one anticipated that many of the participants would meet at Tsingtau under less friendly circumstances. Carl Bormann, "Tagebuch" (really a memoir diary prepared in Japan, 1915-1916), pp. 1-3. Included among the waving Englishmen were a few active soldiers. Until the declaration of war the two groups had been the closest friends. They did everything together while they both actively disliked the French and openly hated the Russians. Interview with Brigadier (ret.) H. D. Somerville, March, 1973; letter from Major General (ret.) Dudley Johnson, August 5, 1971. The guard activities were taken over by the suddenly mustered merchants left in the city. They served well, although their different socioeconomic positions, unmilitary waistlines, and uncertain weapons knowledge elicited many humorous comments.

13. The careful Prange, fearing difficulties with the enemy, kept the breech mechanisms himself. These heavy items he entrusted to a Chinese coolie, who carried them on a nondescript wagon to a remote rail station, drove it onto a flat railway car, and rode the tandem arrangement to Tsinanfu. Here a German sergeant who, unknown to the coolie, had followed everything from some distance, took over the cargo. He ordered a special engine which simply hitched up the single car, still with its horses and wagon, and took them into Tsingtau. There the coolie drove his wagon off the rail car to a happy and economically rewarding reception.

14. Otto Prange, "14 Jahre Soldat im Lande der aufgehenden Sonne" (an unpublished memoir), pp. 11-12; Kurt Assmann, *Die Kämpfe der kaiserlichen Marine in den deutschen Kolonien* (Berlin: E. S. Mittler & Sohn,

1935), p. 21. This volume in the German official history, *Der Krieg zur See, 1914-1918,* is a poor rendering of Meyer-Waldeck's final report on the Tsingtau campaign. Despite the long time involved with its preparation Assmann did not do sufficient research in his own archives. A possible explanation comes from his limited research time. Assmann started his service with the German naval archives in 1933 and was in charge of the office. See the useful survey by G. Sandhofer, "Official History in the German Navy to 1945," *Official Histories; Essays and Bibliographies from Around the World,* ed. Robin Higham (Manhattan: Kansas State University Library, 1972), pp. 147-152.

The howitzers were most important to the Tsingtau defenses because most of their guns were flat trajectory. While the Germans were happy with them, they missed thirty-six modern Krupp field pieces. The weapons, ordered earlier by the Chinese, were in Tientsin awaiting Chinese payment for the final transfer. The Germans insisted that they owned the guns, until the money consummated the transaction. This time the apprehensive Chinese authorities, under extreme French pressure, delayed any response until it was too late for a decision. Telegramm Peking an Tsingtau (Abschrift) 8.8.1914; Vollerthun, *Der Kampf um Tsingtau,* p. 19; Assmann, *Die Kämpfe,* p. 21.

15. In Japan the departees received their most memorable send-off. The scenes of departing soldiers provided many vignettes for history. There were crowds of French, British, Austrians, and Germans leaving for the war; in many instances they departed on the same ships. The Japanese supported the Germans with an unexpected warmth. By the hundreds they crowded Yokohama and Kobe, shouting "banzai" and "sayonnara" to the Germans. They gave the departees presents of food and drink which sustained them for many weeks. The Germans reported these experiences in Tsingtau as clear indications of popular Japanese support for their cause. Kurt Meissner, "Memorien," p. 1; Jefferson Jones, *The Fall of Tsingtau, with a Study of Japan's Ambitions in China* (Boston: Houghton Mifflin Company, 1913), p. 17. One can trust Jones' report only of what he actually observed himself. Otherwise, most of his facts are incorrect. The book is redeemed, in part, by some fine photographs.

16. Perhaps the most adventuresome effort was that of Hans Brauer, who deserted the French Foreign Legion in Tonking on July 22 and fled to Yuenanfu. There he received money from the local consulate and marched on through the heart of China. After thirty-one days he reached Suefu in the heart of the Yangtze. From there he traveled, disguised as a Chinese coolie, by sampan over Chungking to Hankou. Changing his disguise to that of a French peddler, he took the train to Tsinanfu, which he reached in early September. By that time he could no longer continue toward Tsingtau. Abandoning the train, he walked some eighty miles until he reached the shores of Cape Jaeschke. As he signaled a German patrol boat on September 16, a small Japanese scouting party caught him. The Germans opened fire immediately and pinned the Japanese down until Brauer dashed into the

water and swam out to the boat in a hail of gunfire. He reached Tsingtau that evening. Vollerthun, *Der Kampf um Tsingtau*, p. 29, letter from Ed Leipold, December 23, 1972; discussion with Hans Ehlers, November 14, 1972.

Another interesting experience was that of a German sailor aboard a British merchantman in Newchwang. The British refused to release him when the German consul demanded his freedom. They finally agreed to let the American consul make the decision. He decided that no one would want an enemy aboard ship. The sailor hurriedly departed for Tsingtau. Julius Jaspersen, *Do Mau. Arbeit und Abenteuer eines deutschen Chinakaufmanns* (Leipzig: Verlag E. A. Seemann, 1936), p. 216.

    17. Meissner, "Memoiren," p. 2.

    18. This genuine concern for military obligation and civilian activity had other bureaucratic facets. The Tsingtau authorities thought that the various German consuls should make the decision about releasing individuals from their military obligations. The majority of the consulates in Asia wanted the Tsingtau officials to assume the responsibility for such decisions. Despite an extensive, and obviously hurried, exchange over the question, they did not resolve the issue. The same confusion occurred in the individual's relationship with his military district in Germany. In many cases, the home authorities claimed that the men in question owed their allegiances to their domestic district rather than to Meyer-Waldeck and should return home for duty. The resulting administrative chaos was solved only by the decisions of the moment and the passage of time. Alfred Meyer-Waldeck, "Bericht uber die Armierung und Belagerung Tsingtau," pp. 9-10; Assmann, *Die Kämpfe,* p. 19.

    19. In particular, the numberous tavern owners gave their supplies away as a much appreciated patriotic gesture. Ed Leipold, "Memoiren," Teil III, p. 3.

    20. Discussion with Kapitanleutnant a. D. Fred Mensing, July 14, 1971; K. E. Selow-Serman, *Kapitanleutnant Mollers letzte Fahrt* (Berlin: August Scherl, 1917), pp. 40-42.

    21. See *ibid.* for a detailed, if romanticized, version of this trip. It is also in Walter von Schoen, *Auf Vorposten für Deutschland. Unsere Kolonien im Weltkrieg* (Berlin: Ullstein, 1935), pp. 19-20; discussion with Paul Kley, May 12, 1969. Among the crew members, Lieutenant German von Wenckstern had the most exciting trip. Taken ill in Canton, he could not leave with the others. Although still unwell, he started for Tsingtau on August 12. Using river boats, smapans, trains, horses, and foot, he reached Tsingtau after an arduous 400 mile trip. In the city he promptly hired a ricksha to take him to the reporting station. There he saluted and promptly collapsed, and spent a good share of the next few weeks in bed. Letter, German von Wenckstern to his mother, 4 September 1914; German von Wenckstern, "Memoiren" (prepared by Carmen von Wenckstern), chapter 3, p. 2.

    22. He had orders reassigning him to Shanghai for intelligence

activities. His ship was still not in the best condition. On June 16 the English steamer, *Longwoo*, unable to see in a dense fog, had rammed the *Jaguar*, tearing a large hole in the latter's side. Since it was above the waterline, he patched it with sailcloth and remained in service. In Shanghai he sought repairs in the British shipyard, but they would not complete them.

23. Christian Vogelfänger, "Tagebuch" 28 July through 2 August; Christian Vogelfänger, "Wie kam die Jaguar nach Tsingtau, 1914." The other ships had equally harrowing experiences. Following a long run of narrow escapes, both the *Otter* and the *Vaterland* reached Nanking. En route the latter vessel dispatched most of the crew for Tsingtau. They reached Hong Kong and the steamer *Michael Jepson* just before she hurriedly, and successfully, departed for the German colony. The rest travelled by rail via Tientsin. The crews disarmed the two ships (sending some of the munitions and stores to Tsingtau by rail, sinking the rest at various locations), moved and moored them in a small stream six kilometers below Nanking, and, ostensibly, sold them to a native buyer (who renamed the *Otter, Munchen*, and the *Vaterland*, the *Landesvater*). The Chinese authorities seized them in 1917. The remaining crew members, in civilian dress, and in small groups, took the train for Tsingtau. They arrived there with few difficulties. H. Seuffert, "Bericht über die Kriegsfahrt des Flusskanonbootes' Otter von Serifu nach Nanking vom 2. bis 8.8. 1914"; W. Michaelis, "Bericht über S. M. Kanonenboot 'Vaterland' von Ende Juni 1914 bis zur Desarmierung."

24. The *Gouverneur Jaeschke* and *O.I.D. Ahlers* eventually reached their destinations. The British battleship *Triumph* captured the *Frisia*, while the French armored cruiser, *Dupleix*, picked up the *Senegambia* and the *C. Fred Laeisz*. For a variety of reasons the others did not reach their destinations. Assmann, *Die Kämpfe*, pp. 37-38; Raeder, Erich Raeder, *Der kreuzerkrieg in den ausländischen Gewässern*, Band I: *Das Kreuzergeschwader* (Berlin: E. S. Mittler & Sohn, 1922), pp. 88-99; Korvetenkapitan a.D. Friedrich Crusemann, "Handbuch," Band I. The other "Etappe" offices had limited success. There simply were not enough places for procuring the needed supplies. Unfortunately the records of the Etappe service were destroyed in 1919 for security reasons. Letter from Obrarchivrat Sandhofer, Bundesarchiv-Militärchiv, 29 October 1973.

25. Afterward Sachse had three steamers left in port for future use. They were the *Ellen Rickmers, Durendart*, and *Michael Jebsen*.

26. The original *Cormoran*, despite every human effort, could not be made ready for sea. On August 5 she had undertaken a trial run which had ended in disaster. Additional repairs were not possible. Given that fact, her captain, Adalbert Zuckschwerdt, quickly grasped the *Rjasan* as his sole possibility. "Kriegstagebuch den Tsingtauer Werft," 31 July-5 August. For a useful account of the *Cormoran*'s romantic odyssey, see Herb Ward's *Flight of the Cormoran* (New York: Vantage Press, 1971). The seizure of the *Rjasan* was not viewed with pleasure by the Japanese, who saw the German action as an invasion of their neutral waters and sovereign rights.

27. Kessinger, "Geschichte," p. 48.

28. Hans Lipinski "Tagebuch," 11 August 1914; letter from Jakob Neumaier, November 10, 1971. Jakob Neumaier, "Tagebuch," pp. 8-9. This is not a diary, but a splendid narrative of one man's experiences in the campaign. It is in the Historische Sammlung, Marineschule Mürwik.

29. Gustav Hass, "Bericht uber die Tatigkeit der Seefrontenwerke während des Kampfes um Tsingtau," pp. 1-2, 1-12. The shells, passing over the city, introduced the inhabitants to the unpleasant realities of war. As the shells passed over, they shook the foundations, rattled the windows of most houses, and frightened the inhabitants.

30. They also possessed adequate manpower. The large number of reservists allowed an extra allotment of men for the coastal defenses. The authorities accommodated the extra men by erecting huge tents behind the installations or by allowing the men to stay in nearby barracks. Since Hui tschuen huk battery was the only one with electric lights and spacious accommodations, the men elsewhere suffered morale problems after weeks in their dank cement housing. Ibid., p. 13; Hans Pauer, "Tagebuch," 31 July-6 August. Brigadier D.H.S. Somerville kindly allowed me to use this record which his men captured in Tsingtau.

31. Kessinger, "Geschichte," pp. 52-53; Oberst a.D. Licht, "Bericht über die Armierunge Tsingtaus, 1914," pp. 1-2.

32. Kessinger, "Geschichte," p. 139.

33. Although Meyer-Waldeck's staff had many plans for night illumination, it did not possess the requisite means. The nine searchlights, which were eventually impressed into service, came from purchase in Shanghai, transfer from the inner wharfs, and removal from the vessels still in port. One antiquated model appeared in the local high school. The motors for rotating them came from equally diverse places. Meyer-Waldeck, "Bericht," pp. 32-33; Anlage 3.

34. Several European homes near Yuniusan had already been destroyed for the same reasons. They provided a precedent, although the need required none. Kessinger, "Geschichte," pp. 149-151. A proposal to destroy the more extensive Syfang village did not obtain Meyer-Waldeck's approval. Vollerthun, *Der Kampf um Tsingtau*, p. 71.

35. The hand grenade supply was just as insufficient. With inadequate explosives and fuses for this task, Soldan's helpers filled bottles and cans with nails and metal scraps, powder drawn from bullets, and string fuses. The latter were timed for three seconds, which, combined with their obvious unreliability, made them unpopular to everyone who had to use them. Kessinger, "Geschichte," p. 149.

36. The barbed wire in the water quickly became a time and morale-wasting endeavor, as the tides constantly eroded the supports while covering the wire with sand. Eventually the engineers in the company devised cement boxes which kept the wire in place. Jaspersen, *Do Mau*, p. 221.

37. At the last minute they added eight Austrian machine guns, which a policeman had discovered by accident in the basement of a Tsingtau merchant. Apparently someone was transferring them, with ammunition, to

China without official permission. No one asked any questions. Assmann, *Kämpfe*, p. 34; Leipold "Memoiren," III, p. 4.

38. Licht, "Bericht uber die Armierung," pp. 3-6; Ernst Soldan, "Tatigkeit der Marine-Pionier Kompagnie mit Anlagen," pp. 3-9; Bericht des Hauptmanns Schaumburg (Ursprunglich in Brieform)," 19 November 1914, p. 29. This latter report comes through the kindness of Otto Kempin, Gesellschaft Graf Waldersee.

39. "Kladde zum Kriegstagebuch der Marine-Fliegerstation Tsingtau (Abschrift)," 2 August 1914; Leipold, "Memoiren," II, pp. 11-12. The pieces of the wreck were taken to the dockyard shops. Plüschow, in conjunction with the harbor authorities, hoped to rebuild it in the course of the next few months.

40. On one of his first flights Plüschow crashed and smashed his propeller. Discovering that there was no replacement, he made his own. At first the replacement came apart as well, and he finally had to fly the aircraft 100 rpm slower to keep it airborne.

Every takeoff was an adventure. The aircraft possessed two seats, but the weight problem eliminated taking an observer aloft. Normally he took off toward the south, which carried him over a cliff. Once free of the earth, he circled upward. In order to observe efficiently he cut his engine, steered with his feet and good faith, hung a map on the steering wheel, and glided along taking notes. The few times he took off to the hilly north, against the prevailing winds, he used two heavy men whom he dragged along until the motor accelerated properly and lifted off. The heavy men then fell the two or three meters to earth. As Plüschow pointed out, he selected them because they were the best upholstered men in Tsingtau. Gunther Plüschow, *Die Abenteuer des Fliegers von Tsingtau. Meine Erlebnisse in drei Erdteilen* (Berlin: Ullstein, 1916), pp. 46, 64-66; Leipold, "Memoiren," II, 13. Leipold was one of Plüschow's ground crew.

41. *Amtsblatt fur das Schutzgebiet Kiautschou*, 1. August 1914. He followed the declaration with a wide range of others dealing with security, economics, private property, train service, and so on.

42. A precise breakdown of the number and type of shells is in Assmann, *Kämpfe*, pp. 108-109.

43. "Bericht uber die Tatigkeit des Artillerie- und Minendepots während der Belagerung von Tsingtau," p. 2; Assmann, *Kämpfe*, pp. 36-37; Kessinger, "Geschichte," p. 80.

44. In the Shantung area silver was often transferred in bars, which foreigners, because of the bars resemblance to Chinese footware, termed "shoes." The value depended upon the silver content, which was not consistent; therefore, this medium of exchange demanded a measure of trust between transacting parties.

45. "Telegramm Peking an Tsingtau. 13. August 1914" has a synopsis of such events.

46. The singular exception was the Standard Oil Company, which had large petroleum stores in Tsingtau. After some discussion, the Germans

purchased all of the gasoline at the market value. They also accepted liability for damages to other company properties in the city. Willys Peck [American Consul. Tsingtau] to John V. A. MacMurray [Charge d'Affaires, American Embassy, Peking] August 3, 5 1941 U. S. Department of State, File 862a Kiauchau, National Archives. Hereafter cited as D/S File 862a.

The arrival of the motorship *Tschingpo* from Shanghai with a cargo of gasoline eliminated any worry about their supplies. Kessinger, "Geschichte," p. 115. In view of the bulk and of its location, the Germans shifted the oil stored in barrels to the train station. They could do nothing with the great storage tanks and decided against letting the oil run into the bay. "Bericht über die Tatigkeit des Artillerie-und Minendepots während der Belagerung von Tsingtau," p. 4. The other large foreign merchant, the British-American Tobacco Company, owned 400 cases of "Pirate" cigarettes (valued at $200 per case), which the American Consul, W. R. Peck, successfully extricated for them. Although Peck had only arrived in Tsingtau on August 1 he persuaded the Germans to ship the cases, at their expense, to Tientsin.

47. An interesting, albeit superficial, general survey of the postal system is Josef Schlimgen, *Tsingtau, Juli-November 1914, die Kriegspost des deutschen Kiautschou-Gebietes* (Bonn: Arbeitsgemeinschaft der Sammler Deutscher Kolonialwertzeichen, 1971). Another is Helmut Muller, "Kiautschou Postbeforderung kurz von Kriegsausbruch und während des Krieges und der Belagerung," in the Historische Sammburg, Marineschule Mürwik.

48. Karl Coupette, "Die Signalstation und Kustenfunkeinrichtung Tsingtau im Kriege 1914," p. 4. The British and French lodged a protest against this use of neutral territory, but the Germans pointed out the French wireless in the city which served the same purpose for the French in Asia.

49. This service was the result of a careful test made in the spring of 1914. The handlers had established stations throughout the mountains and in various remote posts, and the system had worked perfectly. During poor weather the normal means of communication (wireless, heligraphic, foot) failed completely, making the carrier pigeon the sole possibility for transporting information.

50. Vollerthun, *Der Kampf im Tsingtau*, p. 22; Kessinger, "Geschichte," pp. 174, 184.

51. The incident occasioned some concern among the Americans. Fortunately for the Germans the ship's owner, William Katz, was in Tsingtau at the time and was most accommodating to his friends. The various exchanges are in the American Consular Service papers for Tsingtau. In particular Willys Peck to John van A. MacMurray, August 1, 1914 and August 3, 1914. D/S File 862a. The *Hanametal* eventually departed for Tientsin. En route the British seized her as a war prize.

52. Assmann, *Kämpfe*, p. 40. Timme set up security controls against pilferage and also established the distribution machinery for long-term rationing.

53. The German efforts to seize the various foreign bank holdings proved abortive. In every case the bankers had already dispatched their funds to Tientsin or deposited them in the Deutsch-Asiatische Bank for subsequent withdrawal from other branches in China. Peck to MacMurray, August 3, 1914. D/S File 862a.

54. When, for whatever reason, the expected money was not paid, the Chinese rioted. Often they could be subdued only by physical force. Meissner, "Memorien," p. 3; Interview with Ed Leipold, June, 1973. Obviously the sizeable numbers of laborers demanded various security controls. At first the Germans employed identity cards for trustworthy individuals who crossed the barbed wire lines. Then they turned to a stamping system, employing indelible marks on the chest or arm. Eventually they just stopped free movement in and out of the city for all but the most essential people— food handlers, essential hand workers, and intelligence agents. Kessinger, "Geschichte," pp. 169-170; Meyer-Waldeck, "Bericht," pp. 44-46; "Kriegstagebuch der Tsingtauer Werft," 7. VIII. 14.

55. Vollerthun, *Der Kampf um Tsingtau*, pp. 40-43 has the best published description of the popular mood.

56. The information, coming from two sources reflected the speed with which some communications could move among distant points. Telegram, E. O. Shanghai to Tsingtau, 7 August 1914; Telegram, Marine Attaché Tokyo to Tsingtau, 7 August 1914; "Brief an Herr Dorpmuller von Hauptmann Schaumburg, 19. XI. 14. Despite many rumors to the contrary, Meyer-Waldeck refused to believe that Fukushima had misused his earlier visit to support aggressive plans. Meyer-Waldeck, "Bericht," p. 15.

57. "Abschrift des Telegramms aus Nagasaki von 9.8. 1914; aus Schimonoschi vom 9.8.14; aus Yokuhama von 9.VIII. 14; aus Schanghai von 10.VIII.14; aus Seoul von 10.8.1914."

58. Vollerthun, *Der Kampf um Tsingtau*, p. 34. He also heard that the Japanese had proposed recognition of Chinese territorial integrity to the Chinese authorities because they planned their landing for Lai-chou. "Telegramm aus Peking vom 11.VII. (1914)." The French diplomats in China had already started buying up all the literature and maps on Tsingtau. "Abschrift des Telegramms aus Tsianfu von 12.8.1914." An abortive attempt to employ a German spy on the Japanese is recorded in Jaspersen, *Do Mau,* p. 218.

59. Meyer-Waldeck invited a member of the Japanese consulate in Tientsin to investigate the charges. The man received no official complaints in the city, but his visit did not change the press's shrill attitude. Vollerthun, *Der Kampf um Tsingtau*, p. 35.

60. Ibid., p. 37. Much of the reason for the chaos came from reports indicating that American influence had changed Japanese intentions. Additionally, not all of the official reports arrived in proper sequence. "Abschrift des Telegramms aus Peking vom 13.8.14"; Assmann, *Kämpfe,* p. 24.

61. The Japanese ultimatum evidenced both the completeness of their demands and the totality of their historical sense. In 1894 the Japanese, at some cost, had beaten the Chinese in war. The subsequent Peace Treaty of

Shimonoseki had provided Japan with a goodly portion of the Liao tung peninsula and a significant holding in Manchuria. It also acknowledged the emergence of Japanese power and the concomitant decline of Chinese authority. Russia, France, and Germany did not find the agreement in their best interests and fired off missives, couched as "friendly advice," telling the Japanese not to take so much territory. The Japanese eventually settled for a financial payment. But, in particular, the German role, given the Germans' limited power in Asia, rankled the Japanese. They had not forgotten the harsh tenor of the German note, and they modeled their own upon it. A translation of the Japanese note is in Peter Lowe, *Great Britain and Japan, 1911-1915; a Study of British Far Eastern Policy* (London: Macmillan, 1969), p. 218.

   62. Kessinger, "Geschichte," p. 207; Meyer-Waldeck, "Berichte," pp. 18-19.

   63. Meyer-Waldeck, "Bericht," Anlagen, 6, 7. That evening the Protestant minister, Wilhelm Winter, conducted a joint service in Christ Church. He carefully reviewed the news from home, their own concerns, and ended with a passionate declaration of faith in ultimate victory. As he put it, "und ist die Lage auch noch so verzweifelt, wo der unerschutterliche Wille vorhanden, da kann auch uns der Sieg nicht fehlen." Vollerthun, *Der Kampf um Tsingtau*, p. 61; letter from W. Seufert to Ed Leipold, 26 February 1964. The bells which rang out afterwards made their last sound. They did not play again during the siege.

CHAPTER III: The Japanese Land

   1. From "Die jungen Seesoldaten."
   2. The flow of reservists continued on a declining scale for several weeks. Despite the growing efficiency of the enemy, individuals contrived ways to slip into Tsingtau. For some weeks this growth boosted morale (the group was often termed "the real legacy of Tsingtau") and encouraged continued optimism.
   3. "Bericht des Hauptmanns Schaumburg," p. 29.
   4. Under the terms of the 1898 understanding, the Chinese guaranteed a neutralized fifty-kilometer-wide belt around the German protectorate. While the Chinese possessed full sovereignty over the area, they, like the Germans, could not employ troops in it without the agreement of the other party. A Japanese landing here would seriously challenge Chinese-German relations and delay any defensive response. The invaders could

postpone the legal and moral niceties, since they had neither agreements nor fears about the outcome.

5. In the actual event Meyer-Waldeck's version proved most accurate.

6. In both cases the troops had serious difficulties adjusting to their new equipment. Formation movements by men unused to bicycle riding provided command problems for the officers. The ponies posed a similar challenge in addition to the unusual riding requirements. This lack of experience brought some amusement as many men fell off the ponies but also increased frustration as control proved difficult. Kessinger, "Geschichte," pp. 208-209.

7. They had, nonetheless, a good situation. The Shantung vegetable crop that year had been a very good one and the transporting junks, sheltered in Schatsykou, provided an accessible food source. Furthermore, the local customs agent, a retired pirate with some knowledge of German, entertained them with countless stories of his experiences. "Personlicher Bericht des Herrn Hugo Ponsel," p. 2.

8. Kessinger, "Geschichte," pp. 209f.

9. Ibid., pp. 153-154.

10. The best explanation for the organization and placement of the Tsingtau forces is in Klehmet, *Tsingtau*, pp. 24-28. The sixth company soon achieved a local notoriety in the garrison. In part this came from their personnel composition. Among the lower ranks were many successful businessmen, officials, and professional men whose military experience was not commensurate with their civilian accomplishments. In part it stemmed from their many assignments. They carried the cement, moved the fodder, drove the supply wagons, guarded the Governor's villa, and built their own defensives. They were sincere, if not militarily proficient. As a result, they obtained a widespread reputation as the "unfit for military service" company; a designation they carried with some pride. Meissner, "Memorien," pp. 2-3.

11. "Tatigkeitsbericht der B.B. Batterie (Bismarckberg) in Tsingtau für die Zeit vom 31. Juli bis 7. November 1914," 1.3. August; Hans Lipinski, "Tagebuch," 11-17 August; Hans Pauer, "Tagebuch," 3,6,12, 20 August 1914.

12. The ship moved out behind the Japanese steamer, *Rissai Maru*, which had entered the harbor, picked up the last Japanese civilians, and departed within the space of two hours.

13. "Wie die Englander die Fluchtlinge von Paklat behandelten," a report in a file compiled by the Auswärtiges Amt of papers from the German consuls in Shanghai and Tientsin, Rudolf Zollner (Master of the *Paklat*), "Bericht," 14 November 1914; Rudolf Zollner, "Declaration Before the Prize Court in Hong Kong," 10 October 1914; "Bericht des Marineunterarztes Leopold Schutz uber seine Wahrnehmungen und Erfahrungen wahrend der kriegeriochen Vorgange in Schutzgebiet Kiautschau," 24.V.15. Letter from Heinrich Groning based on the notes of his wife, a participant, January 1973; Prange, "14 Jahre Soldat," p. 13. The British, who had just suffered some

dead and wounded in their first encounter with the Germans, did not accord the women and children a proper reception. A weak cover story concerning an "enormous quality (of) silver bullion aboard the ship" received some notoriety. Radio interception of message to *Daily Mail*. London from Bate, Tientsin "August 26, 1914." There are no records validating the claim. Admiralty records deposited in the Public Record Office, London (hereafter cited as Adm), 137/35.

14. Meyer-Waldeck, "Bericht," p. 69; Vollerthun, *Der Kampf um Tsingtau*, pp. 46-47.

15. The destroyer, *Kennet*, was actually part of a flotilla including the *Colne, Welland*, and *Jed*, cruising some fourteen miles south of Tai kung tau. They had just separated to establish a screen for two German steamers they expected would be leaving Tsingtau that night. The *Kennet* was en route to her position when she sighted the *S-90* and alerted the others, who closed at full speed but did not reach the action. "Report of Commander H.M.S. 'Colne' to Commander-in-Chief China Station," 30 August 1914, Adm 137/35.

16. "Report, Lieutenant Commander F.A.H. Russel to Commander-in-Chief, H.M.S. 'Minotaur,' 24 August 1914, Adm 137/35; letter by first officer, *S-90* to a friend on S.S. *Longmoon*, n.d., in Adm 137/35; Fregatten-kapitan a.D. Brunner, "Das Gefecht bei Tai kung tau am 22. August 1914," Fritz Schmidt, "Tagebuch," August 22, 1914; Jakob Neumaier, "Tagebuch," pp. 10-11. In the engagement the Germans fired 250 shells and the British 300 shells.

17. Assmann, *Kämpfe*, p. 26; Kessinger, "Geschichte," pp. 67, 69; "Kriegstagebuch der Tsingtauer Werft," 22, 23, 24. VIII. 14.

18. Few people appreciated his difficulty. His military power was highly limited, but he could bring on an unwanted war for his country through the slightest error. Makoviz fully understood this problem and searched with incredible care for the thin wire through the diplomatic underbrush. "Vorfallenheitsbericht S.M. Shiffles'Kaiserin Elisabeth' für die Zeit vom 1.- 15. August 1914. (Res Nr. 140) Tsingtau, am 15. August 1914," Kriegsarchiv Wien, file OK 2171-16.

19. During the conference they spoke about the possibility of sending the *Kaiserin Elisabeth* to von Spee's squadron. Ultimately they decided against the idea. The ship was too old, too slow, and used too much coal, and lacked sufficient fire power to offset these deficiencies. Eventually she would end up interned in a neutral harbor or as a needless sacrifice to a superior foe. "S.M.S. 'Kaiserin Elisabeth' Res. Nrs. 401 Vollfallenheits-bericht fur die Zeit vom 16/VIII bis 31/VIII 1914," Kriegsarchiv Wien, file OK2171-16; Sokol, *Osterreich-Ungarns Seekrieg*, p. 775 f 465; Peter Handel-Mazzetti, *Die Ost-Ung. Kriegsmarine vor und im Weltkrieg* (Klagenfurt: Carl Roschnar, n.d.), p. 110.

20. "K.u.k. Marinedetachment in Peking, Res. No 191, an das K.u.k. Kriegsministerium Marinesektion," 31 August 1914; "Beilage 4 zu k.u.k. Marinedetachment in Peking, Res No 206 an das k.u.k. Kriegsministerium,

Marinesektion," 6. Kezember 1915, Kriegsarchiv Wien, file OK 2171-16; Karl Christl, "Bericht," p. 4. The entire issue poses several mysteries. Makoviz did not receive a direct message about the recall. He assumed that it was correct, however, and sent off a telegram to Tientsin with such instructions. It did not arrive, and a letter took eight days. Ibid.; "Bericht des K.u.k. Linienschiffsarztes Dr. Ernst DUB uber S.M.S. 'Kaiserin Elisabeth' und die Kriegsereignisse in Tsingtau," Kriegsarchiv Wien, file OK2171-16.

21. The frantic endeavors of all concerned are reflected in the telegrams and correspondence for the day. They are contained as appendixes in "K.u.k. Marinedetachment in Tientsin Res. Nr. 136 an das k.u.k. Marinedetachement-kommando Peking," 20. Oktober 1914, Kriegsarchiv Wien, file OK 2170-16. This file contains the majority of the correspondence relative to the reception and subsequent efforts to return the crew. The Chinese agreement to wink at the smaller transports is in "K.u.k. osterungar. Gesandschaft in China an Seine Exzellenz der Herrn Minister des Aussern, Peking," 21. September 1914, Kriegsarchiv Wien, file OK 2170-17.

22. The difficulties in reaching this decision had created the original problem. Behind the declaration was the pressure brought on by Austro-Hungarian military leaders. They could not accept the idea of German support in Europe without comparable Austrian support in Asia. See, for example, "Telephondepesche des O.O.K. von 22.8.14," and "Telephondespeche des A.O.K. eingelaufen um Th 2m," 22.8.14, Kriegsarchiv, Wien, file OK2171-17. A view that the intervention came from a chance remark by the German Emperor is not reflected in the archives. See Friedrich Wallisch, *Die Flagge Rot-Weiss-Rot; Männer und Taten der österreichischen Marine in viev Jahrhunderten* (Graz: Verlag Styria, 1956), p. 244.

23. The Austrian authorities in China responded to all questions about these travelers that they were individuals from Harbin and Siberia seeking to help their country. At the same time, they lodged protests that single, unarmed Austrian and Hungarian citizens were subject to harrassment, while armed British and Japanese units did as they pleased. "k.u.k. Marinedetachement in Tientsin Res. Nr. 136 an das k.u.k. Marine-detachementkommando Peking," 20. Oktober 1914, Kriegsarchiv Wien, file OK 2170-16; C. Casapiccola, "S.M.S. Kaiserin Elisabeth 1914 in fernen Osten." His brief report, drawn from his diary notes, reflects the desperate fears of the departees.

24. While these stories received wide attention, the man most feared by the troops trying to reach Tsingtau was R. H. Eckford, the earlier British representative in that city, who had left under such emotional stress. He set up his headquarters at Tsinanfu and ranged along all the rail lines, methodically searching for Germans. Since he had lived in Tsingtau since 1907, he did know a good deal about the German community. The Germans feared and hated him more than any other single person associated with the siege.

25. The last ninety-two could not get through and remained in China. The precise travel dates and departees were: August 29, forty-two men; September 2, twenty men; September 5, sixty men; September 9, seven

men; September 12, sixty-five men; September 13, one hundred men. All
the materials for this story are in "K.u.k. Marinedetachment in Tientsin Res.
Nr. 136 an das k.u.k. Marinedetachmentkommando Peking," 20 Oktober
1914, Kriegsarchiv Wien, file OK 2170-16; "Bericht des k.u.k.
Linienschiffsarztes Dr. Ernst DUB uber S.M.S. "Kaiserin Elisabeth" und
die Kriegsereignisse in Tsingtau," Kriegsarchiv Wien, file OK 2170-17.

    26. Willis Peck, "Autobiography," p. 15, Hoover Institution.

    27. Neumaier, "Tagebuch," pp. 12-13.

    28. He also feared an incident because of the high anti-Japanese feeling
in the garrison. Many Germans were most bitter against the Japanese whom
they believed guilty of betrayal, venality, and unpardonable greed. In return
for an unknown price, they had sold their honor to the British.

    29. He issued the declaration in English:

> I hereby declare that on the 27th day of August of the 3rd year of
> Taisho (1914) the blockade of the whole coastline between the point of
> 120° 10' east longitude and 35° 54' north latitude, and the point of 120°
> 36' east longitude and 36° 7' north latitude, i.e., the whole coastline of
> the leased territory of Kiaochow is established and will be maintained
> with the naval force under my command and will continue to be in such
> state of blockade and that the ships of friendly and neutral powers are
> given twenty-four hours grace to leave the blockaded areas and that all
> measures authorized by the international law and respective treaties
> between the Empire of Japan and the different neutral powers will be
> enforced on behalf of His Imperial Japanese Majesty's Government
> against all vessels which may attempt to violate the blockade.
> Given on board of his Imperial Japanese Majesty's ship "SUVO"
> the twenty seventh day of the eighth month of the third year of Taisho.
>
> S. Kato

A German translation is in Assmann, *Kämpfe*, p. 48. Copies are also in
FO 271/2017 and Peck to MacMurray, August 27, 1914. D/S File 862a.

    30. In part the Japanese were taken in by some decoy guns made from
wood scraps and stove pipes. The incident helped the former lightlighthouse
keeper, August von Thielen, with his domestic problems. When he had
delayed moving his family away from their home near Yuniusan, in order to
complete his engineering projects on the "hay stacks" and Yuniusan, his wife
had become most angry over his tardiness. As they drove off one of the
automobile's wheels had fallen into a hole, scattering all their possessions and
shattering her patience. Mrs. von Thielen had demanded official punishment for her husband because of both the personal discomfort and loss of
family property. When his commanding officer, Lieutenant Hans Lipinski,
had refused to do so, she left in a huff for Tientsin. But when the news of this
incident reached her, she wrote her husband, seeking forgiveness for doubt-
ing his abilities. Hans Lipinski, "Tagebuch," 28. August 1914.

    31. Jakob Neumaier, "Tagebuch," p. 13. At the time the Japanese

"victory" received considerable notoriety as an indication of their superiority over the defenders. Hanyu, Shunsuke, "Der Weltkrieg," p. 17. This is a German translation made by Walter Stecher in a Japanese prison camp. The original, *Shinten dochi sekai taisen shi*, was published in 1915. Despite some effort I have not been able to locate a copy. The second edition, published in 1920, is much changed from the original version.

    32. Assmann, *Kämpfe*, p. 52. Subsequent experience indicated that the engineers did not fully understand the power of dynamite, their only available explosive, nor the elasticity or strength of the iron construction employed in Shantung, Ernst Soldan "Tatigkeit der Marine-Pioneer Kompagnie mit Anlagen," p. 6.

    33. The Japanese had no explanation for the accident. Once the *Schiotayen* did go aground, their investigation, conducted under difficult circumstances, indicated the serious damage. They removed the Emperor's picture, the flag and all their weapons, maps, and codebooks. The crew assembled on deck, solemnly sang the national hymn, "Kimigayo," and quietly hurried over a rope bridge to a neighboring destroyer. Ibid., p. 27. The feat, conducted in a driving rain, in the dark, and without human loss, testified to the Japanese navy's superior seamanship.

    34. Kessinger, "Bericht," pp. 120-121; Vogelfanger, "Tagebuch," August 31, 1914.

    35. Vollerthun, *Der Kampf um Tsingtau*, p. 80.

    36. A moving description of the Chinese disaster is in W. T. Uhlenhuth, "Tsingtau Tagebuch," August 31. He describes the human terror, the physical catastrophe, and the pervasive fear in the most gripping terms. The original is in the Marineschule Mürwick, Historische Sammlung.

    37. Odd and obvious witticisms included questions about the size of the Japanese submarine force, the need to christen the infantry works with naval names for their possible flotation, the possibility of sailing home, and the need for life jackets when Shantung floated away. Willi Nickchen, "Tagebuch," 1-4. September 1914; Hans Farling, "Tagebuch," 1.-5. September 1914; Hans Pauer, "Tagebuch," 31. August- 4. September; Jacob Neumaier, "Tagebuch," pp. 15-17; Assmann, *Kämpfe*, p. 51; "Kriegstagebuch Batterie VII," 4.-9. IX 1914. A further concern was dysentery which ran through the garrison on an unprecedented scale. The soldiers exhausted the supply of port wine, the folk rememdy against this ailment. Hans Lipinski, "Tagebuch," 6. Sept. 14.

    38. "Tatigkeitsbericht der B.B. Batterie (Bismarckberg) in Tsingtau," 5. September; "Kriegstagebuch des Kommandeurs des III. Seebataillons," 5.9.14; Willi Nickchen, "Tagebuch," 5 September 1914; Kessinger, "Bericht, I, Bis zur Einschliessung Tsingtau," 6.9.1914. He reconstructed this report, in diary format, after the war. The opinions and explanations are valuable but the dating is often in error.

    Wade's aircraft, a Farman, had a simple radio, a machine gun, a crude bomb sight, and bombs improvised from artillery shells. He flew from the seaplane tender *Wakamiyo Maru* which had arrived with the blockading squadron. The ship carried four Farman aircraft. Toshikazu Ohmae and Roger Pineau, "Japanese Naval Aviation," *United States Naval Institute Proceedings,* 98 (December, 1972), 70. A more detailed explanation on the ship is in the note by R. D. Layman, "Japanese Naval Aviation," *United Stwsnaval Institute Proceedings*, 99 (September, 1973), 95; Interview of Vice Admiral (ret) three of the five aircraft used over the city had seventy-horsepower engines which did perform well. Eventually the naval aircraft flew forty-seven missions. A detailed account which includes a log of the flights and the reports is in Nippon Kaigun koku shi hen sen iinkai, *Nippon Kaigun koku-shi*, Vol. 4, *Sen shi hen* (Tokyo: Jiji Press, 1969), pp. 23-65.

39. The entire issue of Japan's declaration of war is not germane to this study. It is covered in Lowe, *Great Britain and Japan, 1911-1915*; Ian H. Nish, *Alliance in Decline; a Study in Anglo-Japanese Relations*, 1908-23 (London: Athlone Press, 1972); R. P. Dua, *Anglo-Japanese Relations During the First World War* (New Delhi: S. Chand, 1972). The three books provide complementary accounts which fully detail the frenetic diplomatic exchanges concerning Japanese participation. All of them barely touch on the campaign and when they do, make errors.

40. Excellent descriptions of the German military influence on Japan are in Ernst Presseisen, *Before Aggression; Europeans Prepare the Japanese Army* (Tucson: University of Arizona Press, 1965); Georg Kerst, *Jacob Meckel; sein Leben sein Wirken in Deutschland und Japan* (Göttingen: Musterschmidt Verlag, 1970). The most influential German in training the Japanese army was Major Jakob Meckel whose highly influential command dictum included: "Your neighbor's army may outnumber you. His weapons may be more modern than yours. His military morale may be higher than yours. But do not concede the foremost place in military command to anyone." Ito Masanori, *Gumbatsu kobo shi* (Tokyo: Bungei Shunju Shirsha, 1957), I, p. 74.

The war was not that popular in Japan. It is the only conflict which left no enduring war songs, few heroic tales, and a limited number of books. In terms of the normal after products of war this conflict brought only a slight ripple. Imai Seiichi, *Taisho demokurashii*, 23 *Nihon no rehishi* (Tokyo: Chuo koron sha, 1966), p. 121.

41. A brief summary is in L. B. Robertson, "The Capture of Tsingtao," *The Army Quarterly* 35 (October 1937- January 1938), pp. 338-339.

42. This unit had its headquarters in Kurume and had two brigades, the Twenty-third (Omura) and the Twenty-fourth (Kurume). The former had the Forty-sixth and Fifty-fifth Regiments, while the latter controlled the Forth-eighth and Fifty-sixth Regiments. With them the unit had the Twenty-second Cavalry Regiment, the Twenty-fourth Field Artillery Regiment, and several other support units.

43. Yamada was in the middle of his remarkable career, one which would make him Minister of War. See "Notes on the Japanese XVIIIth Division," 18.-8-14, in W.O. 106/663; D. S. Robertson, "Notes on the

Preliminary Movements of the Japanese Expeditionary Force for the Capture of Tsingtau," p. 1. [Hereafter cited as Robertson, "Notes"], W.O. 106/666; the handwritten notes on the Japanese leaders, p. 12, in W.O. 106/661. The latter come from Lieutenant Colonel Everard Calthrop [Hereafter cited as Calthrop, "Notes"] who was not able to put them into a formal report.

    44. T. Nagasaki, "Hufgeklirr," p. 3 (24. VIII). This 1915 translation by Walter Stecher is of a very rare diary kept by an officer in the Twenty-second Cavalry Regiment. The original is unavailable.

    45. Calthrop, "Notes," p. 65, W.O. 106/661. They did not require the British 1913 assault plan, which the latter sent them in September. This proposal called for a landing in Laoshan Bay and the investment of the city, and listed the troops, equipment, and shipping needed for the undertaking. "Military Appreciation for a Combined Naval and Military Attack on TSING TAO," n.d. (but either December 1912 or January 1913), W.O. 106/660; "War Office to the General Officer Commanding, North China," 14 Sept. 1914, W.O. 106/663.

    46. Rikugun Sanbo Honbu (ed.), *Nichidoku Senshi* (Tokyo: Kaikosha, 1916), I, 86. This extensive official history contains copies of most key documents. I have cited it normally because it is more accessible than the original papers. Nonetheless, I have examined the surviving Japanese documents as a check upon the published account. The key surviving record files (many were lost during the Second World War) are in the Ministry of Defence, Tokyo. The most important ones are Seito homen senki and Senji Shorui. Mr. Takeharu Shima, Chief of the Japanese Military Historical Office kindly provided me access to these papers and Lieutenant Colonel (ret) G. Yamazaki was most helpful with suggestions and research help. I am deeply indebted to both men for their time, consideration, and aid.

    The Japanese possessed all the required knowledge of the German military strength in the Shantung area. Proof of their knowledge is in [no author] "Shina ni okeru Doitsu Seiryoku." Copies are in the Japanese archives and in WO 106/668.

    47. Robertson, "Notes," p. 2, W.O. 106/666; lecture by Colonel Watari, Japanese Military Attaché, Washington, D. C., before the Marine Corps School at Quantico, Virginia, n.d. (but clearly in early 1930), p. 4. [Hereafter cited as Watari, "Lecture"]. United States National Archives, Record Group 45: Naval Records Collection of the Office of Naval Records and Library Subject File 1911-1927, #WA-7 (Japanese Siege of Tsingtao). Hubert Brand, "Siege of Tsing-Tao. Report on Anglo-Japanese Naval Operations. August-November 1914," 30 November 1914, Section III, p. 1. [Hereafter cited as Brand "Report"], Adm. 137/35. This report by the British Naval Attaché in Tokyo, who served as the liaison man between the British and Japanese fleet units, is a model of military narration.

    The detailed plan called for a rapid, leap-frog advance inland. As soon as a representative force secured a landing point, they should move on Pingtu with dispatch. Once they had a brigade in that area, they would occupy

Tsimo and extend their line across the peninsula. This much should require two weeks. Thereafter they could take up advance positions with Litsun as the key point and await the siege troops coming from Laoshan. *Nichidoku Senshi*, I, 117-118.

48. From there the military leaders had a special cable to Japan, a modern telegraph office, and all the essential equipment for supporting the landing. It was some 300 miles from the operational front, but otherwise provided a superb staging area. Brand "Report," III, p. 2, Adm. 137/35.

49. The Second Squadron consisted of several old battleships captured in the Russo-Japanese War and some native-built cruisers: the battleships *Suwo* (ex *Pobjeda*), 12,900 tons with four 30,5-cm guns; *Iwami* (ex *Drel*), 13,700 tons with four 30,5-cm guns; *Tango* (ex *Poltawa*) with four 30,5-cm guns; the old coastal armored ships *Okinoschima* (ex *Apraxin*), 4,200 tons with three 25-cm guns; *Mishima* (ex *Senyawin*), 4,200 tons with four 25-cm guns. With these units were three armored cruisers (*Iwate, Tokiwa, Yakumo*) all close to 10,000 tons with four 20-cm guns, and eight light cruisers (*Chitose, Tone, Mogami, Yodo, Akashi, Akitsushima, Chiyoda, Takachiho*) of widely ranging size and power. They carried at least two 12-cm or larger guns each. In addition were two destroyers and twenty-seven boats, as well as several repair and supply vessels.

50. The *Emden* remained a highly illusive vessel and the uncoordinated blockade efforts between the British and Japanese had occasioned a three-day period when no one was on watch. At the time the naval leaders of both countries had, erroneously, assumed that the *Emden* had slipped away during this hiatus. Each side blamed the other for the error and created ill-will before starting any cooperative activity. Brand "Report," III, p. 2, Adm. 137/35. Jerram's anger over the vacuum is in a letter to his wife, which is partially reproduced in I. H. Nish, "Admiral Jerram and the German Pacific Fleet 1913-1915," pp. 417-418.

51. The relationships between Japan and Great Britain in 1914 provide a fascinating study in diplomatic history. Both parties, under uncertain circumstances, sought new relationships, new positions, and new influences. For the single-minded Japanese these opportunities opened entirely new vistas and possibilities. For the harassed and committed British the situation was highly unpleasant. They were deeply involved with the political, military, and strategic concerns of Europe. At the same time they needed protection for their political, economic, and strategic position in Asia. The Japanese provided an ideal partner free of European contamination, knowledgeable of the Pacific area, and interested in limited objectives. In realistic terms the British failed to see what the Japanese fully understood. In all the discussions and exchanges relative to Japan's participation, the British tacitly accepted Japan's supremacy in Asia. Both Lowe and Nish have performed a prodigious amount of research on this issue, but both neglect a key facet of 00256the British problem—the flow of military intelligence into London. The British were reading many, but apparently not all, of the messages between Tsingtau and Berlin. This hazy image of German strength and intentions

pushed the authorities into supporting the Japanese entrance with very little thought.

52. The precise circumstances surrounding this plea remain highly uncertain. Regnault professed receiving a telegram from Paris about an interview between Sir Arthur Nicolson and M. Cambon involving Tsingtau. He used this purported encounter as the basis for proposing multinational intervention. The British promptly denied that the two men had even met, much less discussed anything. Unfortunately for their interests they could not jettison the proposal so easily. France and Great Britain possessed neither the military strength nor political will for a major Asian campaign. Regnault forced the British to expand their considerations. See Greene to Grey, 8 August 1914; Grey to Greene, 9 August 1914. FO 37½016.

53. The key ambassadors (Greene in Tokyo and Sir John Jordan in Peking) advocated prompt joint action as a means of protecting the British position in Asia. Jordan to Grey, August 9, 1914; Greene to Grey, August 10, 1914; Greene to Grey, August 11, 1914. FO 37½016.

54. Grey to Greene, August 12, 1914. Adm. 137/35; Grey to Sir G. Buchanan (St. Petersburgh), August 14, 1914. W.O. 106/663.

55. Greene to Grey, August 15, 1914. W.O. 106/663; Greene to Grey, August 18, 1914. Adm. 137/35. The same note offered Japanese transportation for the British troops. Clearly the Japanese understood Great Britain's commitment to end difficulties in Europe.

56. The French had collected a token contingent of troops in Tientsin for this possibility, while the Russians had some fifty men in North China. Greene to Grey, August 18, 1914; Grey to Greene, August 20, 1914. FO 37½017. Grey recognized the respective national aspirations very clearly but could not antagonize Japan. He likewise anticipated the victors taking the spoils of war when he wrote a brief minute for the record:

> . . . I would tell him [the Japanese Ambassador in London] quite frankly, though I could only say it privately and unofficially that, after this war, if Germany was beaten, France, Russia and ourselves would naturally get compensation in parts of the world other than China. The only compensation that Japan would get would be in the region of China. It would therefore be unfair for any of us to put forward claims, depriving Japan of compensation for the blood and treasure that she might have to spend. . .

Minute by Grey on a draft telegram by [Beilby] Alston [Foreign Office Official] to Greene, August 20, 1914. Elsewhere he wrote, "It cannot be expected that Japan will spend blood and treasure in Kiao-Chou and get nothing for it—not even the remains of the German lease." Minute by Grey, c19 Aug. 1914, F.O. 37½019.

57. Grey to Jordan, August 16, 1914; "Note from B. B. Cubitt to Under-Secretary of State for Foreign Affairs." Adm 137/35.

58. Paraphrase Telegram from G.O.C.N. China to War Office, 20

August, 1914; Paraphrase Telegram from Secretary of State to G.O.C.N. China, 20 August 1914. W.O. 106/663. The same command subordination directive went to the Navy. Admiralty to Under Secretary of State, Foreign Office, 22 August 1914. Adm. 137/35.

59. Paraphrase Telegram to G.O.C. North China, 21 August 1914. Adm 137/35.

60. Greene to Grey, August 22, 1914. W.O. 106/663. The Chinese, too weak to protest, were not against a convenient arrangement allowing British transit. They obviously understood their weak situation. Grey, however, was already on record against the German violation of Belgian neutrality and could ill-afford any British violation of China's territorial integrity. Grey to Greene, August 14, 1914. F.O. 37½/016; Jordan to Grey, August 21, 1914. W.O. 106/663. The Chinese difficulties are discussed in Madeleine Chi, *China Diplomacy, 1914-1918* (Cambridge: Harvard University Press, 1970), Chapter I. Her book replaces the still useful, but old, Thomas E. LaFargue, *China and the World War* (Stanford: Stanford University Press, 1937).

Grey had not fully recovered from his dismay over the independent Japanese action. The American ambassador in London, Walter Hines Page, reported Grey's position:

Sir Edward Grey has explained to me confidentially that the Japanese government acted on their own account when they sent their ultimatum to Germany. They did not confer with the British government about it but only informed the British government after they decided to send it.

Page to [William J.] Bryan [Secretary of State], August 18, 1914. SD 763.72/508.

61. Robertson, a brilliant linguist, had served much of his career in semidiplomatic posts in the Far East. His assignment came from the confusion in staff appointments brought on by the European conflict. He served as a temporary replacement for the recently arrived British military attaché in Tokyo, Lieutenant Colonel Everard Calthrop. The latter had arrived in Japan on August 14, two days after the five resident language officers had departed for home. There was no one left for the attaché function until these men could be recalled when their ship arrived in Hawaii. Letter to the Military Attaché, Tokyo from Homan [?], Colonel, General Staff, 27 August 1914. W.O. 106/663.

62. *Nichidoku Senshi*, I, 96. Takahashi subsequently returned to the area as a permanent observer-coordinator until September 3, when he joined Kamio's staff.

63. Kamio bade them goodbye and then hurried to Tokyo for a brief presentation to the Emperor. Hany J "Weltkrieg," p. 20, describes the ceremony. Afterward Kamio left for Hakho ho where he spoke with Kato about the blockade and their plans.

64. The captain subsequently reported the landing to the British authorities. Consul [?] to Admiralty, 3 September 1914. Adm. 137/35.

65. Concurrently they distributed leaflets with a brief proclamation for the populace. It explained the reasons for the landing, placing full responsibility for the conflict upon the Germans, and underscored Japan's interest in a peaceful solution. A brief sentence, at the end, indicated that any interruption of the Japanese operations would be treated with the utmost harshness, and that the interpretation of such interruptions belonged to the Japanese. Hanyu, "Weltkrieg," p. 23.

66. The sole opposition was verbal. The Chinese Magistrate in Tsuhifu had given the resident Japanese Consul a note referring to the Hague Conventions and neutrality rules. He withdrew it shortly afterwards. On September 4 the Chinese offered a Circular Note to the various legations in Peking. In it they complained about the landing but did so in obtuse terms, reflecting their weak military position. Greene to Grey, September 3, 1914; Jordan to Grey, September 4, 1914. W.O. 106/663. The Japanese had already initiated general discussions with Peking relative to their landing area on August 20. Once more the Chinese, in an impotent position, sought various limitations on the war zone, but finally conceded to the Japanese desire for an extensive military area. In the end the Chinese agreed to the Japanese demands and then massed troops along the new zones' boundary to defend their neutrality.

67. Nagasaki, "Hufgeklirr," p. 6.

68. Watari, "Lecture," p. 10. Such conditions brought the column moving on Tschauyuan to a standstill. A small party garrisoned the area, while the others returned to the main force.

69. Nagasaki, "Hufgeklirr," pp. 7-11. One small aid was the arrival of the first Japanese spies from Tsingtau. Two men, one the servant in the Japanese military attaché's office in Peking, the other the secretary of the Japanese club in Tsingtau, reached Pingtu at the same time. They had arrived in that city shortly after the Japanese ultimatum and had carefully studied the defensive preparations. Disguised as mourners, they visited various temples and grave sites in the German defensive area. After completing this mission, they shifted to Tsimo and watched German patrols moving about. When the Chinese suddenly revealed their presence, they fled to Pingtu. Ibid.

70. *Nichidoks Senshi*, p. 96.

71. For a short distance from the landing point the proximity of the troop movements to the sea made supply shipments relatively easy. Using impressed Chinese junks and labor, the Japanese supply personnel landed foodstuffs on the beaches, shifted them with locally impressed carts and workmen, and established storage areas along the road. But, once the troops marched inland, they were dependent upon miry roads. There were insufficient carts in the area and those hastily brought from Korea were not enough to offset the shortage. Robertson, "Notes," p. 4. W.O. 106/666.

72. *Nichidoku Senshi*, I, 122-150; Nagasaki, "Hufgeklirr," p. 12. The latter has an account of the engagement on pp. 14-15. Chikami's concerns were well-founded. When the Japanese first entered the city, one of the

officers received a visiting card from one Wakikawa Funichita, with an invitation to follow the Chinese bearer. With some hesitation he did so, and found that Wakikawa had been a translator in Tientsin. He had received orders to Tsimo as a Japanese secret agent and had served there in that capacity. Wakikawa provided the troops with a careful accounting of German movements throughout the area. Ibid., pp. 17-20.

73. For the participants the entire affair was most trying. Because of possible German opposition at Laoshan, secrecy was important. The same concern required a sudden appearance offshore and speedy landing. For the men, totally ignorant of their future, the prospect of more time in confined areas aboard bucking ships was not pleasant.

74. Even this report was open to some challenge. While the river was little more than a wide, shallow waterway, the high vegetation and sandy banks made cavalry reconnaissance difficult.

75. Both men enjoyed superb personal reputations among their men. Sakuma, a simple man who exemplified Japanese military virtues, avoided saki, and honored his Samurai ancestors, was mourned by many. The same was true of Baron Riedesel, a reservist, who had been in the German diplomatic embassy in Peking. His selfless action was in character. Hanyu, "Weltkrieg," p. 45.

76. One of the eerie, unreal aspects of this small drama was the behavior of the Chinese. In Liu ting a colorful wedding procession with drums, gongs, and flags moved through the streets, the gaily dressed participants proceeding on their way irrespective of the flying bullets. In the fields the farmers kept at their work until the bullets came too close, when they took cover for a few minutes, and then stolidly returned to their labors. Uhlenhuth, "Tsingtau Tagebuch," 17.-18. September 1914. A similar response to the insanity of war took place in the Bismarck battery. One of the men quietly observed during an exercise, "Why should we fire when the Japanese or English come? We could just let them in and settle the issues over a glass of beer in the canteen." There was no response. Neumaier, "Tagebuch," p. 12.

CHAPTER IV: The Japanese Advance

1. The spirit within Tsingtau continued high, although the situation was not optimistic. They had many encouraging messages, no immediate threat, and no serious problems. Throughout August and early September they received many telegrams, letters, and other messages exhorting them to do their best. Moreover, the news of many European victories gave them

hope for an international solution before the Japanese assault. The most delightful message was one from Tientsin:

Deutschland siegt weiter, wir sind heiter,
grussen aufs beste, Euch in der Feste!

Nickchen "Tagebuch," 1. September 1914; Hans Farling "Tagebuch," p. 10; Oberstabsartz Prafcke, "Bericht über Kiautschou, Ostasien und Heimreise," 4. VII. 15.

2. Befehl (Nr. 223) fur die Landfront f.d. 5.9.1914.

3. Plüschow, realizing the danger of having his hangar in the open, promptly started construction on a new hangar at the other end of the field. The new building, under a rocky overhang, was completely camouflaged against aerial observation. Plüschow also built a mock aircraft of wood, tin, and sailcloth, which he displayed in different positions before his old installation. The trick worked throughout the siege, as the Japanese constantly tried to destroy the wrong building. Plüschow, *Die Abenteuer*, p. 73.

4. Nickchen "Tagebuch," 6 September 1914. Hans Kersten, "Bericht," p. 6. After the aircraft disappeared from sight, the Germans busied themselves with picking up the spent rifle shells. Each man had to give a precise accounting for his own shells. Ibid.

5. Kessinger, "Geschichte," p. 78. Vollerthun, *Der Kampf um Tsingtau*, pp. 89-90; Hans Farling, "Tagebuch," p. Hans Kersten "Bericht," p. 9. Karl Coupette "Die Signalstation and Kustenfunkeinrichtung," p. 2; Kriegstagebuch der Tsingtauer Werft., 6. IX. 14.

6. Kladde zum Kriegstagebuch der Marine-Fliegerstation Tsingtau (Abschrift), 13.9.14; Vollerthun, *Im Kampf um Tsingtau*, p. 85; letter from Ed Leipold, 27 Dezember 1972.

7. Kessinger, "Geschichte," pp. 176-181.

8. Ibid., pp. 220-221.

9. There is some discrepancy in the descriptions of the changed German thinking and new assignments. Kessinger, "Bericht, I, Bis zur Einschliessung Tsingtau," 11.9.1914 places the German decisiveness and troop shift somewhat earlier than does Kuhlo, "Kurze Beschreibung der Tatigkeit der Ostasiatischen Marine-Detachment während der Belagerung von Tsingtau, 1914," pp. 27-28. From the latter's description one observes some professional tension and personal rancor between Kuhlo and von Kessinger. The version in Kessinger, "Geschichte," p. 231, provides a more sensible explanation which moves between the other views.

10. The conclusions were essentially the same ones which von Kessinger had presented, a few days earlier, before the Governor. There were, as everyone recognized, too many places to defend with their meager resources. The Japanese, with their legendary reputation for night movement, could slip by the scattered defenders and turn on them at daybreak.

11. Kuhlo, "Kurze Beschreibung," p. 28; Kessinger, "Bericht," 16.9.14; Kessinger, "Geschichte," p. 220 f. A precise listing of the units and their location is in Assmann, *Kämpfe*, pp. 58-59.

12. They put in telephone and mirror-signalling connections to Tsing-tau, in addition to provisions, water, and munitions for three weeks. In addition to the demolition work, the occupation force used oil and soap to grease various possible ascent routes.

13. Kessinger, "Geschichte," pp. 247-248; Otto Sarnow, "Tagebuch," 26.-28. Sept. 1914 and his introduction to the diary. Sarnow was one of party. Just why the Germans took so long in recognizing the geographic dominance of Prince Heinrich Mountain remains a mystery.

14. The units had embarked in Japan on September 13. Because of the congestion, both that in Japan and that anticipated in Lau schan, the trans-port authorities had carefully stretched out the entire loading program. The final embarkation took place on September 29. *Nichidoku Senshi*, I, 99.

15. *Nichidoku Senshi*, I, 189-190; Brand, "Report," II, pp. 5-6.

16. G. Nash and G. Gipps, "Narrative of the Events in Connection with the Siege, Blockade, and Reduction of the Fortress of Tsingtau," Adm. 137/35.

17. As they moved ashore, the blockade force made various false landing demonstrations along the coast and fired a desultory bombardment at various points. The *Iwate, Yakumo*, five destroyers, and a few miscellane-ous vessels participated in these activities. Brand "Report," II, p. 7.

18. *Nichidoku Senshi*, I, 193-201; Watari, "Lecture," pp. 14-16. Both accounts are based upon Kamaji's report of the action.

19. Horiuchi reported his success to Kamio, indicating the landing achievements and the inland movement. He did not point out the difficulties of his troops. *Nichidoku Senshi*, I, 203-205.

20. *Nichidoku Senshi*, I, 209-211; Kessinger, "Geschichte," p. 238; Interview with Hans Ehlers, June, 1973; Kessinger, "Bericht," 19.9.1914. The Germans believed that the Japanese fired haphazardly, rather than employing aimed, disciplined rifle fire. As a result, their shots usually went high. There is no like explanation for the German problems. This action was the first for everyone, which may be the best explanation.

21. Steinbruck, "Bericht uber die Sprengung der Cicilienbrucke am 19. Sept. 1914.," 21. September 1914; Manfred Zimmermann, "Bericht," 25. X. 15. The German demolition teams ranged throughout the protecto-rate, destroying bridges, train tracks, and natural objects. Their major assignment was impeding Japanese progress. They did very well with this mission, excluding bridge demolition, where they usually destroyed only the middle span supports, dropping that section to the ground. The Japanese engineers then jacked it back up and into place with little loss of time.

22. E. Dithmar, "Die Kampfe im Vorgelande der Festung Tsingtau im September 1914," *Marine Rundschau*, XI (Nov. 1935), p. 484. The study is actually one written by von Kessinger.

23. Concurrently they prepared for their ultimate withdrawal. The engineers placed demolition charges in the water works and government buildings in Litsun. Kuhlo brought the tiny steamer, *Habicht*, to station behind the Tsangkow Heights.

24. *Nichidoku Senshi*, I, 237-240. The Germans, unable to bring any of the enemy down, tried to keep them above 2,000 meters which, they hoped, would impede effective observation. Meyer-Waldeck, "Bericht," p. 77.

25. Kessinger, "Geschichte," p. 242; Vollerthun, *Der Kampf um Tsingtau*, p. 102; *Nichidoku Senshi*, I, 224-229. Among the personal effects left in haste were some picture postcards and individual photographs of Japanese soldiers. On the back was the name of the photographer, Yakahashi, with the remark, "My new address will be on the Friedrich strasse (his old store)." The men laughed at the industry of their old friend. E. J. Voskamp, *Aus dem belagerten Tsingtau* (Berlin: Buchhandlung der Berliner evag. Missionsgesellschaft 1915), p. 12.

26. At that time they captured a train bearing the director of the rail line. The Germans believed that since he was a civilian heading a Chinese enterprise, he should not come under military control. This view received no Japanese support. They subjected the director, Karl Schmidt, to various indignities. Assmann, *Kämpfe*, pp. 57-58; Hany u, "Weltkrieg," p. 56.

27. This politically explosive issue reflected Japan's determination for general control of the entire Shantung area. Their position, which they could base upon an amazingly precise list of Chinese transgressions of neutrality, allowed them a far more aggressive attitude toward Chinese territory. Unquestionably the Chinese authorities had allowed various German activities. The Japanese used this knowledge to further their interests and to go beyond their designated military limits. On moral grounds they could muster a weak defense; on political power issues they had a stronger position. The issue clearly provides no simple answer. *Nichidoku Senshi*, I, 237-239; Hanyu, "Weltkrieg," pp. 56-57, 60-64. The last pages are a list of Chinese abuses. A splendidly concise discussion is in Chi, *China Diplomacy, 1914-1918*, pp. 14-25. More contentious is the view of John T. Pratt, *War and Politics in China* (London: Jonathan Cape, 1943), pp. 177-179. Concurrently the Japanese strengthened their garrison in Kiautschou and moved strong patrols out along the rail line to assure full control.

28. The *Triumph*, some 13,000 tons, had been built in 1903-1904 for the Chilean Navy. The British Navy had purchased the ship before her completion. She carried four 10-inch and fourteen 7.5-inch guns. Descended from a long and distinguished line of *Triumphs*, she had moved to Hong Kong in 1913 as a depot ship.

29. Captain Maurice Fitzmaurice took men where he could find them and often virtually impressed men into his service. See, for example, Arthur, B.W., "With H.M.S. Triumph at Tsingtau," *Blackwoods Magazine* CXCIX (May 1916), 579. The story of the soldiers' service aboard ship is in Everard Wyrall, *The History of the Duke of Cornwall's Light Infantry, 1914-1919* (London: Methuen, 1932), pp. 6-8.

30. For their training the men already possessed the advantage of success. En route northward they had captured the German steamer, *Frisia*, with some $120,000 in gold. They had also picked up another steamer by using the ruse of hoisting the German Naval Ensign.

31. The pages of Brand's "Report" all reflect the open, pleasant understanding between both parties. His subsequent felicitous letters were formal acknowledgments of a happy relationship. Certainly the Japanese were careful in their relations with their allies. Kato was always considerate of British feelings and desires. See "Instruction to the Commanding Officers of the British Ships" [from Kato], 12 Sept. 1914. Adm. 137/35.

32. He had served as military attaché in Belgium, Holland, Norway, Sweden, and Denmark, as a liaison officer with numerous foreign delegations, and as the potential commander of all foreign military groups in Tientsin.

33. My observations here are founded upon an extensive correspondence with individuals who knew Barnardiston. Included were Captain Malcolm Kennedy and Mrs. Derek Cooper, the only daughter of the General. While I wish to acknowledge my gratitude, I do not want to associate them with my opinions. His surviving papers consist, essentially, of social invitations, congratulatory messages, and various menus. Letter from Librarian, University of London, Kings College, 27 October 1971.

34. In the British Army the regiment served as the basic tactical unit. Normally a regular regiment possessed four battalions of infantry, and one to three battalions of special reservists. The normal battalion rotated from post to post, in the overseas possessions and in the mother country. At home they trained recruits continually in order to keep up their overall strength and general readiness. Soldiers stationed aboard needed to be twenty or more years of age and to have at least a year of home service. The depot station for the South Wales Borderers was Wales, and its soldiers were a mixture of the south Welsh and men from the London area.

35. General Officer Commanding, North China to War Office, 14 September 1914; Note from Sir Eduard Barrow, India Office, 15 September 1914; Paraphrase from War Office to G.O.C. Tientsin, 16.9.1914. W.O. 106/603.

36. In organization the Indian troops were generally formed into two models. One, of regimental size, represented a unit from a single tribe; the other was a regiment in which the companies came from different tribes. Normally they did not possess modern equipment. In this case the Thirty-sixth Sikhs came from the Jalendhar area and formed a unit of the first type. The military observers of the time considered them among India's best soldiers. Unfortunately the records of their campaign have disappeared. Letter from KML Saxena, Historical Section, Ministry of Defence, India, 4 December 1970; letter from M. I. Moir, India Office Records, 22 April 1971; letter Stephen P. Cohen, 26 November 1973.

37. *Nichidoku Senshi*, I, 65-66. Barnardiston fully understood the concerns of coalition warfare. General Officer Commanding, North China Command, to War Office, September 18, 1914. F)37½/017.

38. *Nichidoku Senshi*, I, 73. On the British side, Barnardiston received instructions that he should be cooperative and provide the Japanese with the prewar British operational plan against Tsingtau. War Office to the

General Officer Commanding, North China, 14. Sept. 1914. W.O. 106/663.

39. Interview with Brigadier Desmond Somerville, February 1973; R. K. Beaumont-Walker, "The Siege of Tsintao Campaign, August—November 1914 [a report written in 1922]," p. 2. He reports a meeting with a friend, a Lieutenant Wendt of Kuhlo's command, after the European declaration of war. Wendt asked, "What are you people going to do here?" Beaumont-Walker responded, "I don't know what we're going to do but we don't want to fight you chaps because you are friends of ours." They did not meet again. Ibid., p. 3.

40. They loaded at Tientsin through fear of the neutrality issue. The movement of armed men by rail over Chinese territory might provoke an unwanted confrontation. General Officer Commanding, North China Command, to War Office, September 18, 1914. F.O. 37½017.

41. Desmond Somerville, "Diary," 22 September 1914.

42. G. Nash and G. Gipps, "Narrative of the Events in Connection with the Siege, Blockade, and Reduction of the Fortress of Tsingtau," p. 1. Adm 137/35. A copy of this report is in The British National Maritime Museum, Greenwich. Somerville, "Diary," 23 September 1914; R. T. Eckford, "Report on the Events Leading Up to the Capture of Tsingtau," pp. 1-2. F.O. 371/2381. This highly critical report caused British diplomats some embarrassment since it circulated among several foreign diplomats before the London officials could suppress it.

The small-scale Decauville railway was an interesting surprise to the British. It arrived in sections consisting of two light rails bolted to about nine flat iron ties. Virtually anyone could assemble them when placing them on a roadbed. The roadbed required little work beyond smoothing, but it did require adjacent walking space for the men constructing the railway. Each car was flat (about 0.9 x 1 meter) and light enough to be lifted without difficulty. During construction each car carried at least four track sections. As the men emplaced these sections, they moved the car forward until it was empty. Then they simply lifted it off the rails and placed the car to the side. When all the cars were empty, they quickly put them all back on the rails and hurried them back for other loads. The cars had hand-operated brakes, which allowed easy control on down grades. They could carry extensive loads and, with various sidings and short lines to given points, allowed the Japanese a remarkable mobility. The readily available Chinese labor supply permitted construction without extensive Japanese manpower losses. They planned a construction rate of eight miles per day. J. A. Irons, "Japanese-German War in Kiaouchou, China—1914," February 23, 1915, in United States Army Military Research Collection, pp. 9-10. The Japanese moved an average 300 flat cars with 150 tons of material each day. A round trip required four days. Headquarters, Tsingtao Garrison [?], "Proceedure of the Operations against the fortifications of Tsingtao," trans. Allan F. McLean, in United States Army Military Research Collection, p. 7.

43. A pleasant, if not entirely accurate, description is in C. T. Atkinson, *The History of the South Wales Borderers, 1914-1918* (London: Medici

Society, 1931), p. 74. The Chinese carts brought with them were another challenge. The men disassembled them aboardship, sent them ashore, and then tried to assemble them on the beaches. Since the original builders had not mass-produced the carts, the parts were not interchangeable.

44. Calthrop, from Tokyo, replaced Robertson, who had orders for home. He was a brilliant linguist who translated Chinese and Japanese books, spoke idiomatic Japanese, and understood Oriental culture. After his 1915 death in France, his family presented his sword to the Japanese Staff College as a memento of his great love for Japan. Letter from Malcolm Kennedy, April 2, 1971; F.S.G. Piggott, *Broken Thread* (Aldershot: Gale & Polden, 1950), p. 90.

45. N. W. Barnardiston to the Secretary, War Office, 9 October 1914, p. 3. W.O. 106/667. [Hereafter cited as Barnardiston, Repott 2].

46. Kamio expressed appreciation for the reasons behind the British request but could not honor them. Their unit was small and he explained the limited road network must be used with care. The British troops must depend upon the Japanese supply lines rather than an independent system. *Nichidoku Senshi*, I, 251-254.

47. Barnardiston, Report 2, p. 3. W.O. 106/667; Eckford, "Report," pp. 2-3; Somerville, "Diary," September 24-25; D. G. Johnson, "Narrative of Events in Connection with the Siege and Capture of the German Naval Base and Fortress of Tsingtau in North China 1914," p. 3. The British soldiers were bitter over what they considered a conspiritorial effort against their campaign participation. However, there is no evidence in the Japanese records of a conscious policy against the British. There was only one road, and the surrounding terrain, still soggy from the rains, allowed no cross-country movement. Once in Chimo, the British received limited supplies from the Japanese, which helped sustain them. Despite this aid, the troops remained on half rations. Barnardiston, Report 2, p. 3.

48. Calthrop, "Notes," W.O. 106/661. The Japanese were fearful that any written orders might fall into German hands. They used oral communication as a safeguard, leaving a written record for the archives. Subsequently their fears were confirmed when a flash flood overwhelmed a depot located in a stream bed, and some secret documents washed into Kiautschou Bay. The Germans did recover them but could not understand their significance. Watari, "Lecture," p. 10.

49. Robertson, "Notes," W.O. 106/666.

50. Kessinger, "Bericht," I, 25.9.1914.

51. Vogelfanger, "Tagebuch," 26. Sept. 14; Meyer-Waldeck, "Bericht," p. 78.

52. The Japanese also obtained information through their patrols and two prisoners-of-war, but these details provided confirmation rather than new leads. The aerial intelligence was decisive. Major-General (?) Machida, "A Minute Report of the Siege of Tsingtau" (n.d., no translator), p. 7. This report compiled by the Japanese Military Attaché in Peking is in the US Army Military Research Collection.

53. *Nichidoku Senshi*, I, 243-248. The Germans suspected the existence of a refined espionage system and used its probable contributions as an explanation for their subsequent defeat. Assmann, *Kämpfe*, p. 61. They had supporting evidence, in that the mine locations were often marked with small white pebbles, that the Japanese avoided all ambushes, and that the Japanese found the locations of gaps in the German lines with ridiculous ease.

Despite their constant search, high reward ($300), and warning descriptions of spies (for example the worn spots on the feet occasioned by different sandals), the Germans did not catch any spies. Meyer-Waldeck, "Bericht," p. 77.

54. Ibid., pp. 177-180; letter from Lieutenant General (ret) Iida Sada, October 24, 1972. The timetable was clear and precise, with the departure times for every unit carefully set down. *Nichidoku Senshi*, I, 261.

55. Kessinger, "Geschichte," pp. 254-255; Schaumburg, "Bericht," p. 14. The role and importance of the Chinese workers in these endeavors cannot be reconstructed from the surviving records. Both sides used them extensively, but the documents do not reflect their numbers, their activities, or their significance. The Japanese clearly impressed them in great numbers.

56. Kessinger, "Geschichte," p. 255. In his defense one must suggest that the Japanese did encounter serious difficulties with their communications and with the poor roads. Artillery units, in particular, snarled the communications. In their eagerness to get ahead of schedule or to maintain it, they ruthlessly stole Chinese laborers from one another, used the sweet-potato stalks for road beds (which, often left an incredible morass for following troops), and destroyed the road bed without consideration for the general effort. *Nichidoku Senshi*, I, 267-268. Kuhlo erred in not taking into account the size of the Japanese commitment, the impatience of the Japanese troops for battle, and the lack of any aggressive German response.

57. Kuhlo, "Kurze Beschreibung," p. 39; Kessinger, "Geschichte," pp. 259-260.

58. German reports indicated an assault force well beyond the total Japanese strength in Shantung. Apparently no one reflected upon or questioned the astronomical claims.

59. Vollerthun, *Der Kampf um Tsingtau*, pp. 105-106; Merk, "Bericht über die Ereignisse," pp. 2-3.

60. Kessinger, "Bericht," I, 26.9.14; Hugo Ponsel, "Personlicher Bericht," p. 4. Their departure was a difficult physical challenge. It was not, however, under enemy pressure or fire as many authors, most notable Vollerthun, *Der Kampf um Tsingtau*, p. 106, would have it.

61. His aircraft reported reconnaissance findings almost continuously. Normally he employed one or two aircraft which flew over the enemy lines, made notes on clip boards, and dropped the information near the affected units or by Kamio's headquarters. The time delay for information was, therefore, minimal. *Nichidoku Senshi*, I, 277-278.

62. With the destruction of the water works, Tsingtau fell back on the

Haipo water system and the city pumps. Thereafter the city administration regulated all water usage, a challenging assignment. A good description of the problems and the decisions is in the anonymous "Weitere Regelung der Wasserversorgung." An interesting technical description of the destruction is in Hans Odermann, "Bericht uber die Sprengung des Wasserwerkes Litsun."

63. *Nichidoku Senshi*, I, 334f.

64. One had a machine-gun bullet hole and damage to the pilot's seat, another had five bullet holes, and the third had twenty-nine bullet holes in the fuselage. Hanyu, "Weltkrieg," pp. 72-73.

65. Vogelfänger, "Tagebuch," 26.-28. September 1914; Winkler, "Tagebuch," 26.-27.-9.14.

66. Kessinger, "Geschichte," p. 268.

67. Voskamp, *Aus dem belagerten Tsingtau*, p. 17.

68. Kriegstagebuch des Kommandeurs des II. S. B., 27.9. 1914; Vollerthun, *Kampf um Tsingtau*, p. 100; Sarnow, "Tagebuch," 27.Sept.1914. Already, however, the Germans had committed the cardinal error of revealing their presence on the mountain peak. They stood up to make their observations, and one man unsuccessfully fired several shots at some distant Japanese. Ibid. By day's end the puff of exploding shells ominously appeared on the side of the hill.

69. Meyer-Waldeck, "Bericht," pp. 80—1; Kuhlo, "Kurze Beschreibung," pp. 43-45; Dithmar, "Die Kampfe im Vorgelande," p. 486.

70. "Befehl [No. 245] fur die Landfront fur den 27.9.14"; also *Nichidoku Senshi*, I, 395.

71. Anders had the First Company of the East Asiatic Naval Detachment and platoons from two other companies, the troops from Schatsykou, and some miscellaneous men. Kuhlo had two companies from the East Asiatic Naval Detachment in addition to various platoon-size units and the artillery pieces. Kessinger, "Geschichte," pp. 269-270; "Befehl [No. 246] für die Landfront fur den 28.9.14; Kriegstagebuch des Kommandeurs des III. S. B. 28.9.1914.

72. *Nichidoku Senshi*, I, 373-375.

73. Ibid., p. 377. By that time he thought that both the British troops and the Japanese siege artillery would be ready for commitment. The latter had started ashore on September 23, and the first guns moved into line on September 26.

74. Schaumburg, "Bericht," p. 15.

75. This Japanese bureaucratic uncertainty about siege warfare disrupted the Germans' thought. They felt certain that the Japanese would attack the previous day in support of the general struggle. Nash and Gipps, "Narrative," p. 5.

76. The Germans took some pleasure in the order of the battle line. They remembered earlier peacetime circumstances when Japanese vessels needed British pilots to negotiate familiar terrain. The Germans had watched the fully qualified Japanese captains with the long, pipe-smoking Anglo-

Saxons standing next to them. Throughout the Japanese captain did the work and had the responsibility, but the symbol of British superiority remained on the bridge as a reminder of power relationships. Now the Japanese dictated the terms and the British ship appeared last in line.

77. Brand, "Report," Adm. 137/35. That same day the cruisers *Tokiwa* and *Yakumo* landed troops in Schatsykou Bay. They found the destroyed German guns, in addition to a supply of some 600 useful shells. Ultimately one of the guns went to the *Triumph* as a campaign trophy. A proposed attack for the next day fell through because of other developments. Nash and Gipps, "narrative," p. 6.

78. For reasons which still remain uncertain, a significant portion of the shells did not explode upon impact. The huge steel balls rolled around like misshapen bowling balls, banging into the walls, spinning off various obstructions, crashing into crevices.

79. "Bismarck Battery Tagebuch"; Nickchen, "Tagebuch," p. 32.

80. Bertkau, "Bericht," p. 15; Vollerthun, *Der Kampf um Tsingtau*, p. 113.

81. Schaumburg, "Bericht," p. 10; Kriegstagebuch, Batterie 7, 28.9.1914. German artillerymen carried their shells back but disposed of them in the many ravines. Interview with Vizeadmiral a.D. Herbert Straehler, June, 1973.

82. Ibid.; interview with Hans Ehlers, November, 1972.

83. Hao, *Weltkrieg*, 55.

84. The timing for these events remains unclear. The Japanese records put everything much earlier than do the German accounts although they agree that the surrender came about noon. Kessinger, "Geschichte," pp. 285-287; Kriegstagebuch des Kommandeurs des III. S. B., 27.-28.9.1914; Sarnow, "Tagebuch," 27.-28 September 1914. The latter, as he moved down the hill toward a prison camp, reflected upon a comrade's comment on the Kaiser's directive to hold out, "We will not get out of this mouse trap." A sergeant and eleven men did fight their way back to Tsingtau but they were not to be separated from Sarnow very long.

The brief description in Assmann, *Kämpfe*, p. 64, is inaccurate. His suggestion that the Japanese wore white arm bands, which confused the defenders, has no support in the documents.

85. *Nichidoku Senshi*, I, 428-429.

86. Ibid., I, 441-444; Nagasaki, "Hufgeklirr," p. 30.

87. Kriegstagebuch der Tsingtauer Werft, 28.IX.14. The gunboats *Luchs* and *Iltis* went down shortly thereafter.

88. Discussion with Hans Ehlers. Few of the men had contemplated such matters but Rudiger's observations forced acceptance of the realistic fact. There were three mass grave sites ready for the anticipated losses from the Japanese attack. Vollerthun, *Der Kampf um Tsingtau*, p. 135. Rudiger survived the campaign.

CHAPTER V: A Desperate Position

1. Meyer-Waldeck, "Bericht," p. 92.

2. Vollerthun, *Der Kampf um Tsingtau*, p. 118; Kessinger, "Bericht," II, "Bis zum Fall Tsingtau," 28.9.14. The Chinese agent reports informed him regularly that the heavy Japanese losses (a complete fabrication), the miserable weather, and the difficult terrain had eroded Japanese morale. Meyer-Waldeck, "Bericht," p. 89.

3. Kessinger, "Bericht," II, 28.9.14. His decisions here were not popular with everyone. Many staff officers thought that the de.ienders should demonstrate more activity. They believed that the use of a huge, visible work force might induce the Japanese to misjudge both the defenses and the defenders. Kessinger, "Geschichte," p. 298.

4. She had, as well, surrendered her main mast to the dock area some time before anyone considered the observation possibility. The mast eventually found its way to Peking, where it served as a German war monument for many years.

5. In an effort to improve both his ship's morale and her effectiveness, the *Jaguar*'s captain, von Bodecker, had earlier told his men, "Children, the first man who sees a valuable target and reports it, will have a bottle of champagne from me!" For the crew this was sufficient inducement. It cost von Bodecker many bottles. Interview with Christian Vogelfänger, June 1973.

6. Winkler, "Tagebuch," 30 September 1914; Vogelfänger, "Tagebuch," 4 Okt. 1914.

7. The most notable accomplishment was the Jaquar's report of Japanese activity in Litsun. Only the Austrian battery of two 15 cm. guns could reach that far. They fired several rounds, driving the Japanese into precipitant flight. This battery, named the "Austrian Life Insurance Battery" because of its well-designed and concealed position, received an equal accolade from the Japanese, who termed it "the Litsun Express." Kessinger, "Geschichte," p. 302.

8. Kessinger, "Geschichte," p. 326; Vogelfanger, "Tagebuch," 4 Okt. 1914; "Der Ehrentag des Jaguar"; Eine Erinnerung an einen alten Tsingtau-Kamp en von von Kapitanleutnant Brunner." This much-circulated piece appeared originally in the *Deutschen Zeitung fur China*, October 4, 1915. The *Jaguar* would have had more serious troubles had not one of its early shells hit the telephone cable connecting the Japanese batteries with their

observation post. A visual substitute arrangement failed completely. The Japanese finally resorted to a messenger service, which proved insufficient for the assignment. *Nichidoku Senshi*, I, 469-471.

9. Bodecker himself suffered from the defeat. Shortly after this withdrawal, he saved the life of a sailor who fell overboard, almost losing his own life in the process. The two events brought severe depression and his eventual relief.

10. Leipold, "Bericht," II, p. 5; Nickchen, "Tagebuch," October 5, 1914; Kessinger, "Geschichte," p. 344.

11. Interview with Hans Ehlers, June, 1973; Kessinger, "Geschichte," p. 327. As the balloon headed out to sea, it passed over the Japanese fleet. They were somewhat mystified by the object but took it under fire for practice. Sato ordered a destroyer to follow it, but the ship was late getting under way and lost the balloon. Brand "Report," Adm. 137/35.

11. Kessinger, "Geschichte," pp. 310-311; Interview with Ed Leipold, June, 1973; Plüschow, *Die Abenteuer*, pp. 66-70. After a particularly harrowing experience Plüschow found a large piece of bomb, affixed his calling card to it, and painted on, "All best greetings to the enemy colleagues. Why do you throw such hard objects? How easily they can go into an eye! That one should not do." He dropped it during his next flight over the Japanese lines. Ibid., p. 74.

12. Kessinger, "Geschichte," p. 312.

13. Kessinger, "Geschichte," p. 312; Vollerthun, *Der Kampf um Tsingtau*, p. 132; Ehlers, "Geschichte von Tsingtau," p. 101. When apprehended by the Japanese, these agents received the briefest of trials and immediate execution. Suspicion was sufficient grounds for the death sentence. Somerville, "Diary," 30 Sept. 1914.

14. The surviving reports provide some interesting material, but they are fragmentary. The total return must remain lost to history.

15. This decision, essentially that of Von Kessinger, was not well liked by various staff members. The others argued that the Japanese were more at home in the darkness and that a moving column had no fear for artillery. Several staff officers availed themselves of their rights to note their opposition in the official diary; this was the sole instance of such intense feeling throughout the siege. Kessinger, "Bericht," II, "Anlagen."

16. Kessinger, "Geschichte," p. 322; Befehl (No. 249) fur die Landfront fur 2.10.14.

17. Schaumburg, Bericht, p. 34; Vollerthun, *Der Kampf um Tsingtau*, p. 122; Somerville, Diary, 2-3 October 1914.

18. The Germans sent out a small patrol equipped with Red Cross Arm Bands and a large red lantern for picking up their dead and wounded. They did not get very far, since the nervous Japanese opened a heavy rifle fire upon them. Assmann, *Kämpfe*, pp. 66-69; Kessinger, "Geschichte," pp. 325-328; Kuhlo, "Kurze Beschreibung," pp. 60-65. The Germans suspected treason, but the Japanese records indicate that the Germans did surprise them but did not catch them off guard. *Nichidoku Senshi*, I, 460. Two men spent several days concealed in a ravine before they could

work their way back to the German lines. The most romantic escape was that of a sailor named Noss, who found himself by the water. A non-swimmer, he climbed on a barrel and paddled off. He disappeared with the tide, and his friends presumed him lost at sea. At noon the next day a patrol boat, noting a waving figure on Cape Jaeschke, picked him up. He had traveled a goodly distance with the outgoing tide. He brought back a harrowing tale of his experience and the first news of Japanese troops in that area. Kessinger, "Geschichte," p. 74.

19. Oberartzt Bertkau, "Bericht," p. 20.

20. A good explanation of the options is in F. P. Nosworthy, "The Capture of Tsingtau, 1914," *The Journal of the Royal United Service Institution*, 81 (August 1936), 526-527.

21. *Nichidoku Senshi*, I, 455-459.

22. Ibid., I, 480; J. A. Irons, "Japanese-German War in Kiaochou, China—1914," p. 12. This report is in the United States Army Military Research Collection. The ammunition moved with a meticulous schedule which put almost half of the estimated needs in the designated storage areas before the guns arrived in their firing positions.

23. Although incomplete, the railway was already a major operation, with a work force of some 1500 Japanese and 10,000 coolies. The construction authorities provided numerous sidings, which allowed an efficient control of all supplies. They cleverly designed feeder lines, which permitted several auxiliary depots and cut down on resupply time. Since the shells were loaded in Japan, a few skilled experts adjusted the fuses and turned everything over to the labor troops for movement (the coolies provided the motive power). These careful preparations allowed a superlative field performance. McLean, trans., p. 6; Machida, "Minute Report," p. 11.

24. The carts and wheelbarrows were easily obtained, easily maintained, and easily disposed of. They required no adapting to local conditions and did little damage to the roads. In this sense they were far superior to the heavy artillery pieces, which moved forward by horse power, tore up the road beds unmercifully, and held up the following batteries for extensive periods.

25. *Nichidoku Senshi*, I, 101, 513-515.

26. The entire question of Kamio's interest with this fresh unit remains unclear. Certainly the records do not reflect any view, but his prompt request for them, and his subsequent speedy reassignment, provide grounds for suspecting that he wanted greater certainty of victory than political or territorial gain. Conversation with Takeharu Shima, Director of the Japanese Military Archives, September, 1972. At the same time Japanese intentions toward the railroad and Chinese territory were already a matter of record. The Japanese diplomats paid no attention to the Chinese protests. Chi, *China Diplomacy, 1914-1918*, pp. 19-24 has a succinct account which explains the problem.

27. *Nichidoku Senshi*, I, 477f.

28. On October 25 they presented him with a flawless map. It con-

tained very few errors and none of any significance. Irons, "Japanese-German War," p. 22.

29. Hermann Lange received a shoulder wound on October 5. He had not bothered to seek cover when the Japanese passed over him. Karl Christl, "Tagebuch," 5. Okt. 1914. Thereafter the Germans received strict instructions to take cover during an air raid.

The number of Chinese killed remains unknown. In the spirit of the times, no one reported or recorded their losses.

30. *Nichidoku Senshi*, I, 501-510. In fact, his requirements included a precise list of the tools, ammunition, and equipment items which each individual would carry with him.

31. Lance Corporal Thomas was the first British casualty. The bullet hit him in the chest and carried the piece of his uniform through the hole. Thomas, in shock, observed his condition with equanimity but the sight and report of his wound bothered his colleagues. Beaumont Walker, Report, p. 7.

The two allies did not share any basic friendship for one another. While the Japanese troops could plead ignorance of their European colleagues, the British brought with them the prejudices of Tientsin. They regarded the Japanese as an inferior race, as coolies in uniform, whose good opinions it was not necessary to cultivate. The majority of the British troops disliked the expedition because it impeded their movement to Europe and placed them under an oriental commander. Calthrop, "Notes."

32. Subsequently the continued incidence of error, the excellent target presented by the white spot on the helmet, and the prospect of German falsification of the mark, forced the issuance of the Japanese khaki-colored raincoat to all British troops. They also established a simple countersign identification system (Tokyo-London). These devices solved the basic problem, albeit they did not end the incidents. Eckford, Report, p. 6; Somerville, "Diary," 8 Oct. 1914.

33. The Germans maintained their fire on the vacated areas for several days without success. They never ceased looking for the British, whom they blamed for Japan's declaration of war and their own predicament. On October 10 Plüschow found them again and dropped one of his homemade bombs on their camp. It hit near the cookhouse and shattered upon impact, scattering twenty-five sticks of dynamite and miscellaneous collection of iron and horseshoe nails. The troops started shifting their location before Plüschow reached the ground. Beaumont Walker, "Report," p. 7; Plüschow, *Die Abenteuer*, p. 75; letter from Hans Augustesen, 29 October 1973.

The British suffered from other complaints. They dressed in thin, short pants and carried a single blanket. A shortage of wood forced them to expend energy and time in searching for scrap pieces to be used in their fires and construction efforts against the elements.

Food proved a challenge as well. They scrounged whatever they could in the neighborhood, which was never enough. Some groups hired Chinese entrepreneurs (called Boo-Bahs) who provided eggs, chickens, and other essential needs at a price! When they occasionally did get enough supplies, the men gorged themselves and could do little thereafter for several hours. Somerville, "Diary," 9-10 Oct. 1914; Atkinson, *South Wales Borderers*, p. 76.

34. Eckford, Report, p. 5. This exchange involved far more than a simple question of a signature. Barnardiston was clearly worried about the command relationships. On the day before this dispute he had asked his London superiors about his role in the forthcoming surrender negotiations. He assumed that he would be ". . . specifically associated with the commander-in-chief of the Japanese forces in negotiations. . . ." War Office to Foreign Office, 5 October 1914; General Barnardiston to War Office, 4 October 1914. F)371/2017, WO106/663.

35. Minute by Bilby Austin, 6/10/14. FO 371/2017. Subsequently Barnardiston defended himself by pointing out that none of the Japanese pronouncements carried any reference to the British presence. A note signed by the "Independent Commander of the Eighteenth Division" did not reflect such status. Barnardiston insisted that his participation must be made and maintained as a matter of public record. Barnardiston to War Office, 20.10.1914. WO 106/663.

36. The reason for this delay remains uncertain. Despite the official papers, which indicate the unequivocal nature of the decision and the need for its prompt dispatch, the answer, unfortunately, did not go out in good time. Minute by Bilby Austin, 6/10/14. FO 371/2017.

37. An English copy is in WO 106/661. That he signed the document in such fashion was viewed, in London, as a courtesy. The British had second thoughts. On October 26 the British Army Council expressed its desire that Kamio address the Germans as the "Commander-in-Chief Allied Forces" rather than as the "General Officer Commanding Independent Eighteenth Division." Foreign Office to Sir C. Greene, October 26, 1914 (copy) WO 106/663. The Admiralty then asked the same consideration from Admiral Kato. Foreign Office to Sir C. Greene, October 28, 1914. WO 106/663.

38. Already on October 3 and 5 the two sides had exchanged information on prisoners and enemy dead. On October 12 they had also accepted a four-hour armistice for burying the German dead from the October 2 sortie. The pause went off without difficulty. In fact, the Japanese buried their enemies with full military honors and laid wreaths upon the graves. Somerville, "Diary," 14 Oct. 1914.

39. Kessinger, "Geschichte," p. 332; Hanyu, "Weltkrieg," pp. 79-80; Nickchen, "Tagebuch."

40. He had received orders on October 5 to report in Tientsin. As he pointed out in his response, "Danger in going greater than in remaining unless arranged by Legation with Japanese troops." The Japanese proposal allowed his departure, together with two happy Chinese servants. One American, A. M. Brace, a newspaperman, remained in the city, while the Germans refused exit to another man, Edgar Kopp. They believed that he and eleven Indians possessed too much military information. Peck to Paul

S. Reinsch, American Minister Peking, October 14, 1914. D/S File 862a. The other German women and children elected to stay in Tsingtau.

41. Peck found the ceremonies highly moving and unusual in the middle of a war. Peck to Secretary of State, October 1, 1914 (must be November 1) D/S File 862a; Meyer-Waldeck, Bericht, p. 93.

42. A much-repeated story, for which there is no documentary evidence, is that the Japanese semaphored the message, "Are you now ready, gentlemen?" The reply came from a German sniper, whose bullet cut some hairs in the signaler's mustache. Neville Hildritch, "The Siege of Tsingtau," p. 8, U.S. Army Military Research Collection.

43. In reality the Germans had sown a mere 296 mines. The Japanese gave them a totally unexpected respect, assuming that there were many more.

44. This base was an old factory building which provided space for workshops, storage, living quarters, and, finally, a Japanese bath house. They quickly planted trees and plants which gave it a highly unwarlike appearance. Brand, "Report," II, p. 17. The Japanese had to take the *Wakamiya Maru* back to Japan for repairs. They packed her up in time to take her aircraft home in late November. After the war, in 1920, the Japanese Navy put a landing platform over the forecastle. Lieutenant (later Vice Admiral) Torao Kuwabara made the first Japanese shipboard flight from the platform. The *Wakamiya Maru* served as a naval unit until April 1, 1930. Discussions with Vice Admiral (ret) Torao Kuwabara, September, 1972.

45. These losses incensed the Japanese, who decided that the Chinese junks in the area must be secretly laying mines at night. They destroyed all the junks in the area on October 1.

46. Ibid., p. 14.

47. The *Iwate*, *Yakumo*, and *Tokiwa* left on October 2 for Sasebo.

48. One of *Suwo*'s shells, a 12-inch dud, fell into the Moltke area, tore through the door of an officer's small quarters and came to rest under his bed. The officer had stepped out for a call of nature, just ahead of the shell. Kessinger, "Geschichte," p. 209.

49. The original intention was an operation on October 13. Kato postponed it a day on very short notice for unknown reasons. Brand, "Report," II, p. 18.

50. All the world's navies employed listing for range extension. A ship's crew simply flooded various compartments and shifted the coal in various other compartments. They could heel the ship up to five percent and, by combining this list with the wave action, or normal roll of the ship, they could increase the gun range several thousand yards. The most important defensive risk in listing was the exposure of the ship's unarmored section below the water line. The offensive disadvantage was that the shells' trajectory approximated that of a land howitzer, which required greater accuracy in hitting a target. The *Suwo*'s guns had a better elevation level than those of the *Triumph* ($240°$ against $139°$) which made her a better subject for the effort.

51. Beyond the obviously superb German marksmanship, the explana-

tion for the success was relatively simple. After the September 28 bombard-ment, the Germans altered the carriage and recoil supports of a gun, increas-ing its range. Nonetheless, a hit, on the first shot, at an extreme range, with only the mast as a target, was impressive shooting. Assmann, *Kämpfe*, p. 71. The many subsequent tales, repeated by various authors, (both German and British) about people swimming out and moving buoys or about the guns firing short as an entrapment make unfortunate reading.

52. The list of damages testifies to the impressive power of 24-cm shells. It is in "Letter of Proceedings from Captain Fitzmaurice to Vice Admiral Kato," 16 October 1914. Other descriptions are in Brand, "Report," I, p. 6 and "Report," II, p. 18. Photographs of the damage are in "The Naval Fighting off Tsing-Tau: the Damage to a British Battleship," *The Sphere* (Jan. 16, 1918), pp. 80-81. A small incident in the war was Kato's gift of money for the family of the dead sailor and his personal visit to the two wounded men. The sailor's body was put aboard the *Usk*, which left for Wei Hai Wei. She steamed slowly, with flag at half mast, through the lines of large ships. As she passed the various ships' companies stood at re-spectful attention. Arthur B. W., "With H.M.S. TRIUMPH at Tsingtau," p. 589.

53. The Germans were exhilarated by the news of the hit. It was better than sinking a Japanese dreadnought. They celebrated the shell with great verve. Many pointed out an old German proverb, "Ja, Ja, the dogs bite the last one."

54. Nash and Gipps, "Narrative," p. 11. The orders are an enclosure to "Letter of Proceedings from Captain Fitzmaurice to Vice Admiral Kato."

55. The Forty-eighth Regiment, the unit already stationed there, sim-ply moved its troops out of the front line so that the new units did not get mixed up with the previous occupants. Fortunately, the Germans did not know about this tactic and did not use their artillery against the shift.

56. Despite their precaution, the number of incidents remained high. The British finally gave up complaining, since they found that the Japanese fired just as often on their own people at night. Ultimately the Japanese assigned one of their men to each British patrol. Since these men seldom spoke any English, the results were often stimulating to everyone involved with a patrol. Barnardiston, Despatch No. 2, 29 October 1914, p. 1; Some-rville, Diary, 12-14 Oct. 1914.

57. *Nichidoku Senshi*, I, 530-533.

58. Watanabe suggested that most of this activity should take place at night. His respect for Plüschow exceeded that for a full regiment; he saw the German flyer as a fundamental threat to Japanese success. To aid Watanabe, Kamio ordered his air force to keep the German flyer away. The former nuisance had grown into a problem. When Plüschow appeared on October 13, four Japanese aircraft drove him off. The next day they did the same thing, and he could not report any new details. Ibid., I, 537, 557-560.

59. *Nichidoku Senshi*, I, 513-553; Somerville, Diary, 17 Oct. 1914; Barnardiston, Despatch No. 2, p. 1; Winkler, "Tagebuch," 16 Okt. 1914.

60. Barnardiston, Dispatch No. 2, p. 2; *Nichidoku Senshi*, I, 562-566.

61. As insurance for this possibility, he brought in additional man-power. Kamio ordered the Twenty-ninth Brigade headquarters and some units from the Thirty-fourth Regiment to the battle zone. Johoji could take over command of the right flank and participate in the final rites. Ibid., I, 567.

62. Arthur B. W., "With H.M.S. TRIUMPH at Tsingtau," p. 590; E. F. Knox, "The Siege of Tsing-Tao," *The Journal of the United Service Institution of India*, XLIV (July 1915), p. 278. The British officers, who wore turbans to make them less conspicuous, did no better. They were all a sorry looking lot.

63. Hilditch, "The Siege of Tsingtau," p. 8; Eckford, "Report," pp. 7-8; Knox, "The Siege of Tsing-Tao," p. 279. Many mule skinners cursed the military decision which had, about six weeks before the war's outbreak, decided to reduce the North China garrison. All 200 mules, properly broken and trained had been sold to local farmers. Ibid.

64. *Nichidoku Senshi*, I, 568-569.

65. As they gradually accepted this idea, German staff officers, remembering the German military influence in Japan, made the wry witti-cism, "Now they have reached page—, paragraph— of the Imperial siege manual." Bertkau, "Bericht," p. 16.

66. The intensity of the work is reflected in the various official diary entries. Kriegstagebuch des Kommandeurs des III.S.B.; Kriegstagebuch IW1; Kriegstagebuch IW4. The Germans often simply covered over ravines instead of digging trenches and then covering them.

67. Meyer-Waldeck made two other decisions he did not enjoy signing. On October 17 he ordered the Chinese dock workers locked up in nearby quarters. They were simply too valuable for the work force and might leave at the first opportunity. At the same moment the Governor began releasing merchants from military service. Ostensibly his action was motivated by their ages and previous contributions to the war effort. In reality he antici-pated the Japanese victory and did not want all German merchants relegated to prison camps. The cost to German financial representation in Asia was too great.

68. Assmann, *Kämpfe*, p. 77.

69. Kessinger, "Geschichte," p. 335; Kriegstagebuch des Komman-deurs des III. S.B., 16.10.14.

70. Nichidoku Senshi I, 414.

71. Wenckstern, "Memoirs," Chapter 4, p. 3; Neumaier, Tagebuch, p. 20; letter from Ernst Falkenhagen, 1.8.71. Another comrade noted in a letter home describing the bombardment, "Oh how quickly one learned running."

72. Neumaier, pp. 21-22; Kriegstagebuch des Kommandeurs des III S.B., 14.10.14. The men soon recovered their sense of humor. They col-lected shell fragments until they could construct a full-sized shell from the pieces. Around it they built a small park with other shell fragments, naval emblems, an anchor, and some miscellaneous naval mementos. Over it they

erected a small banner with the inscription, "Pieces of the Anglo-Japanese Alliance." On the entry portal was a small shield with the phrase, "The Defenders of Tsingtau; a unit, a battalion against an Empire and the other enemies of Germany." Vollerthun, *Der Kampf um Tsingtau*, p. 126; Nickchen, p. 55; Kersten, p. 31.

73. Kriegstagebuch IW1; Kessinger, "Geschichte," p. 333.

74. The idea came to him after the *S-90* put down the last German mines without interception. Clearly the blockade was not as tight nor as attentive as the Germans had considered until this point.

75. Brunner then marched his men inland. Completely lost, he hired some coolies, and, without a translator, he assumed that they would head for food and water. His faith proved correct. After a long march they reached Chinese internment in Nanking. Assmann, *Kämpfe*, pp. 72-75; Fregattenkaptan a.D. Brunner, "Die letzte Fahrt von S.M. Torpedoboot *S-90*;" Fregattenkapitän a.D. Brunner, "Bericht: Marsch der Besatzung S-90," Fritz Schmidt, "Tagebuch," 17.-18.10.1914.

76. The *Takaschio* was an elderly ship, constructed in 1885. For the blockade she served to transport men, messages, and, unfortunately, munitions. More significant than her physical loss was the blow to tradition. She had been an active participant in all of Japan's campaigns since construction.

77. Brand, "Report," II, p. 8. Kato refused all suggestions that they use the army observers along the coast. He insisted that they did not know the difference between a merchantman, a destroyer, and a battleship. After the *Takaschio* disaster, Kato began assigning anchorages, using torpedo nets, and bringing some order to the blockade squadron. Ibid., II, pp. 20-21.

78. Brunner's costly error is difficult to understand, since he was a careful man in all details. When he destroyed his ship, he insisted upon the most thorough job possible.

79. Ibid. Among the Japanese soldiers the action was acclaimed for its surprise, execution, and bravery. Nagasaki, "Hufgeklirr," p. 35. The incredible disorder created among the Japanese for two days was also evidence of the German success. Brand, "Report," Appendix II.

80. Kessinger, "Geschichte," pp. 340-341. In spite of the suddenness of the Japanese reaction, the Germans lost only three men.

81. A further reason for his decision was the low supply level for artillery shells. The constant firing was exhausting all supplies. Kessinger issued strict orders on October 25 limiting the number of shells for each piece, calling for the expenditure of old practice ammunition, and creating a special supply issue for the final assault. Ibid., p. 340. Time was running out for the defenders.

82. The two sides, with a few exceptions, honored the Red Cross flag when they could see it. They often exchanged the personal effects of the fallen, and even returned individuals whose military value seemed dubious.

83. This story had a great effect upon German morale. Diehl became something of a folk hero. Kessinger, "Geschichte," p. 343; Kriegstagebuch IW1, 22.10.14.

84. Assmann, *Kämpfe*, p. 75.

CHAPTER VI: Tsingtau Falls

1. *Nichidoku Senshi*, I, 571-576.

2. They had neglected the water difficulty in their planning. The immense shortage of sandbags was unfortunate, since sandbags allowed the employment of additional manpower during the day and appreciably cut the construction time. A brisk black market in sandbags sprang up, as they spared much back-breaking labor.

3. The British and Japanese continued having abrasive incidents. In particular the British complained about the Japanese practice of shooting first and questioning later. Like the Germans, however, the British had very little respect for Japanese rifle marksmanship. Otherwise the difficulties would have been far more serious.

4. Watanabe wanted a guaranteed ten-day supply of ammunition for every piece: enough for two days at the gun site, a three-day allotment at an intermediate location, and a five-day reserve at the general siege park. *Nichidoku Senshi*, I, 578-580.

5. Ibid., I, 582-587.

6. The details of the Japanese artillery deployment are in Ibid., I, 587f.

7. Ibid., I, 600; interview D. Somerville 1973; *Blackwoods Magazine* 591.

8. The telephone connections between that point and all the major unit headquarters came into use the next day. Since Kamio could contact any one of his subordinate commanders on a direct line, there could be very few uncertainties as to orders. On October 31 Kamio had, after lengthy delays, a cable connection between Lau schan and Nagasaki. The Japanese had tied their own cable line between Nagasaki and Shanghai to the old German Tsingtau-Shanghai. Begun on October 8, they completed the connection just as the besiegers opened the last battle. *Nichidoku Senshi*, I, 111. There was, as a result, a direct flow of information from the lowest command echelon, through Kamio, to the Japanese General Staff.

9. Ibid., I, 614-617. Johoji did not know the terrain and had no time for familiarization, but he found a headquarters area, supervised his troop movements, coordinated the division of boundaries with his neighbors, and assumed control over the communication lines. Moreover, all of these activities took place during the advance against the Germans.

10. Atkinson, p. 78; Beaumont Walker, p. 8; Somerville, Diary, 28-29 Oct. 1914. The British line was particularly difficult because of the water

table; they could not construct the formal trenches desired by the Japanese. The result was some recrimination as the Japanese and the British complained over the results.

11. *Nichidoku Senshi*, I, 622, 630.

12. Vollerthun, *Der Kampf um Tsingtau*, p. 142; interviews with Ed Leipold, Paul Kley, Hermann Kersten, Walter Hermann.

13. *Nichidoku Senshi*, I, 460, 592-596; Beaumont Walker, Report, p. 13; Plüschow, *Der Abenteuer*, p. 83f. They even mounted a machine gun on an airplane against him, albeit without success.

14. The Japanese maintained this same attitude toward their friends. On October 23 some dozen foreign military observers arrived in Lau schan Bay. The reception group treated them with utmost respect, but did not facilitate the visitors' investigations. As one of them pointed out, ". . .nothing was lacking that tended to hamper their movements." They could not visit troops, take photographs, or observe the front. The American, Colonel J. A. Irons, caustically proposed, "From personal experience, it is thought that military observers are nearly as much of a nuisance as newspaper correspondents." Irons, "Japanese-German War," p. 24.

15. Brand, "Report," II, p. 24, III, p. 9. The ships, together with the number of shells fired, included the following: October 25, *Iwami* (30); October 26, *Suwo, Iwami* (71); October 27, *Tango, Okinoshima* (44); October 28, *Tango, Okinoshima* (50). These figures come from a detailed report, "Summary of the Bombardment," which is in Adm. 127/35. It clearly comes from Captain Hubert Brand, but it possesses no acknowledgement of that fact.

16. Ibid., II, p. 24, III, p. 9. In reality the shelling did very little damage. The total damage included a rifle, two cartridge crates, and several telephone lines. The Germans had a good deal of cleaning up, but they had grown used to such activity. Kriegstagebuch des Kommandeurs des III. S.B. 29.10.14; Bertkau, p. 20. An enterprising mathematician suggested that the Allied ships had wasted some two million marks in order to destroy property worth a hundred marks.

17. The *Triumph* had some problems through listing the ship to 7.5 percent. This obstructed the firing of some guns, but the crew corrected it to 5 percent, which then became the general rule. Brand, "Report," II, p. 26; Blackwoods, p. 531. Their opinion of their aim was, again, overly optimistic, albeit they did much better than previously. In particular Redoubt 1 suffered from twenty-six hits in its area, damage which the men had to repair that night. Kriegstagebuch I. W. 1.30 Okt. 1914. One man was slightly wounded. Kessinger, "Geschichte," p. 349.

18. Tatigkeitsbericht der B.B. Batterie (Bismarckberg), 25. Oktober 1914.

19. At the same time they began sinking the small coastal vessels, the harbor craft, and even the dinghies in the same area. The Japanese would not find any shipping when they did take over the harbor. Kriegstagebuch des Tsingtauer Werft, 28. X. 14.

20. Ibid., 29.X.14; *Nichidoku Senshi*, I, 663-664; interview with Hermann Kersten, June, 1973.

21. Interviews with Ed Leipold and Hermann Kersten, June, 1973; Plüschow, *Die Abenteuer*, p. 89.

22. The subsequent events of the day gave the superstitious Germans pause on Saturdays. The Japanese had completed their Shantung landing on a Saturday and had crossed the border into the protectorate on a Saturday. They started the final assault on a Saturday and, as fortune would have it, the city fell on a Saturday. Vollerthun, *Der Kampf um Tsingtau*, p. 143; Interview with Ed Leipold, November, 1972.

23. The men of the Bismarck Battery knocked over their coffee urn in their haste to depart the area. Lieutenant von Wenckstern, busy with his ablutions, dove into a hole. When he returned, some hours later, he found his wash pan filled with holes. The fishermen, who had just pulled in a netful of fish, found three water fountains within fifty meters of their tiny boat. They dropped everything and fled back to shore. Vogelfänger, "Tagebuch," 31.Okt.14; Wenckstern, Kap. 4/S. 7; Tatigkeitsbericht der B.B. Batterie, 31. Oktober; Kessinger, "Geschichte," p. 72.

24. "Proceedure of the Operations," trans. by McLean, p. 7; *Nichidoku Senshi*, I, 681f.

25. In the same area another Austrian gun was lost. The previous night a gun crew had manhandled a 15-cm gun from the Tsingtau battery to the same area. Because of various problems they had arrived late the previous night, had stored the heavy gun by the roadside, and had returned to their barracks. Shortly after dawn the Japanese made a direct hit on the gun, giving the crew something to think about for a long time. Eduard Leipold, "Volltreffer bei Batterie 15 in Tsingtau, 1914," *Nachrichtenblatt der Offizierverein der Marine Infanterie* (Juni 1972), pp. 14-15.

26. Kriegstagebuch der Tsingtauer Werft, 31.10.14. The Chinese workers, confined in the wharf area, were subsequently taken over the Bay by the steamer *Tsimo*, and released from duty. In part this action was motivated by humanitarian instincts, in part by fear of insurrection. Ibid. The Germans did regret not shifting the oil. They had considered doing so for some time but had not made the decision in time. Vollerthun, *Im Kampf um Tsingtau*, p. 150.

27. Brand, "Report," II, p. 27.

28. Where the connection remained intact, the conversation was not encouraging. In response to the normal query, "How are you?" came the common answer, "Thank you, we are still alive. How well you can hear through the telephone." The system carried the awesome banging sounds of the barrage. Vollerthun, *Im Kampf um Tsingtau*, p. 151.

29. In the late afternoon the Japanese batteries all fired a heavy barrage on the city. They pounded the environs for an hour or so, damaging many buildings and frightening the Chinese mercilessly. *Nichidoku Senshi*, I, 682; Discussion with numerous Tsingtau veterans, March 1969.

30. They refined these comments even more on occasion. When a shell

exploded, the stock phrase was, "Attention! Friedrich Krupp and Associates, Essen." When it went "plump," banged around, but did not explode, it was a "Japanese quality manufacture! Lacquer and paste!" A "Darling" was a shell which one did not hear approaching and exploded some fifty to seventy-five meters away, creating only shock waves. Nickchen "Tagebuch," p. 56.

31. They did so because of ammunition shortages, albeit the Germans thought that they needed to cool their gun tubes.

32. It could be exciting as well. In the Bismarck battery a sailor saw a dud 30.5-cm shell. For some reason he seized a spade and started prodding it toward a crevice. Despite all the screams from his colleagues, the man simply kept at his project until the shell fell into the hole. All the observers fell to the ground, held their breath—and then laughed nervously as it failed to explode. Neumaier, "Tagebuch," p. 35.

33. The Japanese records for this day far exceed those for any other phase of the campaign. *Nichidoku Senshi*, I, 678f.

34. In the clear night some Germans found a bit of romance through observing the colorful shrapnel explosions high overhead (in their jargon, "on the Moon") and the glowing hot metal drizzle drifting slowly earthwards. More often the shells burst close overhead, driving the men into the nearest cover in abject terror. Neumaier, "Tagebuch," p. 33.

35. Ibid., p. 34; Vogelfanger, Tagebuch, 2. November 1914. This shift of assignment was not a pleasant undertaking. The men reported to a personnel office in the city where they received their assignments. Afterwards the "sand rabbits," as they were termed, hurried through the dead city, over the torn up landscape, to their front line position. Since the Japanese continued their artillery fire, the trip was difficult. Neumaier, p. 36; Discussion with Tsingtau group.

36. KTB Werft, 31.X.14; Kessinger, "Geschichte," pp. 354-356.

37. *Nichidoku Senshi*, I, 698-702. His instructions throughout the campaign were clear and forceful. They created an image of a professional soldier anxious to achieve his goal but also anxious to do so within the accepted rules. Captain Yamada was likewise interested in the fate of his friend and dropped an airplane-delivered postcard with his best wishes. Bertkau, "Bericht," p. 22.

38. "Procedures of the Operations," trans. McLean, p. 7; *Nichidoku Senshi*, I, 732,737f.

39. Brand, "Report," II, p. 29. They stayed by their range markers although Hui tschuen huk did not fire very often. On one occasion the fort's guns just missed the *Triumph*, which had drifted over the restraining line.

40. Meyer-Waldeck, "Bericht," p. 104; Kessinger, "Geschichte," p. 357; Tatigkeitsbericht der B.B. Batterie, 1. November 14; KTB, IW5, 1.November 1914.

41. German estimates vary, but the percentage of duds must have been between ten and twenty-five percent. Faulty craftsmanship played a major role in saving the defenders.

42. Bormann, "Tagebuch," p. 20; Nickchen, "Tagebuch," p. 58. Hasty

repairs made the wireless serviceable once more despite the extensive building damage.

43. Kessinger, "Geschichte," p. 358.

44. *Nichidoku Senshi*, I, 720-722.

45. Vollerthun, *Der Kampf um Tsingtau*, pp. 152-153; Kessinger, "Geschichte," p. 359.

46. Vollerthun, p. 153; *Nichidoku Senshi*, I, 745-749; Discussion with Tsingtau veterans. Other patrols successfully reconnoitered Redoubt 3 that same night, albeit not in such detail. Combined, these patrols provided the Japanese with a good picture of the German center. Ibid., I, 724. However, the actions caused some confusion for the Japanese as well, since their reports and explanations did not always agree with one another. On November 2 Kamio called the patrol leaders together for a full-scale examination and explanation, looking for clarification rather than a scapegoat. Afterwards he congratulated everyone for the command decisiveness and the collected information. Ibid., I, 745-749.

47. C. Casapiccola, "S.M.S. Kaiserin Elisabeth 1914 in fernen Osten," pp. 12-13. Dub, "Bericht," pp. 28-29. The ship had fired some 3,500 shells against the enemy. Emil Schrott, "In Ostasien von 1913 bis 1920," p. 8. Afterwards they burned the secret papers and disposed of various gun parts which they had removed earlier.

48. The Austrians suffered a good deal from this realization. Letter from Sepp Winkler, August 1972; letter from C. Casapiccola, January 1972.

49. All the tugs, small boats, and large pieces of equipment (mostly motors) disappeared into the Bay. The Germans had some difficulty in this final destruction effort because they ran out of explosives. KTB Werft, 1-2 November.

50. Bertkau, "Bericht," p. 22.

51. Kessinger, "Geschichte," pp. 362-363.

52. *Nichidoku Senshi*, I, 753. The poor weather halted the sea bombardment. Kato feared that the heavy winds would increase the range of Hui tsuen huk's guns while decreasing his own, thereby cutting the safety margin too thin. Brand, "Report," II, p. 28.

53. *Nichidoku Senshi*, I, 738; Calthrop, "Notes." The concussion of the firing tilted the gun platforms and made them both insecure and inaccurate.

54. In spite of the general gloom, one group did hold an impromptu holiday scene near Redoubt 4. They had a huge hog which the unit had picked up in September, and during the bombardment someone found a paper box filled with holiday ornaments. No one asked about the reasons for saving such things. Cutting down a small tree, they deocrated it and sat around quietly singing "Silent Night" under the stars. As they did so two Japanese shells roared in on them, forcing them to the extinguish the candles, quickly dispose of the tree, and seize their rifles. After a pause for many other shells, the men returned to their redoubt for a pork dinner. It was a sumptuous, if unusual, holiday party. Neumaier, "Tagebuch," p. 40.

55. The adjustments did bring some difficulties in Japanese fire plans.

As they moved closer to the front, the congestion created many fears about gun positions. Whenever one piece shifted its location, the neighboring commanders, anticipating a like movement, made all of the necessary preparations for shifting their positions; thereby interrupting their firing activities. *Nichidoku Shenshi*, I, 830-832.

56. Ibid., I, 792f; Kessinger, "Geschichte," pp. 366-367; Assmann, *Kämpfe*, p. 84. For the defenders the loss was more irritating than catastrophic. There were sufficient pumps for water, the difficulty came with the distribution. Carrying water by hand was dangerous, time-consuming, and wasted manpower.

57. Somerville, "Diary," 5-6 November 1914; Atkinson, *The History of the South Wales Borderers*, pp. 81-82. Johnson received a medal, the DSO, for his exploits. This action was also notable for showing the capricious nature of war. One man had a bullet score his back as it passed by. Another had a large coin in his pocket turned into a memorable bullet-enclosing cup, while another thanked his life to a bone-handled knife which absorbed the force of a bullet. Somerville, "Diary," 6 November.

58. *Nichidoku Senshi*, I, 843-845; Assmann, *Kämpfe*, p. 80. The strange dating has thrown many writers (including Assmann) off the actual time. The original German syntax also was somewhat less certain than this corrected version. Several German diaries and the Japanese records place it correctly on November 5.

59. The Germans erroneously thought that the *Triumph* had scored the hit and had, thereby, brought history full circle. Assmann, *Kämpfe*, p. 85. On the bombardment see Brand, "Report," II, p. 29, III, p. 10.

60. Hsiauniwa had not fired a shot against the Japanese while several others, given a similarly poor location, had not expended very many. They furnished men for the front lines. Kessinger, "Geschichte," pp. 369-370; Gustav Muller, "Bericht," p. 3.

61. Bertkau, "Bericht," p. 22.

62. He had received instructions from Meyer-Waldeck the previous day that he must leave the city before the fall. Plüschow did so with several war diaries, official papers, various symbolic items (including the fastenings from the flag pole), and some private letters. He did fly as far as neutral territory in China and eventually reached home after a lengthy, adventurous trip. Plüschow, *Abenteur*, pp. 95-96; Assmann, *Kämpfe*, p. 85; Guenther Plüschow, "Mein letzten Flug in China," (12 November 1914) in possession of Ed Leipold. Plüschow's published account of his travails makes delightful reading, although its accuracy is less certain. The final conversation between Plüschow and Meyer-Waldeck is recorded in Isot Plüschow, *Gunther Plüschow, deutscher Seemann und Flieger* (Berlin: Ulktein, 1936), p. 171.

In addition to sending his most valuable papers out of the protectorate, Meyer-Waldeck ordered the secret burial of other records.

A note on the landing in China and the breakup of the aircraft for use by local missionaries is in Carrell B. Morgan, "An Ancient Taube Found in

China," *Popular Aviation*, 13 (June, 1937), pp. 38, 66. The postal question is discussed in Heinrich Mundorf, "KIAUTSCHOU. Postbeforderung kurz vor Kriegsausbruch und während des Krieges und der Belagerung," and in the Marineschule Mürwik Historische Sammbung.

63. Meyer-Waldeck, "Bericht," pp. 111; Bertkau, "Bericht," p. 23.

64. *Nichidoku Senshi*, I, 895.

65. Hanyu, "Weltkrieg," p. 97.

66. Ehlers, "Bericht," p. 120; Meyer-Waldeck, "Bericht," Anlage 15 (which includes a careful diary of the day's events); Kessinger, "Geschichte," p. 376.

67. Two other posts, manned with machine guns, observed some advancing Japanese but believed that they were of no importance. They did not report their observation.

68. Hanyu, "Weltkrieg," p. 97; Jekizo Nakamura, "Assault on Central Fort, Tsingtao Campaign, 1914" (a speech held before the Emperor), trans. by J. A. Irons in U.S. Army Military Research Collection; Ehlers, "Bericht," p. 143; Assmann, *Kämpfe*, p. 112; Ludwig Dessel, "Tagebuch," 7. November 1914. The entire affair proved ridiculously easy. Many Germans suspected that the attacks succeeded through treason, but the success came simply from initiative, aggressiveness, and good fortune. Also, there was some accuracy in those Germans who called the troops in the captured Redoubt, "the sleeping army." Meisser, "Memoirs," p. 4.

69. *Nichidoku Senshi*, I, 896-897.

70. Paul Kley, "Bericht," p. 6; interview with Paul Kley, June, 1973.

71. Meyer-Waldeck, "Bericht," Annex 15; Paul Kley, "Bericht," p. 7. The *Jaguar*, after firing her last shells, was sunk near the *Kaiserin Elisabeth* by a few explosive charges. She went down slowly. Afterwards the crew smashed the small boats which they used to get ashore.

72. Ehlers report from the survivor, Sergeant Wadarz.

73. During the exchange the Japanese shot the German carrying the white flag as revenge. Naumaier, "Tagebuch," p. 32.

74. Tatigkeitsbericht der B.B. Batterie, 6.November 1914; Assmann, *Kämpfe*, pp. 82-86; Hans Kastner, "Bericht."

75. Assmann, *Kämpfe*, p. 90.

76. "Bericht uber die Tatigkeit des Majors von Kayser als Parlamentar am 7. November 1914."

CHAPTER VII: A Turning Point

1. Normally they also advised the men to destroy their arms before giving up. Kersten, "Bericht," p. 12; Kessinger, "Geschichte," p. 384. The

Germans, in a final flurry of destructive activity, destroyed even the paper money in the bank, the stamps in the post office, the official papers in the city files, and all the battle-flags. There was no money in the government vaults and the Deutsch-Asiatischen Bank holdings were private property. The Germans left very little for the conqueror. Kurt Schultze-Jenn, *Der Kampf um Tsingtau* (Shanghai: Verlag von Max Nossler, 1915), p. 18.

2. Beaumont Walker, p. 11; Somerville, "Diary," 8 November 1914.

3. Discussion with many Tsingtau veterans.

4. His orders were blunt and clear. He held everyone accountable for his own actions and added the injunction that everyone's baggage would be inspected in Japan. *Nichidoku Senshi*, I, 900-902.

5. Vollerthun, *In Kampfum Tsingtau*, p. 171.

6. Vogelfanger "Tagebuch," 7-10 November; Ehlers, p. 149; Bertkau, "Bericht," p. 26.

7. The artillerymen did not do as well. Several gun crews spent the day marching about from one place to another, ultimately ending up at their old positions. They did not always receive the best treatment from their captors. Assmann, *Kämpfe*, p. 96.

8. Kersten, "Memoiren," p. 12; Meyer-Waldeck, "Bericht," p. 119; Kessinger, "Geschichte," p. 396. Not everyone had sufficient clothing for the first night and many men passed the cold, dark hours walking about, telling and retelling their experiences. Wenckstern, "Memoirs," Kpt. 5, p. 2; Meeting with Tsingtau veterans.

9. The delay came through a humorous incident. Lieutenant H. W. Beaumont Walker had put his trousers on a parapet to dry from his previous night's exertions. When he received orders for the march, he could not put on his frozen uniform and delayed the advance until he could wear the half-thawed garment. For his sin, his platoon came last in line rather than leading the British contingent. Beaumont Walker, pp. 11-12; Jones, *The Fall of Tsingtau*, p. 107.

10. Somerville, "Diary," 8 November 1914; Assmann, *Kämpfe*, pp. 95-96; Ehlers, "Bericht," p. 149. The Japanese took little notice of their allies, much to the latter's discomfiture. Certainly their lack of participation, after all the suffering and preparation, was a disappointment to the British troops. Somerville, "Diary," 9 November 1914.

11. The latter's name was not recorded by either the Germans or the Japanese. They merely noted the presence of a British representative, no more.

12. Certainly this rapid action reflected the state of Japanese discipline. Despite the soldiers elation with victory, the confusion, and the numbers of trotroops, he had them out of the city within a very short period.

13. Bericht des Chefs des Stabes, Kapitän zür See Saxer; *Nichidoku Senshi*, I, 1001f. Calthrop was present only through his position as the liaison man in the Japanese headquarters. The Japanese did not even inform Barnardiston that the formal surrender was taking place, much less ask his presence. Calthrop, "Notes"; Somerville, "Diary," 11 November 1914.

The Japanese Emperor, on November 9, ordered the German officers be allowed to keep their swords. Yamanaschi employed an official air during this communication, indicating that the allowances came from the Emperor himself. Calthrop added, "I have also the honor to report that, through the generosity of my sovereign, the German officers may keep their swords." This proved a bit much for Yamanaschi, who coldly responded, "Can you show me the paper authorizing this expression of your King's will?" Ehlers, "Bericht," p. 152; Interview with various Tsingtau veterans. The incident was much reported in the German press.

14. Governmentstagesbefehl (Nr. 321) vom 7. November 1914.

15. Meyer-Waldeck, "Bericht," p. 118. The Kaiser responded through the American Embassy with his recognition for their faithful service and with the award of the Iron Cross, First Class, for Meyer-Waldeck.

16. Winkler, "Tagebuch," 9 November; Interview with Hans Ehlers, June, 1973. The cemetery remained the final resting place for the dead, although subsequently the bodies were disinterred and buried in more formal order, with a large memorial tablet. A gardener, paid by the German government, took care of the small cemetery until the Chinese Communists dismissed him in 1948. Thereafter a veteran of the battle, Fred Bischof, assumed the responsibility. He had settled in Tsingtau after his prison term. The Communists would not let him leave, but did allow him to do the work. Later, after they shifted him to another area, his Chinese wife traveled, under considerable difficulty, to Tsingtau each November 7 to clean up the burial ground and to put flowers on the graves. In 1966, as part of the cultural revolution, the Communists leveled the cemetery for a housing project. *Nachrichtenblatt der Offiziervereinigung der Marine-Infanterie,* 29 (Dezember 1967), p. 19; letter from Wilhelm Seufert, 26 February 1973.

17. Meyer-Waldeck, "Bericht," pp. 119-120; Assmann, *Kämpfe,* pp. 100-101; Calthrop, Notes.

18. Kessinger, "Geschichte," pp. 404-405.

19. Ehlers, "Bericht," p. 153; Discussion with various Tsingtau veterans, June 1969.

20. Farling, "Tagebuch," 7-14 Nov. 1914.

21. Kessinger, "Geschichte," p. 207; Somerville, "Diary," 10 November 1914. Another old friend had better fortune. Takahasi reopened his photography store at his old address. Letter from Willy Jordan, 23 June 1973.

22. They laid their mats, when they had them, wherever they could find a space and ate hard bread and water. Packed like herrings, they managed to survive five days on top of one another. Fatigue, cool weather, and a calm sea made the trip bearable, but no more than that. The total lack of safety; i.e., insufficient lifeboats, poor ship's maintenance, and manifest neglect, did not disturb them since they were too tired to care about such niceties.

23. His problems may well have come from an unfortunate letter he had written two days earlier to Kamio. In the note he had charged the

Japanese with additional acts of looting. The charge upset the Japanese, who simply refused to dignify it with an answer. Kessinger, "Geschichte," pp. 403-404; Meyer-Waldeck, "Bericht," Anlage 15; Vogelfanger, "Tagebuch," 18 November 1914.

24. Some seventy-five prisoners-of-war who were in hospitals and unable to move were eventually sent to Hong Kong. The medical personnel and Red Cross worker.s largely received their freedom and reached Peking without difficulty. Meyer-Waldeck, "Bericht," p. 122.

25. This fulsome exchange is in FO 371/2381 and in WO 106/663. It reflects the entire problem of British participation. No one, in China or London, really understood the issues or problems of involvement, participation, and removal.

26. Wai-chiao Pu to Sir J. Jordan, FO 371/2018.

27. Minute by Balby Alston, 21 November 1914. FO 37½/2018. A note to this paper by Walter Langley supports it without reservation. Behind the decision were clearly several different forces. The war in Europe remained an overriding concern, but the issues of the German Pacific colonies posed another challenge (particularly as they affected Australia). No one could anticipate the adjusting balance of power.

28. Sir C. Greene to Foreign Office, November 20, 1914. FO 37½/2018. At the same moment the Japanese Emperor extended an invitation to Barnardiston to visit Japan before the latter returned home. G.O.C. North China to War Office, 21.XI. 1914; Sir C. Greene to War Office, November 19, 1914. WO 106/663.

29. Somerville, "Diary," 15 November 1914; Beaumont Walker, "Report," p. 15.

30. Calthrop, "Notes," Hanyu, "Weltkrieg," p. 112; Jones, *Fall of Tsingtau*, pp. 108-110. The latter's version of the ceremony is vividly presented, but it does not agree with that of the more linguistically qualified Calthrop.

31. Eckford, "Report," p. 12. The British dependence upon Japanese permission marked a significant adjustment in power relationships. Formerly the British had stood by and made the key decisions for the Japanese, but now the situation allowed the Japanese to trade places, roles, and power. They would make the decisions.

32. As they departed, their Japanese liaison officer, Major Huwatashi, gave a moving speech indicating his pleasure at serving with them. He concluded with three loud "Banzais," shouted at the top of his voice. Somerville, "Diary," 20 November 1914.

33. The *Triumph* had departed on November 12. G.O.C. N. China to Troopers, London, 20 November 1914. WO 106/662; "Itinerary of H.M.S. Triumph and Narrative of her Proceedings from the Fall of Tsingtau to the Commencement of the Operations at the lardanelles" *Naval Review* (vol III), pp. 645-646. Beaumont Walker, "Report," p. 14; Somerville, "Diary," 18-19 November. In leaving, Fitzmaurice presented a piece of plate to the flagship as a token of appreciation for a pleasant association. As she departed,

the *Triumph* fired a twenty-one gun salute and steamed about the various Japanese naval units, and her crew cheered wildly without orders. The naval relationship had been a pleasant one.

The Sikhs remained in Tsingtau for some time. While the London authorities evidenced every desire to shift them to Hong Kong, they delayed and postponed the effective date, without explanation. The Japanese finally tired of the delays and reported, on December 19, that the loading facilities would not be available after December 28. The Sikhs departed on Christmas Day. G.O.C. North China to War Office, 19-12-1914. WO 106/664.

34. The Japanese press descriptions of the time were ecstatic. The most interesting, albeit unintentionally revealing, was one which described the reception as, ". . . one of the events which will live in history as setting the seal upon the charter of Japan, entitling her to enter the ring of the World Powers upon equal terms." *The Times History of the War*, p. 426.

35. Two members of his staff, Major H. G. Pringle and Captain C.D.H. Moore, received the same order, but the Fourth and Fifth class respectively.

36. The British Ambassador saw Barnardiston's visit in a different light. Jordan thought that the entire affair had been conceived by the Japanese Foreign Ministry to eliminate any rancor or resentment created by the campaign. The parades, medals, and publicity had, in his view, no purpose beyond obscuring the real issue, i.e., the Japanese presence in China. J. Jordan to W. Langley, 5 March 1915. FO 371/2381. Given the increasing tension between the two powers over the ownership of Germany's Pacific possessions, Jordan's views would seem accurate.

The same suspicious observation may be made about the ultimate view of history. In a well-chronicled war, the British did not publish an official account of the campaign, nor did they even contemplate the possibility.

37. Hanyu, "Weltkrieg," p. 109.

38. A British study in 1914 suggested that Japanese power would actually decline in the near future. The author also thought that Russia would prove a much improved competitor with Japan in the years ahead. Lieutenant Colonel Somerville, Report, in Greene to Grey, 23 Jan 1914. FO 371/2010.

39. The Japanese clearly appreciated their accomplishment. They made an impressive analysis of the community's history, commercial position, and economic potential in September 1915. This report pointed out the German-made changes: between 1899 and 1912 the value of cargo moving throught Tsingtau had increased twenty times. In 1897 no ships visited the harbor; in 1912, 902 ships did so. The compilers of the report foresaw unlimited possibilities for improvement. This report was a confidential Japanese army survey which came into American hands. Peck to Secretary of State, September 30, 1915 D/S File 862a. The congratulatory telegram from the *Usk* to the *Triumph* on November 7 came very close to the truth when it suggested that "they had removed the . . . brightest jewel in the Kaiser's crown."

40. The Japanese were unhappy with the Germans for taking Kiauchou, for aiding the Russians (albeit on a limited scale), and for penetrating the Chinese economic market. This disgruntlement was more pique than anger. The Germans erred in not making friends rather than acquaintenacesacquaintences in Tokyo.

41. Thomas E. LaFargue, *China and the World War* (Stanford: Stanford University Press, 1937), p. 18; Vollerthun, *Der Kampf um Tsingtau*, p. 40. Ironically many firms continued their former activities for new owners. The most interesting one, perhaps is the old *Germania* brewery. Immediately after the conquest the Japanese put it back into service. Today the brewery, still using the same methods, formulas, and buildings, produces Tsingtau beer. The European importer is Hans Augustesen, whose family established the firm. Letter from Hans Augustesen, January 26, 1974; *Frankfurter Allgsmeine Zeitung*, 4. August 1973.

42. William R. Louis, *Great Britain and Germany's Lost Colonies, 1914-1919 (Oxford: Oxford University Press, 1967) has some interesting material on this subject.*

43. H. G. W. Woodhead, *Adventures in Far Eastern Journalism, a Record of Thirty-Three Years' Experience* (Tokyo: Hokuseido Press, 1935), p. 67; Calthrop, "Notes," Sugawara Sagael, *Chintao koryaku shoshi* (?, 1925), pp. 96-97.

44. Hilditch, "Report," p. 7. Apparently the same source observed that ". . . the masterful attack and successful siege of Tsingtau is but an example of the ultimate fate of Manila." Ibid., p. 14. The Japanese carried out the siege without changing their military readiness at home. In November they executed their normal peace-time maneuvers.

45. These lessons were not lost on Brigadier Nosworthy, whose brief account of the battle was imperfect in fact, but whose professional commentary provides a useful prediction of the coming Second World War. Nosworthy, "The Capture of Tsingtau," pp. 528-530.

46. W.S.C. to Triumph, Nov. 3, 1914; "Triumph" to Admiralty, 6.11.14. Adm. 137/35.

47. Brand, "Report," Conclusion.

48. All observers evidenced amazement over the artillery damage. The smashed trenches, the cracked redoubts, and the demolished forests all proved the authority of the steel barrage.

49. Somerville, "Diary," 15 November 1914; Irons, "Japanese-German War," p. 16; Landers, "Report," p. 22. They were unanimous on Japanese sanitation and secrecy—a total lack of the former and intense pursuit of the latter.

50. Walter Hermann, Letter of December 14, 1972. Together with this instructive incident the Japanese provided another sign of their power. When the difficult British diplomat, Eckford, returned to his residence, he found it occupied by the Japanese who had planted their flag in the front yard. He found accommodations elsewhere. An English advertisement in the *Shanghai Daily News*, obviously prepaid, read "Tsingtau, a splendid health resort," ran out on November. 8. Jaspersen, *Do Mau*, p. 222.

Bibliography

I. UNPUBLISHED RECORDS

A. Archives

Bundesarchiv-Militärarchiv, Freiburg

There are fifty-three folios on the siege. They include a potpourri of records—original diaries and records, papers prepared in Japanese prison camps, reports made in peacetime, private correspondence and accounts. They include Governor Meyer-Waldeck's final report, the official war diary, diaries of all the defensive works, the various artillery batteries, the infantry companies, and all of the independent commands. Additionally there are numerous private letters, individual reports, newspaper clippings and miscellaneous documents.

Public Record Office, London

In the Foreign Office papers the series FO371 contains the general correspondence relating to Japan and China, FO 395 has the News Department correspondence, and FO 228 holds the Tokyo embassy papers.

Among the War Office files there are nine volumes, WO 106/660 through 668. They include all the army papers on the campaign.

The Admiralty records are in ADM 137/35. These papers are in good order and cover the period 30 July to 20 November 1914.

Österreich Staatsarchiv, Kriegsarchiv, Wien

The Austrian archives contain two extensive files OK 2171-16 and 17. They have several lengthy reports concerning the Austrian participation in Tsingtau. There is, unfortunately, no material on the Austrian contribution to the land struggle.

Shenshi shitsu, Defense Agency, Tokyo

The Japanese records include several internal histories written for staff study. Included are "Taisho 4—nen naishi 9—nen seneki kaigun senshi"; "Seito homen senki"; "Senji Shorui." Some miscellaneous papers are on Reels: T318, R86 and T319, R87 of the Library of Congress microfilm collection of the Japanese military archives. Many of these latter documents were not in the Defense Agency holdings.

United States, National Archives, Washington, D.C.

The American records are divided among various agencies. Among the diplomatic files are the "Records of the Department of State Relating to Internal Affairs of Germany, 1910-1929," file 862a Kiauchou which hold most of the diplomatic papers. Scattered in Record Group 84 are other reports which must be searched out by date.

The Record Group 45: "Naval Records Collection of the Office of Naval Records and Library Subject File, 1911-1927, WA-7 (Japanese Siege of Tsingtao, 1914)" contains a miscellaneous collection of translations, observations, newspaper clippings, and speeches made by participants. It is, despite its lack of unity, a valuable source of information.

United States Army Military Research Collection, Carlisle, Pennsylvania

Because of its former activities with the Army's War College this collection houses the American Army's records. Included are military attaché reports, several student papers on the siege, and some translations.

National Maritime Museum, Greenwich, Connecticut

This collection has two little used, but important sources. One is the papers of Admiral Sir Thomas H. Jerram and the other is George Gipps, "Journal kept in H.M.S. *Triumph*, China squadron, including the siege of Tsingtao, 1 August 1914 - January 1915.

Hoover Institution, Stanford, California

In addition to its incomparable collection of the published materials the Hoover Institution has the "Autobiography" of Willys R. Peck.

B. Private Diaries

Carl Bormann, Karl Christl, Ludwig Dessel, Hans Farling, Julius Jaspersen, Hans Kastner, Hans Lipinski, Jacob Neumaier, Willi Nickchen, Hans Pauer, Otto Sarnow, Fritz Schmidt, Desmond Sommerville, W.T. Uhlenhuth, Christian Vogelfänger, and Sepp Winkler.

C. Miscellaneous

Beaumont-Walker, R.K., "The Siege of Tsingtao Campaign, August-November 1914."

Bertkau, Oberartzt, "Bericht des Stabartzes Dr. Bertkau über die Belagerung von Tsingtau."

Bischof, Fred, "Plaudereien am Kamin—Erinnerung an Infanteriewerk 5."

Brunner, Fregattenkapitän a. D., "Das Gefecht bei Tai kung tau am 22. August 1914."

Casapiccola, C., "S.M.S. Kaiserin Elisabeth 1914 im fernen Osten (Verteidigung von Tsingtau)."

Christl, Karl, "Memoiren."

Ehlers, Hans, "Geschichte von Tsingtau."

Hermann, Walter, "Erinnerungen."

Hinrichs, Georg, "Die Erste Reise. Ostasiatische Erinnerungen eines Fahrenmannes."

Johnson, D. G., "Narrative of Events in Connection with the Siege and Capture of the German Naval Base and Fortress of TSINGTAU in North China 1914."

Kastner, Hans, "Bericht über die Belagerung von Tsingtau."

Kersten, Hermann, "Vortrag am 7. November 1960."

Kersten, Hermann, "Memoirs."

Kersten, Hermann, "Kladde zum Kriegstagebuch der Marine-Fliegerstation Tsingtau."

Kley, Paul, "Memoirs."

Kramer, C. F., "Auszug aus meinem Bericht über eine Reise zu Schiff um den Erdball."

Leipold, Ed., "Ausfahrt des Truppentransportschiffs, *Patrizia* [sic] 1914 nach Tsingtau/Kiautschou, China."

Leipold, Ed., "Bei der Besatzung in Tsingtau im deutschen Pachtgebiet Kiautschou in China 1914."

Leipold, Ed., "Memoirs."

Leipold, Ed., "Meine Kriegsdienstzeit in Tsingtau-Kiautschou 1914."

Meissner, Kurt, "Memoirs."

Müller, Gustav, "Bericht."

Müller, Helmut, "Kiautschou-Postbeförderung kurz vor Kriegsausbruch und während des Krieges und der Belagerung."

Odermann, Hans, "Bericht über die Sprengung des Wasserwerk Litsun."

Plüschow, Gunther, "Bericht über die Belagerung."

Ponsel, Hugo, "Persönlicher Bericht."

Präfcke, Oberstabsartz, "Bericht über Kiautschou, Ostasien und Heimreise."

Prange, Otto, "14 Jahre Soldat im Lande der aufgehenden Sonne."

Puls, Georg, "Erinnerungen an Tsingtau."

Schaumburg, Hauptmann, "Bericht des Hauptmanns Schaumburg (ursprunglich in Briefform)."

Schrott, Emil, "In Ostasien von 1913 bis 1920."

Schutz, Leopold, "Bericht des Marineunterartzes Leopold Schutz über seine Wahrnehmungen und Erfahrungen während der kriegerischen Vorgange in Schutzgebiet Kiautschau."

Stegemann, Otto, "Memoirs."

Wenckstern, German von, "Letters to his mother."

Wenckstern, German von, "Memoirs."

Zimmermann, Manfred, "Bericht."

D. Correspondence

Hans Augustesen, Fred Bischof, Heinrich Bredemeier, Richard Bueschel, Stephen Cohen, Mrs. Derek Cooper, Stephen Cohen, Ludwig Dessel, Hans Ehlers, Ernst Falkenhagen, Alexander Franke, Dagmar Frowein, Walter Hermann, Stefan Hules, Dudley Johnson, Willy Jordan, Malcolm Kennedy, Paul Kley, Torao Kuwabara, Heinrich Lankenau, J. D. Lawson, Gertrud Leffler, Ed Leipold, Ursula Lipinski, Kurt Meissner, Fred Mensing, Robert Mikesh, M. I. Moir, Gustav Müller, Jacob Neumeier, Georg Puls, K. M. L. Saxens, Josef Schlingen, Emil Schrott, Karlgeorg Schuster, Reinhold Schwörke, M. von Senden, Desmond Sommerville, Otto Stegemann, Sven Talgert, Karl Vesper, Christian Vogelfänger, Friedrich Zanzinger.

E. Unpublished doctoral dissertations

Baker, Dwight, "Germany and the Far East, 1895 to 1908," Berkeley, 1927.

Bennett, N. R., "The Anglo-Japanese Alliance and the Dominions, 1902-1922," London, 1966.

Lau Kitching, "Sir John Jordan and the Affairs of China, 1906-16," London, 1968.

Ming-Chu Bee, Benjamin, "The Leasing of Kiachow; a Study in Diplomacy and Imperialism," Harvard 1935.

Peter, Eldmar, "Die Bedeutung Chinas in der deutschen Ostasien-Politik, 1911-17," Hamburg 1965.

II. PUBLISHED MATERIALS

A. Monographs

Alckens, August. *Tsingtau, 1914*. München: v.Lama, 1938.

Assmann, Kurt. *Die Kämpfe der kaiserlichen Marine in den deutschen Kolonien*. Berlin: E. S. Mittler & Sohn, 1935.

Atkinson, C. T. *The History of the South Wales Borderers, 1914-1918*. London: Medici Society, 1931

Behme, F., and M. Krieger. *Guide to Tsingtau and Its Surroundings*. Wolfenbüttel: H. Wessel, 1905.

Bennett, Geoffrey. *Coronel and the Falklands*. London: B. T. Batsford, 1970.

Brauer, Otto. *Kreuzerfahrten des Prinz Eitel-Friedrich*. Berlin: August Scherl, 1930.

Chi, Madeleine. *China Diplomacy, 1914-1918*. Cambridge: Harvard University Press, 1970.

Dane, Edmund. *British Campaigns in Africa and the Pacific 1914-1918*. London: Hodder and Stoughton, 1919.

Dua, R. P. *Anglo-Japanese Relations During the First World War*. New Delhi: S. Chand & Co., 1972.

Godshall, Wilson L. *Tsingtau under Three Flags*. Shanghai: Commercial Press, 1929.

Gottberg, Otto von. *Die Helden von Tsingtau*. Berlin, Wien: Ullstein, 1915.

Handel-Mazzetti, Peter. *Die Ost.-Ung. Kriegsmarine vor und im Weltkrieg*. Klagenfurt: Carl Roschnar, n.d.

Heeren, John. *On the Shantung Front*. New York: Board of Foreign

Missions of the Presbyterian Church in the United States of America, 1940.

Higham, Robin (ed.) *Official Histories, Essays and Bibliographies from around the World*. Manhattan: Kansas State University Library, 1970.

Hoyt, Edwin P. *The Last Cruise of the Emden*. New York: Macmillan, 1966.

Huguenin, C. *Geschichte des III. See-Bataillons*. Tsingtau: Adolf Haupt, 1912.

Isakov, Ivan. *Operacija Japoncev protiv Cindao v 1914 g...* Moscow: Gos.Voen. Izdat., 1936.

Ito, Masanori. *Gumbatsu kobo shi.* Tokyo: Bungei Shunju Shinsha, 1957-59.

Jaspersen, Julius. *Do Mau. Arbeit und Abenteuer eines deutschen Chinakaufmanns*. Leipzig: E. A. Seemann, 1936.

Jones, Jefferson, *The Fall of Tsingtau. With a study of Japan's ambitions in China*. Boston & New York: Houghton Mifflin Co., 1915.

Kerst, Georg. *Jacob Meckel; sein Leben sein Wirken in Deutschland und Japan*. Göttingen: Musterschmidt Verlag 1970.

Klehmet, *Tsingtau. Rückblick auf d. Geschichte, bes. d. Belagerund u. d. Falles d. Festung*. Berlin: Bath, 1931.

Kropff, H.v. *Deutsche Soldaten in Kiautschau*. Leipzig: Arnd, n.d.

Kuechler, Kurt. *Die letzten Tage von Tsingtau*. Heilbronn: Salzer, 1916.

LaFargue, Thomas E. *China and the World War*. Stanford, California: Stanford University Press, 1937.

Louis, William R. *Great Britain and Germany's Lost Colonies 1914-1919*. Oxford: Clarendon Press, 1967.

Lowe, Peter. *Great Britain and Japan, 1911-1915; a Study of British Far Eastern Policy*. London: Macmillan, 1969.

Mohr, F. W. *Handbuch für das Schutzgebiet Kiautschou*. Tsingtau: Deutsch-Chinesiscen Druckerei, 1911.

Nish, Jan H. *Alliance in Decline; a Study in Anglo-Japanese Relations, 1908-23*. London: Athlone Press, 1972.

Norem, Ralph. *Kiachow Leased Territory*. Berkeley: University of California, 1936.

Piggott, F. S. G. *Broken Thread; an Autobiography*. Aldershot: Gale & Polden Ltd., 1950.

Plüschow, Gunther. *Die Abenteuer des Fliegers von Tsingtau. Meine Erlebnisse in drei Erdteilen.* Berlin: Ullstein, 1917.

Plüschow, Isot. *Gunther Plüschow, deutscher Seemann und Flieger. Das Bild seines Lebens.* Berlin: Ullstein, 1933.

Pochhammer, Hans. *Before Jutland; Admiral von Spee's Last Voyage. Coronel and the Battle of the Falklands.* London: Jarrolds, 1931.

Pratt, John T. *War and Politics in China.* London: Jonathan Cape, 1943.

Presseisen, Ernst L. *Before Aggression; Europeans Prepare the Japanese Army.* Tucson: University of Arizona Press, 1965.

Raeder, Eric. *Der kreuzerkrieg in den ausländischen gewässern.* Berlin: E. S. Mittler * Sohn, 1922-1937.

Schlimgen, Josef. *Tsingtau, Juli-November 1914; die Kriegspost des deutschen Kiautschou-Gebietes.* Bonn: Arbeitsgemeinschaft der Sammler Deutscher Kolonialwertzeichen, 1971.

Schoen, Walter von. *Auf Vorposten für Deutschland. Unsere Kolonien im Weltkrieg.* Berlin: Ullstein, 1935.

Schrecker, John E. *Imperialism and Chinese Nationalism; Germany in Shantung.* Cambridge: Harvard University, 1971.

Schultze-Jena, Kurt. *Der Kampf um Tsingtau.* Shanghai: Verlag von Max Nössler, 1915.

Selow-Serman, K. E. *Kapitänleutnant Möllers letzte Fahrt.* Berlin: August Scherl, 1917.

Sokol, Hans. *Osterreich-Ungarns Seekrieg 1914-18.* Zurich: Amalthea Verlag, c 1933.

Steinberg, Jonathan. *Tirpitz and the Birth of the German Battle Fleet: Yesterday's Deterrent.* London: Macdonald, 1965.

Vollerthun, Waldemar. *Der Kampf um Tsingtau. Eine Episode aus dem Weltkrieg 1914-1918 nach Tagebuchblättern.* Leipzig: Hirzel, 1920.

Voskamp, D. *Aus dem belagerten Tsingtau.* Berlin: Buch. d. Berliner Evang. Missionsges, 1915.

Wallisch, Friedrich. *Die Flage Rot-Weiss-Rot. Männer und Toten der österreichischen Marine* in vier Jahrhunderten. Graz: Verlag Styria, 1956.

Walter, Robert. *Tsingtau unterm Feuer.* Weimar: Kiepenheur, 1915.

Ward, Herb. *Flight of the Cormoran*. New York: Vantage Press, 1971.

Wilhelm, Richard. *Aus Tsingtaus schweren Tagen im Weltkrieg 1914.* Berlin: Hutten-Verlag, 1915.

Woodhead, H.G.W. *Adventures in Far Eastern Journalism; a Record of thirty-three years' Experience*. Tokyo: Hokuseido Press, 1935.

Wyrall, Everard. *The History of the Duke of Cornwall's Light Infantry, 1914-1919*. London: Methuen, 1932.

B. Articles

Dithmar, G. "Die Kämpfe im Vorgelände der Festung Tsingtau im September 1914," *Marine Rundschau*, II (November 1935), 482-488.

Hicks, Charles R. "Genesis of the Shantung War Zone, China, 1914," *The Historian* 8-10 (1945-1948), 19-25.

Gipps, George. "Narrative of the Events in Connection with the Siege, Blockade and Reduction of the Fortress of Tsingtau," *Naval Review*, III, 322-334.

Grosse, Ernst. "Die Belagerung Tsingtaus," in Grosse. *Ostasiatische Erinnerungen* Munich, 1938, pp. 126-140.

"Itinerary of H.M.S. Triumph and Narrative of Her Proceedings, from the Fall of Tsingtau to the Commencement of the Operations at the Dardanelles," *Naval Review*, III, 644-648.

Jones, Clifford. "Japanese Landing at Tsing-tao," *Coast Artillery Journal*, No. 2 (1928), 145-149.

Kersten, Hermann. "Der Kampf im Kiautschou-Gebiet 1914," *Mitteilungsblatt des Traditionsverbandes ehemaliger Kolonial und Überseetruppen,* No. 18 (June 1961), 6-10.

Knox, E. F. "The Siege of Tsing-Tao," *The Journal of the United Service Institution of India*, XLIV (July 1915), 267-291.

Layman, R. D. "Japanese Naval Aviation," *United States Naval Proceedings* 99 (September 1973), 95.

Leipold, Eduard. "Volltreffer bei Batterie 15 in Tsingtau, 1914," *Nachrichtenblatt der Offizierverein der Marine Infanterie* (June 1972), 14-15.

Meyer-Waldeck. "Das Schutzgebiet Kiautschou," in *Die deutsche Flotte in grosser Zeit*. 3. Aufl. Berlin, 1926, pp. 141-144.

Morgan, Carrel B. "An Ancient Taube Found in China," *Popular Aviation* (June 1937), 38, 66.

"The Naval Fighting off Tsing-Tau: The Damage to a British Battleship," *The Sphere* (January 16, 1915).

"Naval Operations Against Tsingtau," *Journal of the United States Artillery* (May-June 1916), 89-92.

Nish, I. H. "Admiral Jerram and the German Pacific Fleet 1913-1915," *Mariner's Mirror*, Vol. 56, No. 4 (November 1970), 411-421.

Nosworthy, F. P. "The Capture of Tsingtao, 1914," *The Journal of the Royal United Service Institution*, Vol. 81, No. 523 (August 1936), 517-532.

"Notes from Tsingtau," *Journal of the United States Artillery (Antiaircraft Journal), May/June, 1916, 374-375.*

Perry, Emil B. *"The Siege of Tsingtao," United States Naval Institute Proceedings*, Vol. 55 (January-June 1929), 524-526.

Riedel-Konitz, Otto. "Tsingtau 1914," in *Deutsches Soldatens-Jahrbuch*. Jg.12. Munich, 1964, p. 29.

Robertson, L. B. "The Capture of Tsingtao," *The Army Quarterly*, Vol. 35 (October 1937-January 1928), 335-342.

Schrott, Emil. "In Ostasien von 1913 bis 1920," *Römerstädter Ländchen*, (1969), 7-8.

Smith, Bernard. "The Siege of Tsingtau," *The Coast Artillery Journal* (November, December 1934), 405-419.

Steffen, Walter. "Vor 45 Jahren; Das III. Seebataillon in 1. Weltkriege," *Nachrichtenblatt der Offiziervereinigung der Marine-Infanterie*, No. 13 (December 1959), 10-12.

Walters, H. F. "International Manoeuvres at Tientsin, North China, November 12th, 1913," *Army Review*, VI (April 1914), 498-507.

Index

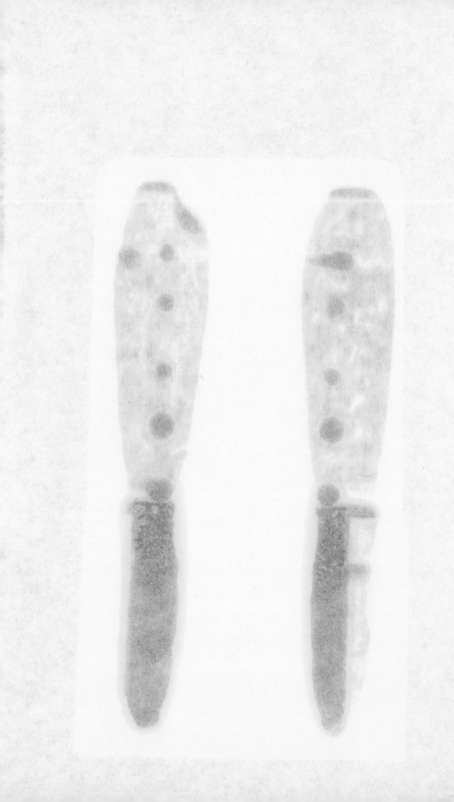